IV. Punctuation

V. Conventions of Form and Appearance

VI. Research and Documentation

VII. Special Types of Writing

The
Little, Brown
Compact
Handbook

Second Edition

Jane E. Aaron
New York University

HarperCollins*College*Publishers

Senior Acquisitions Editor: Patricia Rossi
Developmental Editor: Tom Maeglin
Project Editor: Steven Pisano
Design Manager: Teresa Delgado-Rodriguez
Text Designer: Robin Hoffman
Cover Designer: Kay Petronio
Electronic Production Manager: Mike Kemper
Electronic Page Make-up: Dorothy Bungert/EriBen Graphics
Printer and Binder: R. R. Donnelley & Sons Company
Cover Printer: Coral Graphics

The Little, Brown Compact Handbook, Second Edition

The author and publisher are grateful to the many students who have allowed their work to be reprinted here and to the following:

Excerpt from "Worthy Women Revisited" by Angeline Goreau, *The New York Times*, December 11, 1986. Copyright © 1986 by The New York Times Company. Reprinted by permission. • Excerpt from "The Confounding Enemy of Sleep" by Lawrence A. Mayer, *Fortune*, © 1984 Time Inc. All rights reserved. Reprinted by permission of Fortune, Time Inc. Magazines. • Excerpt from "A Book-Writing Venture" by Kim Yong Ik. Originally published in *The Writer*, October 1965. Copyright © 1965 by Kim Yong Ik. Reprinted by permission of the author. • Excerpt from *Disturbing the Universe* by Freeman J. Dyson. Copyright © 1979 by Freeman J. Dyson. Reprinted by permission of HarperCollins Publishers, Inc. • Excerpt from "The Decline of Quality" by Barbara Tuchman, *The New York Times*, November 2, 1980. Copyright © 1980 by The New York Times Company. Reprinted by permission. • Excerpt from "Search for Yesterday" by Ruth Rosen from *Watching Television* by Todd Gitlin. New York: Pantheon Books, 1986. • "The Bean Eaters" from *Blacks* by Gwendolyn Brooks. The Third World Press, 1987. Reprinted by permission of the author.

Library of Congress Cataloging-in-Publication Data

Aaron, Jane E.
    The Little, Brown compact handbook/Jane E. Aaron—2nd ed.
        p.   cm.
    Includes index.
    ISBN 0-673-99408-2
    1. English language—Grammar—1950-—Handbooks, manuals, etc. 2. English language—Rhetoric—Handbooks, manuals, etc. I. Little, Brown and Company.   II. Title.
PE1112.A23   1995
808'.042—dc20   95-3789
                                                               CIP

95 96 97 98   9 8 7 6 5 4 3 2 1

Preface

❖

Like its predecessor, this writer's handbook weds the breadth and authority of its parent, *The Little, Brown Handbook*, to a convenient and accessible format. Intended for writers of varying experience, *The Little, Brown Compact Handbook* concisely answers questions about the writing process, paragraphs, clarity and style, grammar, research writing, and more.

This second edition, while remaining trim, responds to instructors' and students' needs with changes both large and small.

- ❖ The format is even more convenient. A COMPLETE AT-A-GLANCE CONTENTS now appears inside the back cover. New durable notebook-style DIVIDERS make it easy to flip to any part of the book. And a sturdy COMB BINDING allows the book to lie flat for use.
- ❖ A new chapter on WRITING ARGUMENTS (51) introduces and illustrates assertions, evidence, and assumptions; reasoning and fallacies; and organization. The chapter includes an annotated student essay.
- ❖ A new chapter on WRITING ABOUT LITERATURE (52) comes from Sylvan Barnet, the author of *A Short Guide to Writing About Literature* and other texts. A concise introduction to the essentials of literary analysis, the chapter includes two student papers (one without and one with secondary sources), each accompanied by the literary work it discusses.

❖ NEW OR EXPANDED TOPICS include titling an essay, standard English and dialects, sexist language, parallelism, sentence fragments, and the ellipsis mark.

❖ Pointers for students using ENGLISH AS A SECOND LANGUAGE have nearly doubled in this edition. They are integrated throughout the book's other material on grammar and usage, so that ESL students do not have to distinguish between special ESL problems and those shared by native speakers. Flagged with a small color block (ESL), the pointers are easy to find and easy to skip.

❖ In its discussion of research writing, this edition now emphasizes COMPUTERIZED SOURCES (including key-word searches) and CRITICAL READING OF SOURCES (including evaluation and synthesis). The four substantial chapters on research writing cover project planning, finding and using sources, and documenting sources in either MLA or APA style (with a sample paper in each style).

As before, the handbook strives to minimize terminology and to help students around unavoidable terms. The GUIDE TO THE BOOK inside the front cover pairs a brief contents with questions like those that students ask, using everyday language and examples in place of terms. Similarly, the DETAILED PART OUTLINES at each tabbed divider substitute examples for terms or use examples to clarify terms. Headings with the text do the same. Then the text itself avoids cross-references by defining principal terms in the running text and secondary terms in out-of-the-way white boxes at the bottoms of pages.

Students and instructors alike have many paths into *The Little, Brown Compact Handbook.* For a list and illustration of all the book's reference aids, see FINDING WHAT YOU NEED IN THIS BOOK on the page immediately before the back endpapers.

Supplements

Accompanying *The Little, Brown Compact Handbook* is an array of supplements for students and instructors.

❖ *Exercises to Accompany The Little, Brown Compact Handbook* is a booklet offering activities on everything from paragraph coherence to comma splices to capitals. Representing a wide range of academic disciplines, the exercises are all in connected discourse so that students work at the level of the paragraph rather than the isolated sentence. A separate answer key is also available.

❖ *53rd Street Writer* is a word-processing program (IBM or Macintosh) that includes an on-line *Little, Brown Compact Hand-*

book and *Documentor*, which helps students put citations in correct MLA or APA form. The on-line handbook is also available separately for use with other word-processing programs.

❖ *The Writer's Workshop* is an on-line writing aid for students as they compose essays, arguments, and research papers. Like *53rd Street Writer*, it is accompanied by an on-line handbook and *Documentor* and is available for both IBM and Macintosh computers.

❖ Several references can be packaged with the handbook: *The Oxford American Dictionary*, a hardcover desk dictionary, and the paperback *Funk & Wagnalls Standard Dictionary*, *Roget's Thesaurus*, *Collins Gem Dictionary*, and *Collins Gem Thesaurus*.

❖ The HarperCollins Resources for Instructors and for Students include a range of helpful supplements, such as additional exercises, assessment packages, and an essay anthology.

Acknowledgments

More than two dozen instructors wrote detailed reviews or answered extensive questionnaires to help me revise *The Little, Brown Compact Handbook*. For their thoughtful advice, I thank Cathryn Amdahl, Harrisburg Area Community College; Ruth A. Anderson, Grossmont College; Elsie E. Bock, Lynchburg College; Phyllis Brown Burke, Hartnell College; Joseph Colavito, Northwestern State University of Louisiana; Judith A. Callarman, Cisco Junior College; Suzanne B. Dixon, Carroll Community College; Marilyn M. Fisher, Central Virginia Community College; Phyllis Gleason, Middlesex Community College; John K. Hanes, Duquesne University; Carl E. Henderson, Harford Community College; James M. Ivory, University of North Carolina, Chapel Hill; Janet C. Joseph, Baldwin-Wallace College; Richard J. Larschan, University of Massachusetts, Dartmouth; Terry Long, Ohio State University, Newark; William MacPherson, Essex County College; James Marsden, Bryant College; Sylvia A. Martin, Black Hawk College; Anne Maxham-Kastrinos, Washington State University; Barbara Moran, University of San Francisco; Jerry Olsen, Middlesex Community College; Anne M. Paye, Foothill College; Tami Phenix, University of Cincinnati; Fern Rathsuk, Concordia University; David Sabrio, Texas A&M University, Kingsville; Jocelyn Siler, University of Montana; Kathy O. Smith, Indiana University, Bloomington; Neal Snidow, Butte Community College; Sheila D. Willard, Middlesex Community College; James D. Williams, University of North Carolina, Chapel Hill.

In addition, I'm grateful to Sylvan Barnet, Tufts University, for the new chapter "Reading and Writing About Literature." The chapter abridges a longer chapter in *The Little, Brown Handbook*, which was itself adapted from Sylvan Barnet's *A Short Guide to Writing About Literature*, *Introduction to Literature* (with Morton Berman and William Burto), and *Literature for Composition* (with Morton Berman, William Burto, and Marcia Stubbs).

After several books in various editions, I have come to rely on "my" team at HarperCollins, a talented group that keeps me almost constantly occupied, but not without giving as much themselves. To Patricia Rossi, Ann Stypuloski, Steven Pisano, and Dorothy Bungert, once again, my thanks.

I

The Writing Process and Paragraphs

I

The Writing Process and Paragraphs

❖

1 Subject, Purpose, and Audience

No matter what you are writing, you will be working within a writing situation: writing on a particular subject, for a particular purpose, to a particular audience of readers.

1a Finding your subject

A subject for writing has several basic requirements:

❖ It should be suitable for the assignment.
❖ It should be neither too general nor too limited for the length of paper and deadline assigned.
❖ It should be something you care about.

When you receive a writing assignment, ask yourself these questions about it:

❖ What's wanted from you? Many writing assignments contain words such as *report, summarize, compare, define, analyze, interpret, evaluate,* or *argue.* These words specify the way you are to approach your subject and what your purpose is. (See 1b.)
❖ For whom are you writing? Some assignments will specify your readers, but usually you will have to figure out for yourself whether your audience is your boss, the college community, your instructor, or some other group or individual. (See 1c.)
❖ What kind of research is required? Sometimes an assignment specifies the kinds of sources you are expected to consult, and you can use such information to choose your subject. (If you are unsure whether research is expected, check with your instructor.)
❖ What is the length of the paper? The deadline? Having a week to write three pages or three weeks to write six pages can make a big difference in the subject you select.

Considering these questions will help set some boundaries for your choice of subject. Then, within those boundaries, you can explore your own interests and experiences to narrow the subject so that you can cover it adequately within the space and time assigned. Federal aid to college students could be the subject of a book; the kinds of aid available or why the government should increase aid would be a more appropriate subject for a four-page paper due in a week. Here are some guidelines for narrowing broad subjects:

1b

- ❖ Break your broad subject into as many specific topics as you can think of. Make a list.
- ❖ For each topic that interests you and fits the assignment, roughly sketch out the main ideas and consider how many paragraphs or pages of specific facts, examples, and other details you would need to pin those ideas down. This thinking should give you at least a vague idea of how much work you'd have to do and how long the resulting paper might be.
- ❖ If an interesting and appropriate topic is still too broad, break it down further and repeat the previous step.

1b Defining your purpose

Your PURPOSE in writing is your chief reason for communicating something about your subject to a particular audience of readers. Most writing you do will have one of four main purposes. Occasionally, you will *entertain* readers or *express yourself*—your feelings or ideas—to readers. More often you will *explain* something to readers or *persuade* readers to respect and accept, and sometimes even act on, your well-supported opinion. These purposes often overlap in a single essay, but usually one predominates. And the dominant purpose will influence your particular slant on your subject, the details you choose, and even the words you use.

Many writing assignments narrow the purpose by using a signal word, such as the following:

- ❖ *Report:* Survey, organize, and objectively present the available evidence on the subject.
- ❖ *Summarize:* Concisely state the main points in a text, argument, theory, or other work.
- ❖ *Discuss:* Examine the main points, competing views, or implications of the subject.
- ❖ *Compare and contrast:* Explain the similarities and differences between two subjects. (See also p. 39.)
- ❖ *Define:* Specify the meaning of a term or a concept—distinctive characteristics, boundaries, and so on. (See also pp. 37–38.)
- ❖ *Analyze:* Identify the elements of the subject, and discuss how they work together. (See also p. 38.)
- ❖ *Interpret:* Infer the subject's meaning or implications.
- ❖ *Evaluate:* Judge the quality or significance of the subject, considering pros and cons. (See also pp. 212–13.)
- ❖ *Argue:* Take a position on the subject, and support your position with evidence. (See also pp. 271–81.)

1c   Considering your audience

The readers likely to see your work—your audience—may influence your choice of subject and your definition of purpose. Your audience certainly will influence what you say about your subject and how you say it—for instance, how much background information you give and whether you adopt a serious or a friendly tone.

The box below contains questions that can help you analyze and address your audience. Depending on your writing situation, some questions will be more helpful than others. For instance, your readers' knowledge of your topic will be important to consider if

---

Questions about audience

- ❖ Who *are* my readers?
- ❖ Why are readers going to read my writing? What will they expect?
- ❖ What do I want readers to know or do after reading my work, and how should I make that clear to them?
- ❖ How will readers' characteristics, such as those below, influence their attitudes toward my topic?

  Age or sex
  Occupation: students, professional colleagues, etc.
  Social or economic role: adult children, car buyers, potential employers, etc.
  Economic or educational background
  Ethnic background
  Political, religious, or moral beliefs and values
  Hobbies or activities

- ❖ What do readers already know and *not* know about my topic? How much do I have to tell them?
- ❖ If my topic involves specialized language, how much should I use and define?
- ❖ What ideas, arguments, or information might surprise readers? excite them? offend them? How should I handle these points?
- ❖ What misconceptions might readers have of my topic and/or my approach to the topic? How can I dispel these misconceptions?
- ❖ What is my relationship to my readers? What role and tone should I assume? What role do I want readers to play?
- ❖ What will readers do with my writing? Should I expect them to read every word from the top, to scan for information, or to look for conclusions? Can I help them with a summary, headings, illustrations, or other special features?

2b

you are trying to explain how a particular computer program works, whereas readers' beliefs and values may be important if you are trying to gather support for a change in welfare policy.

2   Invention

Writers use a host of techniques to help invent or discover ideas and information about their subjects. *Whichever of the following techniques you use, do your work in writing, not just in your head.* Your ideas will be retrievable, and the very act of writing will lead you to fresh insights.

2a   Keeping a journal

A journal, or diary of ideas, gives you a place to record your reactions to courses, conversations, movies, and books. It gives you an outlet from the pressures of family, friends, studies, and work. It gives you a private place to find out what you think.

If you write in a journal every day, even for just a few minutes, the routine will loosen up your writing muscles and improve your confidence. And the writing you produce can supply ideas when you are seeking an essay subject or developing an essay. For example, two entries about arguments with your brother may suggest a psychology paper on sibling relations.

2b   Observing your surroundings

Sometimes you can find a good subject or good ideas by looking around you, not in the half-conscious way most of us move from place to place in our daily lives but deliberately, all senses alert. On a bus, for instance, are there certain types of passengers? What seems to be on the driver's mind? To get the most from observation, you should have a tablet and pen or pencil handy for notes and sketches. Back at your desk, study your notes and sketches for oddities or patterns that you'd like to explore further.

2c Freewriting and brainstorming

A good way to find or explore a subject is to write without stopping for a certain amount of time (say, ten minutes) or to a certain length (say, one page). The goal of this FREEWRITING is to generate ideas and information from *within* yourself by going around the part of your mind that doesn't want to write or can't think of anything to write. You let words themselves suggest other words. *What* you write is not important; that you *keep* writing is. Don't stop, even if that means repeating the same words until new words come. Don't go back to reread, don't censor ideas, and don't stop to edit: grammar, punctuation, and spelling are irrelevant at this stage.

The physical act of freewriting may give you access to ideas you were unaware of. For example, the following freewriting by a student, Robert Benday, gave him the subject of writing as a disguise.

> Write to write. Seems pretty obvious, also weird. What to gain by writing? never anything before. Writing seems always—always— Getting corrected for trying too hard to please the teacher, getting corrected for not trying hard enuf. Frustration, nail biting, sometimes getting carried away making sentences to tell stories, not even true stories, *esp.* not true stories, *that* feels like creating something. Writing just pulls the story out of me. The story lets me be someone else, gives me a disguise.

(A later phase of Benday's writing process appears on p. 9.)

Freewriting is also useful to discover ideas about a specific subject, as the following example shows. The writer, Terry Perez, had an assignment to explore some aspect of cultural diversity in the United States. She had just read a statement by the writer Ishmael Reed that conflict among cultural groups "is played up and often encouraged by the media."

> Cultural diversity in the media? The media has a one track mind, cultural diversity is bad. Like Reed says the media makes a big deal of conflict between racial and ethnic groups, it's almost constant in the papers, on TV. TV especially—the news vs. all the white bread programs, the sitcoms and ads. That's a whole other view—*no* conflict, *no* tension. No diversity. So we have all people the same except when they're not, then they're at war. Two unreal pictures.

(An outline and drafts of Perez's paper appear on pp. 14, 17–18, 21–22, and 23–26.)

A method similar to freewriting is BRAINSTORMING—focusing intently on a subject for a fixed amount of time (say, fifteen minutes), pushing yourself to list every idea and detail that comes to mind. Like freewriting, brainstorming requires turning off your internal editor so that you keep moving ahead. Here is an example by a student, Johanna Abrams, on what a summer job can teach:

> summer work teaches—
>> how to look busy while doing nothing
>> how to avoid the sun in summer
>> seriously: discipline, budgeting money, value of money
> which job? Burger King cashier? baby sitter? mail-room clerk?
> mail room: how to sort mail into boxes: this is learning??
> how to survive getting fired—humiliation, outrage
> Mrs. King! the mail-room queen as learning experience
> the shock of getting fired: what to tell parents, friends?
> Mrs. K was so rigid—dumb procedures
> initials instead of names on the mail boxes—confusion!
> Mrs. K's anger, resentment: the disadvantages of being smarter than your boss
> The odd thing about working in an office: a world with its own rules for how to act
> what Mr. D said about the pecking order—big chick (Mrs. K) pecks on little chick (me)
> a job can beat you down—make you be mean to other people

(A later phase of Abrams's writing process appears on p. 13.)

2d   Clustering

Like freewriting and brainstorming, CLUSTERING also draws on free association and rapid, unedited work. But it emphasizes the relations between ideas by combining writing and nonlinear drawing. When clustering, you radiate outward from a center point—your topic. When an idea occurs, you pursue related ideas in a branching structure until they seem exhausted. Then you do the same with other ideas, staying open to connections, continuously branching out or drawing arrows.

The example of clustering on the next page shows how Robert Benday used the technique for ten minutes to expand on the topic of writing as a means of disguise, an idea he arrived at through freewriting (see the preceding page).

2e   Asking questions

Asking yourself a set of questions about your subject—and writing out the answers—can help you look at the topic objectively and see fresh possibilities in it.

2e

CLUSTERING

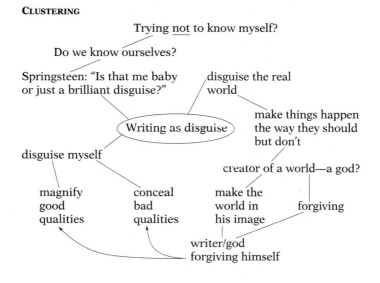

1. Journalist's questions

A journalist with a story to report poses a set of questions:

Who was involved?
What happened, and what were the results?
When did it happen?
Where did it happen?
Why did it happen?
How did it happen?

These questions can also be useful in probing an essay subject, especially if you are telling a story or examining causes and effects.

2. Questions about patterns

We think about and understand a vast range of subjects through patterns such as narration, classification, and comparison and contrast. Asking questions based on the patterns can help you view your topic from many angles. Sometimes you may want to develop an entire essay using just one pattern.

How did it happen? (Narration)
How does it look, sound, feel, smell, taste? (Description)
What are examples of it or reasons for it? (Illustration or support)
What is it? What does it encompass, and what does it exclude?
　(Definition)

What are its parts or characteristics? (Division or analysis)
What groups or categories can it be sorted into? (Classification)
How is it like, or different from, other things? (Comparison and
    contrast)
Why did it happen? What results did or could it have? (Cause-and-
    effect analysis)
How do you do it, or how does it work? (Process analysis)

For more on these patterns, including paragraph-length examples,
see pages 35–40.

2f   Reading and thinking critically

Even when reading is not required by an assignment, it can
help you locate or develop your topic by introducing you to ideas
you didn't know or expanding on what you do know.

People often read passively, absorbing content like blotters, not
interacting with it. To read for ideas, you need to be more active,
probing text and illustrations with your mind. In other words, you
need to *think critically* while you read, questioning the material,
testing it against what you know, building on what it says and what
you yourself think. In this context *critical* does not mean "negative"
but "skeptical," "exacting," "creative."

To read actively and critically, read with a pen or pencil in your
hand. Mark up the material if it's yours, or make separate notes if
it's borrowed. Question what you don't understand or find doubt-
ful. Agree or disagree with the writer's ideas. Highlight or quote
passages you find especially interesting or important. With such
notes you create a record of what the material makes *you* think,
and you begin to organize the material for your own purposes. (For
more on critical reading, see pp. 211–13.)

NOTE Whenever you use the information or ideas of others in
your writing, you must acknowledge your sources in order to avoid
the serious offense of plagiarism. (See pp. 217–19.)

3   Thesis and Organization

Shaping your raw material helps you clear away unneeded
ideas, spot possible gaps, and energize your topic. The two main
operations in shaping material are focusing on a thesis (3a) and organizing ideas (3b).

3a   Conceiving a thesis sentence

3a

Your readers will expect your essay to be focused on and controlled by a main idea, or THESIS. In your final draft you may express this idea in a thesis sentence (or sentences), often at the end of your introduction. A THESIS SENTENCE helps readers in several ways:

- ❖ It narrows the topic to a single idea that you want readers to gain from your essay.
- ❖ It asserts something about the topic, conveying your purpose for writing and your opinion of the topic.
- ❖ It *may* provide a concise preview of how you will arrange your ideas in the essay.

All three thesis sentences below fulfill the first two functions; the last example also fulfills the third.

TOPIC	THESIS SENTENCE
Why the federal government should aid college students	If it hopes to win the technological race, the United States must make higher education possible for any student who qualifies academically.
What public relations is	Although most of us are unaware of the public relations campaigns directed at us, they can significantly affect the way we think and live.
The effects of strip-mining	Strip-mining should be tightly trolled in this region to reduce its pollution of water resources, its permanent destruction of the land, and its devastating effects on people's lives.

A thesis will not usually leap fully formed into your head: you will have to develop and shape the idea as you develop and shape your essay. Still, try to draft a thesis sentence when you have a fairly good stock of ideas. Then it can help you start drafting and can serve as a point of reference when changes inevitably occur.

While you are developing your thesis sentence, ask questions about each attempt:

- ❖ Does it make an *assertion* about your topic?
- ❖ Does it convey your *purpose* and your *opinion?*
- ❖ Is it *limited* to an assertion of only one idea?
- ❖ Is the assertion *specific?*

3b Organizing your ideas

Most essays share a basic pattern of introduction (states the subject), body (develops the subject), and conclusion (pulls the essay's ideas together). Introductions and conclusions are discussed on pages 40–42. Within the body, material may be arranged in an almost infinite number of ways, the choice depending on your subject, purpose, and audience.

1. The general and the specific

To organize material for an essay, you need to distinguish general and specific ideas and see the relations between ideas. GENERAL and SPECIFIC refer to the number of instances or objects included in a group signified by a word. *Plant,* for example, is general because it encompasses all kinds of plants; *rose* is specific because it refers to a certain kind of plant; and *Uncle Dan's prize-winning American Beauty rose* is even more specific. As you arrange your material, pick out the general ideas and then the specific points that support them. Set aside points that seem irrelevant to your key ideas.

2. Outlines

It's not essential to craft a detailed outline before you begin drafting an essay; in fact, too detailed a plan could prevent you from discovering ideas while you draft. Still, even a rough scheme can show you patterns of general and specific, suggest proportions, and highlight gaps or overlaps in coverage.

There are many different kinds of outlines, some more flexible than others.

Scratch or informal outline

A scratch or informal outline includes key general points in the order they will be covered. It may also suggest the specific evidence for them.

Here is Terry Perez's scratch outline for her essay on diversity in the media:

THESIS SENTENCE

Judging from the unrealistic images projected by the media, the United States is a nation either of constant ethnic conflict or of untroubled homogeneity.

Organizing your ideas 13

3b

SCRATCH OUTLINE

Media images—
    Ethnic conflict
        —news stories—examples
        —the real story—examples
    Sameness—homogeneity
        —TV sitcoms and ads: the happy (white) family
        —the real story—examples

A scratch or informal outline may be all you need to begin drafting. Sometimes, though, it may prove too skimpy a guide, and you may want to use it as a preliminary to a more detailed outline. Indeed, Terry Perez used her scratch outline as a base for a detailed formal outline that gave her an even more definite sense of direction (see p. 14).

Tree diagram

In a tree diagram, ideas and details branch out in increasing specificity. Unlike more linear outlines, this diagram can be supplemented and extended indefinitely, so it is easy to alter. The following example was developed from Johanna Abrams's brainstorming about a summer job (p. 8).

THESIS SENTENCE

Two months working in a large government agency taught me that an office's pecking order should be respected.

TREE DIAGRAM

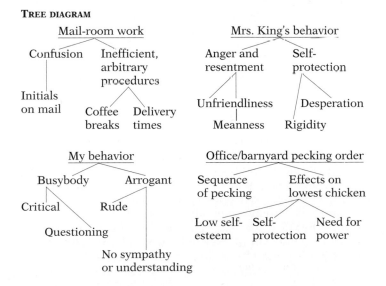

Formal outline

A formal outline not only lays out main ideas and their support but also shows the relative importance of all the essay's elements. Following is Terry Perez's outline, developed from her scratch outline (p. 13). (Perez's first draft from this outline appears on pp. 17–18.)

THESIS SENTENCE

Judging from the unrealistic images projected by the media, the United States is a nation either of constant ethnic conflict or of untroubled homogeneity.

FORMAL OUTLINE

    I. Images of ethnic conflict
       A. News stories
          1. Hispanic-black gang wars
          2. Defaced synagogues
          3. Korean-black disputes
       B. The real story
          1. No war among groups
          2. Coexistence among groups
   II. Images of untroubled homogeneity
       A. Those pictured in TV shows and ads
          1. Mainly white people
          2. Mainly middle-class people
          3. Mainly attractive people
       B. Those missing from TV shows and ads
          1. Ethnic groups
          2. Poor people
          3. Other groups

This example illustrates several principles of outlining that can ensure completeness, balance, and clear relationships.

- ❖ All parts are systematically indented and labeled: Roman numerals (I, II) for primary divisions; indented capital letters (A, B) for secondary divisions; further indented Arabic numerals (1, 2) for supporting examples. (The next level down would be indented further still and labeled with small letters: a, b.)
- ❖ The outline divides the material into several groups. A long list of points at the same level should be broken up into groups.
- ❖ Topics of equal generality appear in parallel headings (with the same indentation and numbering or lettering).
- ❖ All subdivided headings break into at least two parts because a topic cannot logically be divided into only one part.
- ❖ All headings are expressed in parallel grammatical form—in the example, as phrases using a noun or pronoun plus modi-

fiers. This is a topic outline; in a sentence outline all headings are expressed as full sentences.

NOTE Because of its structure, a formal outline can be an excellent tool for analyzing a draft before revising it. See page 19.

3. Unity and coherence

Two qualities of effective writing relate to organization: unity and coherence. When you perceive that someone's writing "flows well," you are probably appreciating these qualities.

To check an outline or draft for UNITY, ask these questions:

❖ Is each section relevant to the main idea (thesis) of the essay?
❖ Within main sections, does each example or detail support the principal idea of that section?

To check your outline or draft for COHERENCE, ask these questions:

❖ Do the ideas follow a clear sequence?
❖ Are the parts of the essay logically connected?
❖ Are the connections clear and smooth?

See also pages 30–35 on unity and coherence in paragraphs.

4 Drafting

Drafting is an occasion for exploration. Don't expect to transcribe solid thoughts into polished prose: solidity and polish will come with revision and editing. Instead, while drafting let the very act of writing help you find and form your meaning.

4a Starting to draft

Beginning a draft sometimes takes courage, even for seasoned professionals. Procrastination may actually help if you let ideas for writing simmer at the same time. At some point, though, you'll have to face the blank paper or computer screen. The following techniques can help you begin:

4b

- Read over what you've already written—notes, outlines, and so on—and immediately start your draft with whatever comes to mind.
- Freewrite (see p. 7).
- Write scribbles or type nonsense until usable words start coming.
- Pretend you're writing to a friend about your topic.
- Conjure up an image that represents your topic—a physical object, a facial expression, two people arguing over something, a giant machine gouging the earth for a mine, whatever. Describe that image.
- Skip the opening and start in the middle. Or write the conclusion.
- Write a paragraph on what you think your essay will be about when you finish it.
- Using your outline, divide your essay into chunks—say, one for the introduction, another for the first example or reason, and so on. Start writing the chunk that seems most eager to be written, the one you understand best or feel most strongly about.

4b   Keeping momentum

Drafting requires momentum: the forward movement opens you to fresh ideas and connections. To keep moving while drafting, try one or more of these techniques:

- Set aside enough time for yourself. (For a brief essay, a first draft is likely to take at least an hour or two.)
- Work in a place where you won't be interrupted.
- Make yourself comfortable.
- If you must stop working, jot a note before leaving the draft, saying what you expect to do next. Then you can pick up where you left off.
- Be as fluid as possible. Spontaneity will allow your attitudes toward your subject to surface naturally in your sentences. It will also make you receptive to ideas and relations you haven't seen before.
- Keep going. Skip over sticky spots; leave a blank if you can't find the right word. If an idea pops out of nowhere but doesn't seem to fit in, quickly jot it down on a separate sheet, or write it into the draft and bracket it for later attention.
- Resist self-criticism. Don't worry about your style, grammar, spelling, and the like. Don't worry what your readers will think. These are very important matters, but save them for revision.

❖ Use your thesis sentence and outline to remind you of your
planned purpose, organization, and content.
❖ But don't feel constrained by your thesis and outline. If your
writing leads you in a more interesting direction, follow.

Write or type your first draft on only one side of the paper,
leave wide margins, and double- or triple-space all lines. Then you
will have room for changes.

4c   Examining a sample first draft

The following is Terry Perez's first draft on the subject of cultural diversity in the media. (Perez's freewriting appears on p. 7 and
her outlines on pp. 13 and 14.) Like most first drafts, this one is
rough, with holes, digressions, and grammatical errors. But it gave
Perez a good start.

                          Title?

    In "America: The Multinational Society," Ishmael Reed

mentions that the communications media sensationalizes the

"conflict between people of different backgrounds." Ei-

ther that, or it depicts Americans as homogeneous. Judg-

ing from the unrealistic images projected by television,

newspapers, and magazines, the U.S. is a nation either of

constant ethnic conflict or untroubled homogeneity.

    It is easy to find examples of the emphasizing of

conflict among ethnic groups. The news is full of stories

of Hispanic gangs fighting black gangs or Korean shopkeep-

ers pitted against black and Hispanic customers. In fact,

New York City, with its dense and ethnically diverse pop-

ulation, regularly supplies stories for other cities' news

media when they run out of local stories of hate and may-

hem. My brother who lives in San Francisco is always com-

plaining about all the New York stories in the news. What

he doesn't realize is that it's not New York's fault, it's

the media's for always playing up the bad news. Bad news

is what the media specializes in--as everyone is always

complaining. When it comes to ethnic relations, this is
certainly the case. All sorts of different people mingle
together peacefully, but not in the media.

   There the only peace belongs to a very narrow band of
people. Especially in television fiction and advertising.
They have usual characteristics: they are white, married
or expecting to be someday, unethnic, white collar, well-
to-do, settled, materialistic, good looking, and thin.
Many, many groups are excluded from this TV type, such as
ethnic groups, poor people, and the handicapped. A certain commercial is typical of TV with the happy prosperous
nuclear family enjoying breakfast together.

   The problem with this media image, with its extremes
of peace and conflict, is that it is untrue. It caters to
the ones who feel that the U.S. should be a "monoculture"
and would be. If only we could battle down the ones who
don't belong or won't. A different picture is possible,
but we aren't getting it.

5   Revising and Editing

During revision—literally "re-seeing"—you shift your focus
outward from yourself and your subject toward your readers, con-
centrating on what will help them respond as you want. It's wise to
revise in at least two stages, one devoted to fundamental meaning
and structure (here called REVISING) and one devoted to word
choice, grammar, punctuation, and other features of the surface
(here called EDITING). Trying to revise and edit in one sweep can be
overwhelming, so each step should be done separately.

5a   Revising

To revise your writing, you have to read it critically (see p. 10),
and that means you have to create some distance between your

draft and yourself. One of the following techniques may help you see your work objectively:

- Take a break after finishing the draft to pursue some other activity. A few hours may be enough; a whole night or day is preferable.
- Ask someone to read and react to your draft.
- Outline your draft. A formal outline, especially, can show where organization is illogical or support is skimpy. (See p. 14.)
- Listen to your draft: read it out loud, read it into a tape recorder and play the tape, or have someone read the draft to you.

Set aside at least as much time to revise your essay as you took to draft it. Plan on going through the draft several times to answer the questions in the checklist below and to resolve any problems you uncover.

Checklist for revision

- What is the central idea, or thesis? Is it expressed?
- Does the body of the essay carry out the purpose and central idea expressed by the thesis sentence (3a)?

    Is the reason for writing apparent, not only in the thesis sentence but throughout the essay?

    If the body of the essay does not carry out the thesis sentence, is the problem more with the thesis sentence (because it does not reflect a new and better direction in the draft) or with the body (because it wanders)?

- Do readers need more information at any point to understand the meaning or appreciate the point of view (1c)?
- Is the essay unified (3b-3)? Does each paragraph and sentence relate clearly to the thesis sentence?
- Is the essay coherent (3b-3)? Is the sequence of ideas clear? Are the relationships within and among parts logical and clear?
- Is each paragraph in the body unified (7a), coherent (7b), and well developed (7c)?
- Does the introduction engage and focus readers' attention (7d-1)? Does the conclusion provide a sense of completion (7d-2)?

A note on titling your essay

The revision stage is a good time to consider a title because attempting to sum up your essay in a phrase can focus your attention sharply on your topic, purpose, and audience.

Here are some suggestions for titling an essay:

❖ A DESCRIPTIVE TITLE is almost always appropriate and is often expected for academic writing. It announces the topic clearly, accurately, and as briefly as possible. The title Terry Perez finally chose, "America's Media Image," is an example. Other examples: "Images of Lost Identity in *North by Northwest*"; "An Experiment in Small-Group Dynamics"; "Why Lincoln Delayed Emancipating the Slaves."

❖ A SUGGESTIVE TITLE—the kind often found in popular magazines—may be appropriate for more informal writing. Examples include "Making Peace" (for an essay on the Peace Corps) and "Royal Pain" (for an essay on Prince Charles of England). For a more suggestive title, Perez might have chosen something like "Distorted Pictures." Such a title conveys the writer's attitudes and main concerns but not the precise topic, thereby pulling readers into the essay to learn more. A source for such a title may be a familiar phrase, a fresh image, or a significant expression from the essay itself.

❖ A title tells readers how big the topic is. For Perez's essay, the title "Watching the Media" or "Cultural Diversity" would have been too broad, whereas "The Media and Cultural Conflict" or "Exclusion in the Media" would have been too narrow.

❖ A title should not restate the assignment or the thesis sentence, as in "What Ishmael Reed Means by Cultural Diversity" or "How I Feel About Cultural Diversity."

For more information on essay titles, see pages 179 (the format of a title in the final paper) and 195 (capitalizing words in a title).

5b   Examining a sample revision

The material below is the first half of Terry Perez's revision (first draft pp. 17–18). Some changes are especially notable. (This list is keyed to the revision by number.)

1. Perez added a descriptive title to give readers a sense of her topic.
2. Perez rewrote and expanded the previous abrupt introduction to give more of a sense of Reed's essay and to make a clearer transition to her additional point about the media (the new sentence beginning *Another false media picture*).
3. Perez added examples and other details to support her general statements. This and the following category of changes occupied most of Perez's attention during revision.

4. In response to a reader's comments, Perez added several concessions and exceptions to balance her strong point of view.
5. Perez cut a digression that her reader had found distracting and irrelevant.

~~Title?~~ America's Media Image   1

Is the United States a "monoculture," a unified, homogeneous   2
society? Many Americans would like it to be or they think that it is
now. But the writer Ishmael Reed says no. His essay is titled "America:
The Multinational Society." In it he speaks out for cultural diversity.
He thinks it makes the nation stronger. In passing he

~~In "America: The Multinational Society," Ishmael Reed~~

mentions that the communications media sensationalize the
                    Another false media picture can be added to Reed's
"conflict between people of different backgrounds." ~~Ei-~~
point. The picture of Americans as socially, economically, and ethnically similar.
~~ther that, or it depicts Americans as homogeneous.~~ Judg-

ing from the unrealistic images projected by television,

newspapers, and magazines, the U.S. is a nation either of

constant ethnic conflict or untroubled homogeneity.

It is easy to find examples of the emphasizing of

conflict among ethnic groups. The news is full of stories
                    swastikas are painted on Jewish synagogues,
of Hispanic gangs fighting black gangs, ~~or~~ Korean shopkeep-   3

ers pitted against black and Hispanic customers. ~~In fact,~~
These are real stories, and all-too-real ethnic conflict should not be covered up. However,
~~New York City, with its dense and ethnically diverse pop-~~   4
these stories are blown out of proportion.
~~ulation, regularly supplies stories for other cities' news~~

~~media when they run out of local stories of hate and may-~~   5

~~hem. My brother who lives in San Francisco is always com-~~

~~plaining about all the New York stories in the news. What~~

~~he doesn't realize is that it's not New York's fault, it's~~

~~the media's for always playing up the bad news. Bad news~~
                                              # E
~~is what the media specializes in--as~~ ¢veryone ~~is~~ always
        that the news media never present enough good news.
complain~~ing~~. When it comes to ethnic relations, this is

certainly the case. ~~All sorts of different people mingle~~

~~together peacefully, but not in the media.~~

Pakistanis, Russians, Mexicans, Chinese, Mayflower descendants, great-   3 *grandchildren of African slaves. All these and more mingle on the nation's streets, attend school together, work together. Integration is very far from complete, severe inequality persists. Real conflict exists. But for the most part, cultural groups are not at war.*   4

5c Editing and proofreading

Editing for style, sense, and correctness may come second to more fundamental revision, but it is far from unimportant. After revising your draft, try the following approaches to editing:

❖ Recopy, retype, or print out your revision so that you can read it easily and have plenty of room for changes.

❖ As you read the new draft, try to imagine yourself encountering it for the first time, as a reader will.

❖ Have a friend read your work. Or, if you share your work in class, listen to the responses of your classmates or instructor.

Checklist for editing

❖ Is the writing clear and effective?

Do the sentences use coordination (8), parallelism (9), and subordination (10) effectively?

Are the sentences varied and detailed (11)?

Are the words appropriate and exact (12)?

Is the writing concise (14)?

❖ Are the sentences grammatically correct?

Are verbs in the correct form (19), tense (20), and mood (21)? Do subjects and verbs agree (23)?

Are pronouns in the correct case (25)? Do pronouns and antecedents agree (26)? Are the antecedents always clear (27)?

Are adjective and adverb forms correct (28)? Are modifiers clear and logical (29)?

Are sentences grammatically complete (30)?

Are sentences punctuated correctly to avoid comma splices and fused sentences (31)?

❖ Is the use of commas, semicolons, colons, apostrophes, and other punctuation correct (33–39)?

❖ Are spelling, hyphenation, capital letters, underlining, and other features correct (41–46)?

❖ As when revising, read the draft aloud, preferably into a tape recorder, listening for awkward rhythms, repetitive sentence patterns, and missing or clumsy transitions.
❖ Be careful to read what you actually see *on the page,* not what you may have intended to write but didn't.

In your editing, work first for clarity and a smooth movement among sentences and then for correctness. Use the questions in the checklist on the facing page to guide your editing, referring to the chapters in parentheses as needed.

After editing your essay, recopy, retype, or print it one last time. Follow the guidelines in Chapter 40 or the wishes of your instructor for an appropriate manuscript form. Be sure to proofread the final essay several times to spot and correct errors. To increase the accuracy of your proofreading, you may need to experiment with ways to keep yourself from relaxing into the rhythm of your prose. Here are a few tricks used by professional proofreaders:

❖ Read the paper aloud, very slowly, and distinctly pronounce exactly what you see.
❖ Place a ruler under each line as you read it.
❖ Read "against copy," comparing your final draft one sentence at a time against the edited draft you copied it from.
❖ Read the essay backward, end to beginning, examining each sentence as a separate unit. (This technique will help keep the content of your writing from distracting you.)

5d Examining a sample editing and a final draft

Excerpts from Terry Perez's edited draft and her complete final draft appear below (first draft pp. 17–18; revision pp. 21–22).

EDITED FIRST PARAGRAPH

Is the United States a "monoculture," a unified, homogeneous society? Many Americans ~~would like it to be~~ think that it is or should be. ~~or they think that it is now.~~ But the writer Ishmael Reed says no. ~~His essay is titled~~ In "America: The Multinational Society ⌃," ~~In it he~~ Reed speaks out for cultural diversity. He thinks it makes the nation stronger. In passing he mentions that the communications media sensationalize the "conflict between people of different backgrounds." To ~~An-~~

Reed's point can be added the media's Other false picture of America,
~~other false media picture of America can be added to Reed's~~
~~point.~~ *t/*he picture of Americans as socially, economically, and ethnically similar. Judging from the unrealistic images projected by television, newspapers, and
magazines, the ~~U.S.~~ *United States* is a nation either of constant ethnic
conflict or ^*of* untroubled homogeneity.

FINAL DRAFT

America's Media Image

Is the United States a "monoculture," a unified,
homogeneous society? Many Americans think that it is or
should be. But the writer Ishmael Reed says no. In
"America: The Multinational Society," Reed speaks out
for cultural diversity. He thinks it makes the nation
stronger. In passing he mentions that the communications
media sensationalize the "conflict between people of
different backgrounds." To Reed's point can be added the
media's other false picture of Americans as socially,
economically, and ethnically similar. Judging from the
unrealistic images projected by television, newspapers, and
magazines, the United States is a nation either of constant
ethnic conflict or of untroubled homogeneity.

It is easy to find examples of the emphasizing of conflict among ethnic groups. The news is full of stories of
Hispanic gangs fighting black gangs, swastikas painted on
Jewish synagogues, Korean shopkeepers pitted against black
and Hispanic customers. It's not that these aren't real
stories, or that all-too-real ethnic conflict should be
covered up. It's just that these stories are blown out of
proportion.

Everyone complains that the news media never present
enough good news. When it comes to ethnic relations, this

is certainly the case. Pakistanis, Russians, Mexicans, Chinese, Mayflower descendants, great-grandchildren of African slaves--all these and more mingle on the nation's streets, attend school together, work together. Granted, integration is very far from complete. Severe inequality persists. Real conflict exists. But for the most part, cultural groups are not at war.

In the media, though, especially television fiction and advertising, the only peace belongs to a very narrow band of people. They are usually white, married or ex-pecting to be someday, unethnic, white collar, well-to-do, settled, materialistic, good looking, and thin. These are but a few of the groups excluded from this TV type (some overlap): Polish-Americans, homeless families, homosexuals, factory workers, Lebanese immigrants, teenage mothers, am-putees, Japanese-Americans, unmarried couples, loners, stay-at-home fathers, transients, mentally handicapped people, elderly pensioners, homely people, fat people, small people.

Exceptions come and go, of course, such as the working-class and overweight Roseanne, the Cosbys, and more recent African-American situation comedies and dramas. However, the norm is easy to recognize. For example, a cereal commercial features a mother who is overseeing her husband's and children's breakfasts. The kitchen is full of the latest appliances and decorations. Everyone is white. Everyone is fit and cute, beautiful, or handsome. Everyone is well dressed and cheerful.

The media's two extremes of peace and conflict create a composite picture of a nation where a "monoculture" is desirable and all but achieved, if only we could battle down the ones who don't belong or won't belong. Imagine a different picture, though. In this one, people coexist who

have diverse backgrounds, interests, incomes, living ar-
rangements, and appearances. Sometimes they stay apart;
sometimes they blend. Sometimes they clash or prey on
each other; sometimes they laugh together. It all happens
now, and we could be watching.

5e Collaborative learning

In many writing courses students work together on writing,
from completing exercises to commenting on each other's work.
This collaborative learning gives experience in reading written
work critically and in reaching others through writing.

If you are a reader of someone else's writing, keep the following principles in mind:

- ❖ Be sure you know what the writer is saying. If necessary, summarize or outline the paper to understand its content.
- ❖ Read closely and critically. (See p. 10.)
- ❖ Unless you have other instructions, address only the most significant problems in the work.
- ❖ Use the revision checklist on page 19 as a guide to what is significant in a piece of writing.
- ❖ Be specific. Explain *why* you are confused or *why* you disagree
  with a conclusion.
- ❖ Remember that you are the reader, not the writer. Resist the
  temptation to edit sentences, add details, or otherwise assume
  responsibility for the paper.
- ❖ Word your comments supportively. Question the writer in a
  way that emphasizes the effect of the work on *you*, the reader
  ("I find this paragraph confusing"), and avoid measuring the
  work against a set of external standards (instead of "This essay
  is poorly organized," say "I have difficulty following your argument").
- ❖ Be positive as well as honest. Instead of saying "This paragraph
  bores me," say "You have an interesting detail here that seems
  buried." And tell the writer what you like about the paper.

When you *receive* the comments of others, whether your classmates or your instructor, you will get more out of the process if you
follow these guidelines:

- ❖ Think of your readers as counselors or coaches who will help
  you see the virtues and flaws in your work and sharpen your
  awareness of readers' needs.

* Read or listen to comments closely.
* Make sure you know what the critic is saying. If you need more information, ask for it.
* Don't become defensive. Letting comments offend you will only erect a barrier to improvement in your writing.
* When comments seem appropriate, revise your work in response to them. You will learn more from the act of revision than from just thinking about changes.
* Though you should be open to suggestions, you are the final authority on your paper. You are free to decline advice when you think it is inappropriate.
* Keep track of problems that recur in your work so that you can give them special attention in new essays.

6 Writing with a Word Processor

A computerized word processor will not think for you, but it can save time and make writing easier. You need not understand computers or have expert typing skills. A user's manual or tutorial will explain the system and the keystrokes for important commands, such as deleting or saving text. You can avoid losing work accidentally by regularly saving or filing what you've written and by making paper back-up copies.

6a Using a word processor for invention and development

All word processors can aid the initial steps of writing. For instance, you can freewrite or brainstorm (see pp. 7–8) and then easily trim or expand the result and even move it directly into a draft. You can free your mind for very creative work by using a technique called INVISIBLE WRITING. Turn the computer screen's brightness control all the way down so that the screen appears blank. The computer will record what you write but keep it from you and thus prevent you from tinkering with your prose. When you're finished freewriting, simply turn up the brightness control to read what you've written and then save or revise it as you see fit.

You can use the computer on a continuing basis to keep a journal (see p. 6) or to make notes on your reading (p. 10). When you are ready to do so, you can transfer journal entries or reading notes (with source information) directly into your draft.

6c

When you come to think about your audience, you can create a standard file of questions by typing the "Questions About Audience" from page 5 into your computer and saving them. For each assignment, duplicate the file and insert appropriate answers between the questions. Save the answers under a new file name, and print a copy for future reference.

A word processor is the ideal tool for shaping and organizing material. Beginning with just a list of ideas, you can isolate the more general points and then use the computer's tab settings to indent the more specific material. Unusable ideas can be deleted; redundant ideas can be merged. Once saved, the outline can be called up and revised as needed to reflect changes in your thinking and writing.

6b   Using a word processor for drafting

Many writers find that a word processor eases the transition from developing ideas to drafting. For instance, you can retrieve notes to the screen and rewrite, delete, or insert as needed.

While drafting, don't stop to correct errors or rewrite—both of which the computer will help you handle easily in a later draft. Use a symbol such as an asterisk (*) to mark gaps or tentative phrasings. Later, you can find these places quickly by instructing the computer to search for the symbol. If it helps, use invisible writing just to keep moving through a draft (see the preceding page).

6c   Using a word processor for revising and editing

The convenience of extensive revising and editing is the greatest advantage of word processing. With a few keystrokes you can add, delete, and move words, lines, and whole passages.

Here are some guidelines for using a word processor as an effective revision tool:

- ❖ Deal with major revisions first: see the revision checklist on page 19. Save editing, formatting the manuscript, and proofreading for later drafts.
- ❖ Use commands for deleting and moving blocks of copy as you would cut and paste a handwritten draft.
- ❖ Save earlier drafts under their own file names in case you need to consult them for ideas or phrasings. Make a duplicate of any draft you want to revise, and work on the duplicate.
- ❖ If you have trouble finding your focus or organizing your

¶
7

paper, print a copy of your entire draft and work on it. Many writers prefer to work on paper copy because it is easier to read and allows a view of the whole. Transferring changes from printed copy to computer is not difficult.

The following guidelines will help you make the most of the machine while editing and proofreading:

❖ Save your drafts on the computer, print your work, and do your editing on a paper copy. Almost everyone finds it much harder to spot errors on the computer screen than on paper. And paper copy may discourage you from overediting to the point where you say less with less life.

❖ After editing, return to the draft in the computer. Either work through the draft line by line or use the search command to find particular words or phrases.

❖ Use the search command as well to find misused words or stylistic problems that tend to crop up in your writing. Such problems might include misused commas; *there are, it is,* and other expletive constructions; *the fact that* and other wordy phrases; and *is, are,* and other forms of *be,* which often occur in wordy constructions and passive sentences. (Programs known as grammar or style checkers can also help identify such problems, but they are too limited to substitute for your own close reading of your work.)

❖ Make sure that you neither omit needed words nor leave in unneeded words when deleting or inserting text on the computer.

❖ If your computer is equipped with one, use a spelling checker to locate errors. Be aware, though, that a spelling checker cannot help with many errors, such as *there* for *their.*

❖ Resist the temptation to view the final draft coming out of the printer as perfect simply because the copy is clean. Always proofread your final draft *carefully.* (See p. 23 for proofreading tips.)

7 Paragraphs

Setting off groups of related sentences in paragraphs with beginning indentions helps you and your readers focus on one idea at a time. Effective paragraphs are unified (7a), coherent (7b), and well developed (7c).

7a   Maintaining paragraph unity

An effective paragraph develops one central idea—in other words, it is UNIFIED. For example:

> Some people really like chili, apparently, but nobody can agree how the stuff should be made. C. V. Wood, twice winner at Terlingua, uses flank steak, pork chops, chicken, and green chilis. My friend Hughes Rudd of CBS News, who imported five hundred pounds of chili powder into Russia as a condition of accepting employment as Moscow correspondent, favors coarse-ground beef. Isadore Bleckman, the cameraman I must live with on the road, insists upon one-inch cubes of stew beef and puts garlic in his chili, an Illinois affectation. An Indian of my acquaintance, Mr. Fulton Batisse, who eats chili for breakfast when he can, uses buffalo meat and plays an Indian drum while it's cooking. I ask you.
>
> —CHARLES KURALT, *Dateline America*

Kuralt's paragraph works because it follows through on the central idea stated in the first sentence, the TOPIC SENTENCE. But what if he had written this way instead?

> Some people really like chili, apparently, but nobody can agree how the stuff should be made. C. V. Wood, twice winner at Terlingua, uses flank steak, pork chops, chicken, and green chilis. My friend Hughes Rudd, who imported five hundred pounds of chili powder into Russia as a condition of accepting employment as Moscow correspondent, favors coarse-ground beef. He had some trouble finding the beef in Moscow, though. He sometimes had to scour all the markets and wait in long lines. For any American used to overstocked supermarkets and department stores, Russia can be quite a shock.

In this altered version, the topic of chili preparation is forgotten midway. In Kuralt's original, by contrast, every sentence after the first develops the topic sentence with examples.

A topic sentence need not always come first in the paragraph, and in some paragraphs the central idea may not be stated at all. But always the idea should govern the paragraph's content as if it were standing guard at the opening.

7b   Achieving paragraph coherence

When a paragraph is COHERENT, readers can see how it holds together: the sentences seem to flow logically and smoothly into one another. Exactly the opposite happens with this paragraph:

¶ coh

7b

The ancient Egyptians were masters of preserving dead people's bodies by making mummies of them. Mummies several thousand years old have been discovered nearly intact. The skin, hair, teeth, finger- and toenails, and facial features of the mummies were evident. It is possible to diagnose the diseases they suffered in life, such as smallpox, arthritis, and nutritional deficiencies. The process was remarkably effective. Sometimes apparent were the fatal afflictions of the dead people: a middle-aged king died from a blow on the head, and polio killed a child king. Mummification consisted of removing the internal organs, applying natural preservatives inside and out, and then wrapping the body in layers of bandages.

The paragraph is hard to read. The sentences lurch instead of gliding from point to point.

The paragraph as it was actually written is much clearer. Not only did the writer arrange information differently; he also built links into his sentences so that they would flow smoothly. The highlighting on the actual paragraph below emphasizes the techniques:

❖ After stating the central idea in a topic sentence, the writer moves to two more specific explanations and illustrates the second with four sentences of examples.
❖ Circled words repeat or restate key terms or concepts.
❖ Boxed words link sentences and clarify relationships.
❖ Underlined phrases are in parallel grammatical form to reflect their parallel content.

Central idea
The ancient Egyptians were masters of preserving dead people's bodies by (making (mummies) of them. [Basically,] (mummifica-

Explanation

tion) consisted of removing the internal organs, applying natural preservatives inside and out, and then wrapping the body in layers of bandages. [And] (the process) was remarkably effective. [Indeed,]

Explanation

(mummies) several thousand years old have been discovered nearly intact. (Their) skin, hair, teeth, finger- and toenails, and facial features are [still] evident. (Their) diseases in life, such as smallpox, arthritis, and nutritional deficiencies, are [still] diagnosable. [Even] (their) fatal afflictions are [still] apparent: a middle-aged king died from a blow on the head; a child king died from polio.

Specific examples

—MITCHELL ROSENBAUM (student), "Lost Arts of the Egyptians"

1. Paragraph organization

A coherent paragraph organizes information so that readers can easily follow along. These are the most common paragraph schemes:

- ❖ GENERAL TO SPECIFIC: sentences downshift from more general statements to more specific ones. (See the paragraph on the preceding page by Rosenbaum.)
- ❖ CLIMACTIC: sentences increase in drama or interest, ending in a climax. (See the paragraph by Lawrence Mayer opposite.)
- ❖ SPATIAL: scans a person, place, or object from top to bottom, from side to side, or in some other way that approximates the way people actually look at things. (See the paragraph by Virginia Woolf on p. 36.)
- ❖ CHRONOLOGICAL: presents events as they occurred in time, earlier to later. (See the paragraph by Kathleen LaFrank on p. 34.)

2. Parallelism

Parallelism helps tie sentences together. In the following paragraph the underlined parallel structures of *She* and a verb link all sentences after the first one. Parallelism also appears *within* many of the sentences. Aphra Behn (1640–89) was the first Englishwoman to write professionally.

> In addition to her busy career as a writer, Aphra Behn also found time to briefly marry and spend a little while in debtor's prison. She found time to take up a career as a spy for the English in their war against the Dutch. She made the long and difficult voyage to Suriname [in South America] and became involved in a slave rebellion there. She plunged into political debate at Will's Coffee House and defended her position from the stage of the Drury Lane Theater. She actively argued for women's rights to be educated and to marry whom they pleased, or not at all. She defied the seventeenth-century dictum that ladies must be "modest" and wrote freely about sex.
>
> —ANGELINE GOREAU, "Aphra Behn"

KEY TERM

PARALLELISM   The use of similar grammatical structures for similar elements of meaning within or among sentences: *The book caused a stir in the media and aroused debate in Congress.* (See also Chapter 9.)

3. Repetition and restatement

Repeating or restating key words helps make a paragraph coherent and also reminds readers what the topic is. In the following paragraph note the underlined repetition of *sleep* and restatement of *adults*.

> Perhaps the simplest fact about sleep is that individual needs for it vary widely. Most adults sleep between seven and nine hours, but occasionally people turn up who need twelve hours or so, while some rare types can get by on three or four. Rarest of all are those legendary types who require almost no sleep at all; respected researchers have recently studied three such people. One of them—a healthy, happy woman in her seventies—sleeps about an hour every two or three days. The other two are men in early middle age, who get by on a few minutes a night. One of them complains about the daily fifteen minutes or so he's forced to "waste" in sleeping.
> —LAWRENCE A. MAYER, "The Confounding Enemy of Sleep"

4. Pronouns

Because pronouns refer to nouns, they can help relate sentences to each other. In the paragraph by Angeline Goreau on the facing page, *she,* substituting for *Aphra Behn,* works just this way.

5. Consistency

Consistency (or the lack of it) occurs primarily in the person and number of nouns and pronouns and in the tense of verbs. Any inconsistencies not required by meaning will interfere with a reader's ability to follow the development of ideas. For example:

SHIFTS IN TENSE

In the Hopi religion, water is the driving force. Since the Hopi lived in the Arizona desert, they needed water urgently for drinking, cooking, and irrigating crops. Their complex beliefs are focused in part on gaining the assistance of supernatural forces in obtaining water. Many of the Hopi kachinas, or spirit essences, were directly concerned with clouds, rain, and snow.

KEY TERMS

PRONOUN   A word that refers to and functions as a noun, such as *I, you, he, she, it, we, they: The patient could not raise her arm.*

TENSE   The form of a verb that indicates the time of its action, such as present (*I run*), past (*I ran*), or future (*I will run*).

SHIFTS IN NUMBER

<u>Kachinas</u> represent spiritually the things and events of the real world, such as cumulus clouds, mischief, cornmeal, and even death. A <u>kachina</u> is not worshipped as a god but regarded as an interested friend. <u>They</u> visit the Hopi from December through July in the form of men who dress in kachina costumes and perform dances and other rituals.

SHIFTS IN PERSON

Unlike the man, the Hopi <u>woman</u> does not keep contact with kachinas through costumes and dancing. Instead, <u>one</u> receives a tihu, or small effigy, of a kachina from the man impersonating the kachina. <u>You</u> are more likely to receive a tihu as a girl approaching marriage, though a child or older woman sometimes receives one, too.

6. Transitional expressions

Transitional expressions such as *therefore, in contrast,* or *meanwhile* can forge specific connections between sentences, as the italicized expressions do in this paragraph:

> Medical science has *thus* succeeded in identifying the hundreds of viruses that can cause the common cold. It has *also* discovered the most effective means of prevention. One person transmits the cold viruses to another most often by hand. *For instance,* an infected person covers his mouth to cough. *Then* he picks up the telephone. *Half an hour later,* his daughter picks up the *same* telephone. *Immediately afterward,* she rubs her eyes. *Within a few days,* she, *too,* has a cold. *And thus* it spreads. To avoid colds, *therefore,* people should wash their hands often and keep their hands away from their faces.
> —KATHLEEN LaFRANK (student), "Colds: Myth and Science"

Here is a list of transitional expressions, arranged by the functions they perform:

TO ADD OR SHOW SEQUENCE

again, also, and, and then, besides, equally important, finally, first, further, furthermore, in addition, in the first place, last, moreover, next, second, still, too.

KEY TERMS

NUMBER   The form of a noun, pronoun, or verb that indicates whether it is singular (one) or plural (more than one): *boy, boys.*

PERSON   The form of a pronoun that indicates whether the subject is speaking (first person: *I, we*), spoken to (second person: *you*), or spoken about (third person: *he, she, it, they*). All nouns are in the third person.

TO COMPARE

also, in the same way, likewise, similarly

TO CONTRAST

although, and yet, but, but at the same time, despite, even so, even though, for all that, however, in contrast, in spite of, nevertheless, notwithstanding, on the contrary, on the other hand, regardless, still, though, yet

TO GIVE EXAMPLES OR INTENSIFY

after all, an illustration of, even, for example, for instance, indeed, in fact, it is true, of course, specifically, that is, to illustrate, truly

TO INDICATE PLACE

above, adjacent to, below, elsewhere, farther on, here, near, nearby, on the other side, opposite to, there, to the east, to the left

TO INDICATE TIME

after a while, afterward, as long as, as soon as, at last, at length, at that time, before, earlier, formerly, immediately, in the meantime, in the past, lately, later, meanwhile, now, presently, shortly, simultaneously, since, so far, soon, subsequently, then, thereafter, until, until now, when

TO REPEAT, SUMMARIZE, OR CONCLUDE

all in all, altogether, as has been said, in brief, in conclusion, in other words, in particular, in short, in simpler terms, in summary, on the whole, that is, therefore, to put it differently, to summarize

TO SHOW CAUSE OR EFFECT

accordingly, as a result, because, consequently, for this purpose, hence, otherwise, since, then, therefore, thereupon, thus, to this end, with this object

7c   Developing paragraphs

An effective, well-developed paragraph always provides the specific information that readers need and expect in order to understand you and to stay interested in what you say. Paragraph length can be a rough gauge of development: anything much shorter than 100 to 150 words may leave readers with a sense of incompleteness.

To develop or shape an idea in a paragraph, one or more of the following patterns may help. (These patterns may also be used to develop entire essays. See pp. 9–10.)

1. Narration

Narration retells a significant sequence of events, usually in the order of their occurrence (that is, chronologically). A narrator is concerned not just with the sequence of events but also with their consequence, their importance to the whole.

> Jill's story is typical for "recruits" to religious cults. She was very lonely in college and appreciated the attention of the nice young men and women who lived in a house near campus. They persuaded her to share their meals and then to move in with them. Between intense bombardments of "love," they deprived her of sleep and sometimes threatened to throw her out. Jill became increasingly confused and dependent, losing touch with any reality besides the one in the group. She dropped out of school and refused to see or communicate with her family. Before long she, too, was preying on lonely college students.
> —HILLARY BEGAS (student), "The Love Bombers"

2. Description

Description details the sensory qualities of a person, scene, thing, or feeling, using concrete and specific words to convey a dominant mood, to illustrate an idea, or to achieve some other purpose.

> The sun struck straight upon the house, making the white walls glare between the dark windows. Their panes, woven thickly with green branches, held circles of impenetrable darkness. Sharp-edged wedges of light lay upon the window-sill and showed inside the room plates with blue rings, cups with curved handles, the bulge of a great bowl, the criss-cross pattern in the rug, and the formidable corners and lines of cabinets and bookcases. Behind their conglomeration hung a zone of shadow in which might be a further shape to be disencumbered of shadow or still denser depths of darkness. —VIRGINIA WOOLF, *The Waves*

3. Illustration or support

An idea may be developed with several specific examples, like those used by Charles Kuralt on page 30, or with a single extended example, as here:

> The language problem that I was attacking loomed larger and larger as I began to learn more. When I would describe in English certain concepts and objects enmeshed in Korean emotion and imagination, I became slowly aware of nuances, of differences between two languages even in simple expression. The remark "Kim entered the house" seems to be simple enough, yet, unless a reader

has a clear visual image of a Korean house, his understanding of the sentence is not complete. When a Korean says he is "in the house," he may be in his courtyard, or on his porch, or in his small room! If I wanted to give a specific picture of entering the house in the Western sense, I had to say "room" instead of house—sometimes. I say "sometimes" because many Koreans entertain their guests on their porches and still are considered to be hospitable, and in the Korean sense, going into the "room" may be a more intimate act than it would be in the English sense. Such problems!

—Kim Yong Ik, "A Book-Writing Venture"

Sometimes you can develop a paragraph by providing your reasons for stating a general idea. For instance:

There are three reasons, quite apart from scientific considerations, that mankind needs to travel in space. The first reason is the need for garbage disposal: we need to transfer industrial processes into space, so that the earth may remain a green and pleasant place for our grandchildren to live in. The second reason is the need to escape material impoverishment: the resources of this planet are finite, and we shall not forgo forever the abundant solar energy and minerals and living space that are spread out all around us. The third reason is our spiritual need for an open frontier: the ultimate purpose of space travel is to bring to humanity not only scientific discoveries and an occasional spectacular show on television but a real expansion of our spirit.

—Freeman Dyson, "Disturbing the Universe"

4. Definition

Defining a complicated, abstract, or controversial term often requires extended explanation. The following definition of the word *quality* comes from an essay asserting that "quality in product and effort has become a vanishing element of current civilization." Notice how the writer pins down her meaning by offering examples and by setting up contrasts with nonquality.

In the hope of possibly reducing the hail of censure which is certain to greet this essay (I am thinking of going to Alaska or possibly Patagonia in the week it is published), let me say that quality, as I understand it, means investment of the best skill and effort possible to produce the finest and most admirable result possible. Its presence or absence in some degree characterizes every man-made object, service, skilled or unskilled labor—laying bricks, painting a picture, ironing shirts, practicing medicine, shoemaking, scholarship, writing a book. You do it well or you do it half-well. Materials are sound and durable or they are sleazy; method is painstaking or whatever is easiest. Quality is achieving or reaching for the highest standard as against being satisfied with the sloppy or fraudulent. It is honesty of purpose as against catering to cheap or sensational sentiment. It does not allow compromise with the second-rate.   —BARBARA TUCHMAN, "The Decline of Quality"

5. Division or analysis

With division or analysis, you separate something into its elements to understand it better—for instance, you might divide a newspaper into its sections, such as national news, regional news, lifestyle, and so on. As in the paragraph below, you may also interpret the meaning and significance of the elements you identify.

> The surface realism of the soap opera conjures up an illusion of "liveness." The domestic settings and easygoing rhythms encourage the viewer to believe that the drama, however ridiculous, is simply an extension of daily life. The conversation is so slow that some have called it "radio with pictures." (Advertisers have always assumed that busy housewives would listen, rather than watch.) Conversation is casual and colloquial, as though one were eavesdropping on neighbors. There is plenty of time to "read" the character's face; close-ups establish intimacy. The sets are comfortably familiar: well-lit interiors of living rooms, restaurants, offices, and hospitals. Daytime soaps have little of the glamour of their prime-time relations. The viewer easily imagines that the conversation is taking place in real time.   —RUTH ROSEN, "Search for Yesterday"

Analysis is a key skill in critical reading of research sources and literature. See pages 211–13 and 282–84.

6. Classification

When you sort many items into groups, you classify the items to see their relations more clearly. For instance:

> In my experience, the parents who hire daytime sitters for their school-age children tend to fall into one of three groups. The first group includes parents who work and want someone to be at home when the children return from school. These parents are looking for an extension of themselves, someone who will give the care they would give if they were at home. The second group includes parents who may be home all day themselves but are too disorganized or too frazzled by their children's demands to handle child care alone. They are looking for an organizer and helpmate. The third and final group includes parents who do not want to be bothered by their children, whether they are home all day or not. Unlike the parents in the first two groups, who care for their children however they can, these parents seek a permanent substitute for themselves.   —NANCY WHITTLE (student), "Modern Parenting"

7. Comparison and contrast

Comparison and contrast may be used separately or together to develop an idea. The following paragraph illustrates one of two common ways of organizing a comparison and contrast: SUBJECT BY SUBJECT, first one subject and then the other.

> Consider the differences also in the behavior of rock and classical music audiences. At a rock concert, the audience members yell, whistle, sing along, and stamp their feet. They may even stand during the entire performance. The better the music, the more active they'll be. At a classical concert, in contrast, the better the performance, the more *still* the audience is. Members of the classical audience are so highly disciplined that they refrain from even clearing their throats or coughing. No matter what effect the powerful music has on their intellects and feelings, they sit on their hands.   —TONY NAHM (student), "Rock and Roll Is Here to Stay"

The next paragraph illustrates the other common organization: POINT BY POINT, with the two subjects discussed side by side and matched feature for feature.

> The first electronic computer, ENIAC, went into operation not even fifty years ago, yet the differences between it and today's home computer are enormous. ENIAC was enormous itself, consisting of forty panels, each two feet wide and four feet deep. Today's PC or Macintosh, by contrast, fits easily on a small table. ENIAC had to be configured by hand, with its programmers taking up to two days to reset switches and cables. Today, the average home user can change programs in an instant. And for all its size and inconvenience, ENIAC was also slow. In its time, its operating speed of 100,000 pulses per second seemed amazingly fast. However, today's home machine can operate at 4 million pulses per second or faster.   —SHIRLEY KAJIWARA (student),
> "The Computers We Deserve"

8. Cause-and-effect analysis

When you use analysis to explain why something happened or what did or may happen, then you are determining causes or effects. In the following paragraph the author looks at the causes of an effect—Japanese collectivism.

> The *shinkansen* or "bullet train" speeds across the rural areas of Japan giving a quick view of cluster after cluster of farmhouses surrounded by rice paddies. This particular pattern did not develop purely by chance, but as a consequence of the technology peculiar to the growing of rice, the staple of the Japanese diet. The growing of rice requires the construction and maintenance of an irrigation

system, something that takes many hands to build. More importantly, the planting and the harvesting of rice can only be done efficiently with the cooperation of twenty or more people. The "bottom line" is that a single family working alone cannot produce enough rice to survive, but a dozen families working together can produce a surplus. Thus the Japanese have had to develop the capacity to work together in harmony, no matter what the forces of disagreement or social disintegration, in order to survive.

—WILLIAM OUCHI, *Theory Z: How American Business Can Meet the Japanese Challenge*

9. Process analysis

When you analyze how to do something or how something works, you explain the steps in a process. For example:

What used to be called "laying on of hands" is now practiced seriously by nurses and doctors. Studies have shown that therapeutic touch, as it is now known, can aid relaxation and ease pain, two effects that may in turn cause physiological healing. A "healer" must first concentrate on helping the patient. Then, hands held a few inches from the patient's body, the healer moves from head to foot. The state of concentration allows the healer to detect energy disturbances in the patient that indicate localized tension, pain, or sickness. With further hand movements, the healer can redirect the energy. Patients report feeling heat from the healer's hands, perhaps indicating an energy transfer between healer and patient.

—LISA KUKLINSKI (student), "Old Ways to Noninvasive Medicine"

7d Writing introductory and concluding paragraphs

1. Introductions

An introduction draws readers from their world into your world.

- ❖ It focuses readers' attention on the topic and arouses their curiosity about what you have to say.
- ❖ It specifies your subject and implies your attitude.
- ❖ Often it states your thesis sentence.
- ❖ It is concise and sincere.

Depending on your purpose and your main idea (thesis), you can use one of the following techniques for opening an essay:

- ❖ State the subject.
- ❖ Use a quotation.
- ❖ Relate an incident.
- ❖ Create a visual image that represents your subject.
- ❖ Ask a question.

- State an opinion.
- Offer a surprising statistic or other fact.
- Outline a view opposite your own.
- Define a word central to your subject.
- Make a historical comparison or contrast.
- Describe a problem or a dilemma.
- In some business or technical writing, summarize your paper.

A very common introduction opens with a statement of the essay's general subject, clarifies or limits the subject in one or more sentences, and then, in the thesis sentence, asserts the point of the essay. (See p. 11 for more on thesis sentences.)

> We Americans are a clean people. We bathe or shower regularly and spend billions of dollars each year on soaps and deodorants to wash away or disguise our dirt and odor. Yet cleanliness is a relatively recent habit with us. From the time of the Puritans until the turn of the twentieth century, bathing in the United States was rare and sometimes even illegal.
> —AMANDA HARRIS (student), "The Cleaning of America"

When writing and revising your introduction, avoid some approaches that are likely to bore readers or make them question your sincerity or control.

- Don't reach back too far with vague generalities or truths, such as those beginning "Throughout human history . . ." or "In today's world. . . ." You may have needed a warm-up paragraph to start drafting, but your readers can do without it.
- Don't start with "The purpose of this essay is . . . ," "In this essay I will . . . ," or any similar flat announcement of your intention or topic.
- Don't refer to the title of the essay in the first sentence—for example, "This is my favorite activity" or "This is a big problem."
- Don't start with "According to Webster . . . " or a similar phrase leading to a dictionary definition. A definition can be an effective springboard to an essay, but this kind of lead-in has become dull with overuse.
- Don't apologize for your opinion or for inadequate knowledge with "I'm not sure if I'm right, but I think . . . ," "I don't know much about this, but . . . ," or similar lines.

2. Conclusions

Your conclusion finishes off your essay and tells readers where you think you have brought them. Usually set off in its own paragraph, the conclusion may consist of a single sentence or a group of sentences. It may take one or more of the following approaches:

- Create a visual image that represents your subject.
- Strike a note of hope or despair.
- Use a quotation.
- Give a symbolic or powerful fact or other detail.
- Recommend a course of action.
- Summarize the paper.
- Echo the approach of the introduction.
- Restate the thesis and reflect on its implications.

The following paragraph concludes the essay on bathing habits whose introduction is on the preceding page. The writer both summarizes her essay and echoes her introduction.

> Thus changed attitudes and advances in plumbing finally freed us to bathe whenever we want. Perhaps partly to make up for our ancestors' bad habits, we have transformed that freedom into a national obsession.
> —AMANDA HARRIS (student), "The Cleaning of America"

Conclusions have several pitfalls you'll want to avoid:

- Don't simply restate your introduction—statement of subject, thesis sentence, and all. Presumably the paragraphs in the body of your essay have contributed something to the opening statements, and it's that something you want to capture in your conclusion. Answer the question "So what?"
- Don't start off in a new direction, with a subject different from or broader than the one your essay has been about.
- Don't conclude more than you reasonably can from the evidence you have presented. If your essay is about your frustrating experience trying to clear a parking ticket, you cannot reasonably conclude that *all* local police forces are too tied up in red tape to be of service to the people.
- Don't apologize for your essay or otherwise cast doubt on it. Don't say, "Even though I'm no expert," or "This may not be convincing, but I believe it's true," or anything similar. Rather, to win your readers' confidence, display confidence.

II

Clarity and Style

❖

II

Clarity and Style

❖

8   Coordination

Use COORDINATION to show that two or more elements in a sentence are equally important in meaning.

❖ Link two main clauses with a comma and a coordinating conjunction, such as *and* or *but*.

Independence Hall in Philadelphia is now restored, but *fifty years ago it was in bad shape.*

coord

8a

❖ Link two main clauses with a semicolon alone or a semicolon and a conjunctive adverb, such as *however*.

The building was standing; however, *it suffered from decay and vandalism.*

❖ Within clauses, link words and phrases with a coordinating conjunction, such as *and* or *or*.

The people and *officials of the nation were indifferent to Independence Hall* or *took it for granted.*

8a   Using coordination to relate equal ideas

Coordination shows the equality between elements, as illustrated above. At the same time that it clarifies meaning, it can also help smooth choppy sentences.

CHOPPY SENTENCES   We should not rely so heavily on oil. Coal and uranium are also overused. We have a substantial energy resource in the moving waters of our rivers. Smaller streams add to the total volume of water. The resource renews itself. Coal and oil are irreplaceable. Uranium is also irreplaceable. The cost of water does not increase much over time. The costs of coal, oil, and uranium rise dramatically.

┌─ KEY TERMS ─────────────────────────────────────

MAIN CLAUSE   A word group that contains a subject and a verb and does not begin with a subordinating word: *The books were expensive.*

COORDINATING CONJUNCTIONS   *And, but, or, nor,* and sometimes *for, so, yet.*

CONJUNCTIVE ADVERBS   Modifiers that describe the relation of the ideas in two clauses, such as *hence, however, indeed,* and *thus.* (See p. 140 for a fuller list.)

IDEAS
COORDINATED

We should not rely so heavily on coal, oil, and uranium, for we have a substantial energy resource in the moving waters of our rivers and streams. Coal, oil, and uranium are irreplaceable and thus subject to dramatic cost increases; water, however, is self-renewing and more stable in cost.

The information in both passages is essentially the same, but the second is shorter and considerably easier to understand because it builds connections among coordinate elements.

8b   Using coordination effectively

Use coordination only to express the *equality* of ideas or details. A string of coordinated elements—especially main clauses—implies that all points are equally important.

EXCESSIVE
COORDINATION

We were near the end of the trip, and the storm kept getting worse, and the snow and ice covered the windshield, and I could hardly see the road ahead, and I knew I should stop, but I kept on driving, and once I barely missed a truck.

Passages with such excessive coordination need editing to emphasize the main points (*the storm kept getting worse* and *I kept on driving*) and to de-emphasize the less important information.

REVISED

As we neared the end of the trip, *the storm kept getting worse*, covering the windshield with snow and ice until I could barely see the road ahead. Even though I knew I should stop, *I kept on driving*, once barely missing a truck. [The revision uses main clauses only for the main ideas, in italics.]

Even within a single sentence, coordination should express a logical equality between ideas.

FAULTY

John Stuart Mill was a nineteenth-century utilitarian, and he believed that actions should be judged by their usefulness or by the happiness they cause. [The two clauses are not separate and equal: the second expands on the first by explaining what a utilitarian such as Mill believed.]

REVISED

John Stuart Mill, *a nineteenth-century utilitarian*, believed that actions should be judged by their usefulness or by the happiness they cause.

9   Parallelism

PARALLELISM is a similarity of grammatical form for similar elements of meaning within a sentence or among sentences.

> The air is dirtied by *factories belching smoke*
>   and
>   *cars spewing exhaust.*

In this example the two italicized phrases have the same function and importance (both specify sources of air pollution), so they also have the same grammatical construction. Parallelism makes form follow meaning.

//
9a

9a   Using parallelism with *and, but, or, nor, yet*

The coordinating conjunctions *and, but, or, nor,* and *yet* always signal a need for parallelism.

> The industrial base is *shifting* and *shrinking.* [Parallel words.]

> Politicians rarely *acknowledge the problem* or *propose alternatives.* [Parallel phrases.]

> Industrial workers are understandably disturbed *that they are losing their jobs* and *that no one seems to care.* [Parallel clauses.]

When sentence elements linked by coordinating conjunctions are not parallel in structure, the sentence is awkward and distracting.

> **NONPARALLEL**   Three reasons why steel companies keep losing money are that their plants are inefficient, high labor costs, and foreign competition is increasing.

> **REVISED**   Three reasons why steel companies keep losing money are *inefficient plants,* high labor costs, and *increasing foreign competition.*

KEY TERM

COORDINATING CONJUNCTIONS Words that connect elements of the same kind and importance: *and, but, or, nor,* and sometimes *for, so, yet.*

NONPARALLEL	Success is difficult even for efficient companies because of the shift away from all manufacturing in the United States <u>and</u> the fact that steel production is shifting toward emerging nations.
REVISED	Success is difficult even for efficient companies because of the shift away from all manufacturing in the United States and *toward steel production in emerging nations.*

All the words required by idiom or grammar must be stated in compound constructions (see also p. 62).

FAULTY	Given training, workers can acquire the skills <u>and</u> interest in other jobs. [Idiom dictates different prepositions with *skills* and *interest.*]
REVISED	Given training, workers can acquire the skills *for* and interest in other jobs.

9b Using parallelism with *both . . . and, either . . . or,* or another correlative conjunction

Correlative conjunctions stress equality and balance between elements. Parallelism confirms the equality.

It is <u>not</u> *a tax bill* <u>but</u> *a tax relief bill,* providing relief <u>not</u> *for the needy* <u>but</u> *for the greedy.*   —FRANKLIN DELANO ROOSEVELT

At the end of the novel, Huck Finn <u>both</u> *rejects society's values by turning down money and a home* <u>and</u> *affirms his own values by setting out for "the territory."*

With correlative conjunctions, the element after the second connector must match the element after the first connector.

NONPARALLEL	Huck Finn learns <u>not only</u> that human beings have an enormous capacity for folly <u>but also</u> enormous dignity. [The first element includes *that human beings have;* the second element does not.]
REVISED	Huck Finn learns that human beings have *not only an enormous capacity for folly* but also enormous dignity. [Repositioning *not only* makes the two elements parallel.]

KEY TERM

CORRELATIVE CONJUNCTIONS   Pairs of words that connect elements of the same kind and importance, such as *both . . . and, either . . . or, neither . . . nor, not . . . but, not only . . . but also, whether . . . or.*

9c   Using parallelism with lists and outlines

The items in a list or outline are coordinate and should be parallel. Parallelism is essential in a formal topic outline (pp. 14–15).

FAULTY	IMPROVED
Changes in Renaissance England	Changes in Renaissance England
1. An extension of trade routes	1. Extension of trade routes
2. Merchant class became more powerful	2. Increasing power of the merchant class
3. The death of feudalism	3. Death of feudalism
4. Upsurging of the arts and sciences	4. Upsurge of the arts and sciences
5. Religious quarrels began	5. Rise of religious quarrels

10   Subordination

Use SUBORDINATION to indicate that some elements in a sentence are less important than others for your meaning. Usually, the main idea appears in the main clause, and supporting details appear in subordinate structures such as the following:

❖ Subordinate clauses beginning with *although, because, if, who (whom), that, which,* or another subordinating word.

Although production costs have declined, they are still high.
Costs, *which include labor and facilities,* are difficult to control.

❖ Phrases.

Despite some decline, production costs are still high.
Costs, *including labor and facilities,* are difficult to control.

KEY TERMS

MAIN CLAUSE   A word group that contains a subject and a verb and does not begin with a subordinating word: *Words can do damage.*

SUBORDINATE CLAUSE   A word group that contains a subject and a verb, begins with a subordinating word such as *because* or *who,* and is not a question: *Words can do damage when they hurt feelings.* (See pp. 77 and 137 for fuller lists of subordinating words.)

PHRASE   A word group that lacks a subject or verb or both: *Words can do damage by hurting feelings.*

sub
10a

❖ Single words.

Declining costs have not matched prices.
Labor costs are difficult to control.

10a Emphasizing main ideas

A string of main clauses can make everything in a passage seem equally important. Subordination with words, phrases, or subordinate clauses will highlight what's important.

STRING OF MAIN CLAUSES	In recent years computer prices have dropped, and production costs have dropped more slowly, and computer manufacturers have had to struggle, for their profits have been shrinking.
REVISED	*Because* production costs have dropped more slowly *than prices* in recent years, computer manufacturers have had to struggle *with shrinking profits.*

Generally, subordinate clauses give the most emphasis to secondary information, phrases give less, and single words give the least.

10b Using subordination effectively

Use subordination only for the less important information in a sentence.

FAULTY	Ms. Angelo was in her first year of teaching, although she was a better instructor than others with many years of experience. [The sentence suggests that Angelo's inexperience is the main idea, whereas the writer intended to stress her skill *despite* her inexperience.]
REVISED	Although Ms. Angelo was in her first year of teaching, *she was a better instructor than others with many years of experience.*

Subordination loses its power to organize and emphasize information when too much loosely related detail crowds into one long sentence.

OVERLOADED	The boats that were moored at the dock when the hurricane, which was one of the worst in three decades, struck were ripped from their moorings, because the owners had not been adequately pre-

pared, since the weather service had predicted the storm would blow out to sea, which they do at this time of year.

REVISED   Struck by one of the worst hurricanes in three decades, *the boats at the dock were ripped from their moorings. The owners were unprepared* because the weather service had said that hurricanes at this time of year blow out to sea. [The details are sorted into two sentences, each with its own main clause.]

11 Variety and Details

Writing that's interesting as well as clear has at least two features: the sentences vary in length and structure, and they are well textured with details.

11a Varying sentence length

In most contemporary writing, sentences tend to vary from about ten to about forty words, with an average of between fifteen and twenty-five words. If your sentences are mostly at one extreme or the other, your readers may have difficulty focusing on main ideas and seeing the relations among them.

- ❖ If most of your sentences contain thirty-five words or more, you probably need to break some up into shorter, simpler sentences.
- ❖ If most of your sentences contain fewer than ten or fifteen words, you probably need to add details to them (p. 53) or combine them through coordination (p. 45) and subordination (p. 49).

11b Varying sentence structure

A passage will be monotonous if all its sentences follow the same pattern, like soldiers marching in a parade. Try these techniques for varying structure.

1. Subordination

A string of main clauses in simple or compound sentences can be especially plodding.

MONOTONOUS   The moon is now drifting away from the earth. It moves away at the rate of about one inch a year. Our days on earth are getting longer, and they grow a thousandth of a second longer every century. A month will someday be forty-seven of our present days long, and we might eventually lose the moon altogether. Such great planetary movement rightly concerns astronomers, but it need not worry us. It will take 50 million years.

var

11b

Enliven such writing—and make the main ideas stand out—by expressing the less important information in subordinate clauses and phrases. In the revision below, italics indicate subordinate structures that used to be main clauses.

REVISED   The moon is now drifting away from the earth *at the rate of about one inch a year. At the rate of a thousandth of a second every century,* our days on earth are getting longer. A month will someday be forty-seven of our present days long, *if we don't eventually lose the moon altogether.* Such great planetary movement rightly concerns astronomers, but it need not worry us. It will take 50 million years.

2. Varied sentence beginnings

Another cause of monotony is an unbroken sequence of sentences beginning with their subjects.

MONOTONOUS   The lawyer cross-examined the witness for two days. The witness had expected to be dismissed within an hour and was visibly irritated. He did not cooperate. He was reprimanded by the judge.

KEY TERMS

MAIN CLAUSE   A word group that contains a subject and a verb and does not begin with a subordinating word: *Tourism is an industry. It brings in over $2 billion a year.*

SUBORDINATE CLAUSE   A word group that contains a subject and verb, begins with a subordinating word such as *because* or *who*, and is not a question: *Tourism is an industry that brings in over $2 billion a year.* (See pp. 77 and 137 for fuller lists of subordinating words.)

PHRASE   A word group that lacks a subject or verb or both: *Tourism is an industry valued at over $2 billion a year.*

Simply beginning some of these sentences with a modifier or conjunction dramatically improves readability.

> **REVISED**   *For two days,* the lawyer cross-examined the witness. *Expecting to be dismissed within an hour,* the witness was visibly irritated. He did not cooperate. *Indeed,* he was reprimanded by the judge.

The italicized expressions represent the most common choices for varying sentence beginnings.

❖ Adverb modifiers, such as *For two days* (modifies the verb *cross-examined*).

❖ Adjective modifiers, such as *Expecting to be dismissed within an hour* (modifies *witness*).

❖ Transitional expressions, such as *Indeed.* (See pp. 34–35 for a list of such expressions.)

11c

3. Varied word order

Occasionally, you can vary a sentence and emphasize it at the same time by inverting the usual order of parts:

> A dozen witnesses testified for the prosecution, and the defense attorney barely questioned eleven of them. *The twelfth, however, he grilled.* [Normal word order: *He grilled the twelfth, however.*]

Inverted sentences used without need are artificial. Use them only when emphasis demands.

11c   Adding details

Relevant details such as facts and examples create the texture and life that keep readers awake and help them grasp your meaning. For instance:

> **FLAT**   Constructed after World War II, Levittown, New York, consisted of thousands of houses in two basic styles. Over the decades, residents have altered the houses so dramatically that the original styles are often unrecognizable.

> **DETAILED**   Constructed *on potato fields* after World War II, Levittown, New York, consisted of *more than 17,000* houses in *Cape Cod and ranch* styles. Over the decades, residents have *added expansive front porches, punched dormer windows through roofs, converted garages to sun porches, and otherwise* altered the houses so dramatically that the original styles are often unrecognizable.

12 Appropriate and Exact Words

The clarity and effectiveness of your writing will depend greatly on the use of words that are appropriate for your writing situation (12a) and that express your meaning exactly (12b).

12a Choosing the appropriate word

Appropriate words suit your writing situation—your subject, purpose, and audience. In most college and career writing you should rely on what's called STANDARD ENGLISH, the written English normally expected and used in schools, businesses, government, and other places where people of diverse backgrounds must communicate with one another. Standard English is "standard" not because it is better than other forms of English but because it is accepted as the common language, much as dimes and quarters are accepted as the common currency.

The vocabulary of standard English is huge, allowing expression of an infinite range of ideas and feelings; but it does exclude words that only some groups of people use, understand, or find inoffensive. Some of these more limited vocabularies should be avoided altogether; others should be used cautiously and in relevant situations, as when aiming for a special effect with an audience you know will appreciate it. Whenever you doubt a word's status, consult a dictionary.

1. Dialect

Like many countries, the United States includes scores of regional, social, or ethnic groups with their own distinct DIALECTS, or versions of English: standard English, Black English, Appalachian English, and Creole are examples. All the dialects of English share many features, but each also has its own vocabulary, pronunciation, and grammar.

If you speak a dialect of English besides standard English, you need to be careful about using your dialect in situations where standard English is the norm, such as in academic or business writing. Otherwise, your readers may not understand your meaning, or they may perceive your usage as incorrect. (Dialects are not wrong in themselves, but forms imported from one dialect into another may still be perceived as wrong.)

Your participation in the community of standard English does not mean you should abandon your own dialect. Of course, you will want to use it with others who speak it. You may want to quote it in an academic paper (as when analyzing or reporting conversation in dialect). And you may want to use it in writing you do for yourself, such as notes and drafts, which should be composed as freely as possible. But edit your drafts carefully to eliminate dialect expressions, especially those which dictionaries label "nonstandard," such as *hisn, hern, hisself, theirselves, them books, them courses, this here school, that there building, knowed, throwed, hadn't ought, could of, didn't never,* and *haven't no.*

appr
12a

2. Slang

SLANG is the language used by a group, such as musicians or computer programmers, to reflect common experiences and to make technical references efficient. The following example is from an essay on the slang of "skaters" (skateboarders):

> Curtis slashed ultra-punk crunchers on his longboard, while the Rube-man flailed his usual Gumbyness on tweaked frontsides and lofty fakie ollies.   —MILES ORKIN, "Mucho Slingage by the Pool"

Among those who understand it, slang may be vivid and forceful. It often occurs in dialogue, and an occasional slang expression can enliven an informal essay. But most slang is too flippant and imprecise for effective communication, and it is generally inappropriate for college or business writing. Notice the gain in seriousness and precision achieved in the following revision.

> **SLANG**   Many students start out *pretty together* but then *get weird.*
>
> **REVISED**   Many students start out *with clear goals* but then *lose their direction.*

3. Colloquial language

COLLOQUIAL LANGUAGE is the everyday spoken language, including expressions such as *get together, go crazy, do the dirty work,* and *get along.*

When you write informally, colloquial language may be appropriate to achieve the casual, relaxed effect of conversation. An occasional colloquial word dropped into otherwise more formal writing can also help you achieve a desired emphasis. But most colloquial language is not precise enough for college or career writing. In such writing you should generally avoid any words and expressions labeled "informal" or "colloquial" in your dictionary.

| COLLOQUIAL | According to a Native American myth, the Great Creator *had a dog hanging around with him* when he created the earth. |
| REVISED | According to a Native American myth, the Great Creator *was accompanied by a dog* when he created the earth. |

4. Technical words

All disciplines and professions rely on specialized language that allows the members to communicate precisely and efficiently with each other. Chemists, for instance, have their *phosphatides,* and literary critics have their *motifs* and *subtexts.* Without explanation technical words are meaningless to nonspecialists. When you are writing for nonspecialists, avoid unnecessary technical terms and carefully define terms you must use.

5. Indirect and pretentious writing

Small, plain, and direct words are almost always preferable to big, showy, or evasive words. Take special care to avoid euphemisms, double-talk, and pretentious writing.

A EUPHEMISM is a presumably inoffensive word that a writer or speaker substitutes for a word deemed potentially offensive or too blunt, such as *passed away* for *died* or *misspeak* for *lie.* Use euphemisms only when you know that blunt, truthful words would needlessly hurt or offend members of your audience.

A kind of euphemism that deliberately evades the truth is DOUBLE-TALK (also called DOUBLESPEAK or WEASEL WORDS): language intended to confuse or to be misunderstood. Today double-talk is unfortunately common in politics and advertising—the *revenue enhancement* that is really a tax, the *peace-keeping function* that is really war making, the *biodegradable* bags that last decades. Double-talk has no place in honest writing.

Euphemism and sometimes double-talk seem to keep company with PRETENTIOUS WRITING, fancy language that is more elaborate than its subject requires. Choose your words for their exactness and economy. The big, ornate word may be tempting, but pass it up. Your readers will be grateful.

| PRETENTIOUS | Many institutions of higher education recognize the need for youth at the threshold of maturity to confront the choice of life's endeavor and thus require students to select a field of concentration. |
| REVISED | Many colleges and universities force students to make decisions about their careers by requiring them to select a major. |

6. Sexist and other biased language

Even when we do not mean it to, our language can reflect and perpetuate hurtful prejudices toward groups of people, especially racial, ethnic, religious, age, and sexual groups. Insulting language reflects more poorly on the user than on the person or persons designated. Unbiased language does not submit to stereotypes. It refers to people as they would wish to be referred to.

Among the most subtle and persistent biased language is sexist language that distinguishes needlessly between men and women in such matters as occupation, ability, behavior, temperament, and maturity. It can wound or irritate readers, and it indicates the writer's thoughtlessness or unfairness. The box below suggests some ways of eliminating sexist language.

appr

12a

Eliminating sexist language

❖ Avoid occupational or social stereotypes.

SEXIST   The considerate doctor commends a nurse when she provides his patients with good care.

REVISED   The considerate doctor commends a nurse *who provides good care for patients.*

SEXIST   The grocery shopper should save her coupons.

REVISED   *Grocery shoppers* should save *their* coupons.

❖ Avoid using *man* or words containing *man* to refer to all human beings. Here are a few alternatives:

businessman	businessperson
chairman	chair, chairperson
congressman	representative in Congress, legislator
craftsman	craftsperson, artisan
layman	layperson
mankind	humankind, humanity, human beings, humans
manmade	handmade, manufactured, synthetic, artificial
manpower	personnel, human resources
policeman	police officer
salesman	salesperson, sales representative

SEXIST   Man has not reached the limits of social justice.

REVISED   *Humankind* (or *Humanity*) has not reached the limits of social justice.

SEXIST   The furniture consists of manmade materials.

REVISED   The furniture consists of *synthetic* materials.

(continued)

Eliminating sexist language
(continued)

❖ Avoid using the generic *he* to refer to both genders. (See also p. 119.)

SEXIST   The person who studies history knows his roots.

REVISED   The person who studies history knows *his or her* roots.

REVISED   *People* who study history know *their* roots.

❖ Avoid demeaning and patronizing language.

SEXIST   Pushy broads are entering almost every occupation.

REVISED   *Women* are entering almost every occupation.

SEXIST   President Reagan came to Nancy's defense.

REVISED   President Reagan came to *Mrs. Reagan's* defense.

exact

12b

12b   Choosing the exact word

To write clearly and effectively, you will want to find the words that fit your meaning exactly and convey your attitude precisely.

1. The right word for your meaning

All words have one or more basic meanings (called DENOTA-TIONS)—the meanings listed in the dictionary, without reference to emotional associations. If readers are to understand you, you must use words according to their established meanings.

❖ Become acquainted with a dictionary. Consult it whenever you are unsure of a word's meaning.

❖ Distinguish between similar-sounding words that have widely different denotations.

INEXACT   Older people often suffer *infirmaries* [places for the sick].

EXACT   Older people often suffer *infirmities* [disabilities].

Some words, called HOMONYMS, sound exactly alike but differ in meaning: for example, *principal/principle* or *rain/reign/rein*. (See pp. 188–89 for a list of commonly confused homonyms.)

❖ Distinguish between words with related but distinct meanings.

INEXACT   Television commercials *continuously* [unceasingly] inter-
                rupt programming.

EXACT   Television commercials *continually* [regularly] interrupt programming.

In addition to their emotion-free meanings, many words also carry associations with specific feelings. These CONNOTATIONS can shape readers' responses and are thus a powerful tool for writers. The following word pairs have related denotations but very different connotations: *desire/lust, firm/stubborn, enthusiasm/mania, pride/vanity, lasting/endless, daring/reckless.*

Several resources can help you track down words with the exact connotations you want:

exact
12b

❖ A dictionary is essential. Besides providing meanings, spellings, and pronunciations, many dictionaries also list and distinguish among SYNONYMS, or words with approximately the same meanings.

❖ A dictionary of synonyms lists and defines synonyms in groups.

❖ A thesaurus lists synonyms but does not distinguish among them. Because it lacks definitions, a thesaurus can only suggest possibilities; you will still need a dictionary to discover the words' connotations. Avoid using a word from a thesaurus unless you have looked it up and are sure of its appropriateness for your meaning.

2. Concrete and specific words

Clear, exact writing balances abstract and general words, which outline ideas and objects, with concrete and specific words, which sharpen and solidify.

❖ ABSTRACT WORDS name qualities and ideas: *beauty, inflation, management, culture, liberal.* CONCRETE WORDS name things we can know by our five senses of sight, hearing, touch, taste, and smell: *sleek, humming, brick, bitter, musty.*

❖ GENERAL WORDS name classes or groups of things, such as *buildings, weather,* or *birds,* and include all the varieties of the class. SPECIFIC WORDS limit a general class, such as *buildings,* by naming one of its varieties, such as *skyscraper, Victorian courthouse,* or *hut.*

Abstract and general words are useful in the broad statements that set the course for your writing.

The wild horse in America has a *romantic* history.

Relations between the sexes today are only a *little* more *relaxed* than they were in the past.

But such statements need development with concrete and specific detail. Look at how such detail turns a vague sentence into an exact one:

VAGUE   The size of his hands made his smallness real. [How big were his hands? How small was he?]

EXACT   Not until I saw his white, doll-like hands did I realize that he stood a full head shorter than most other men.

3. Idioms

exact

12b

IDIOMS are expressions in any language that do not fit the rules for meaning or grammar—for instance, *put up with*, *plug away at*, *make off with*.

Idiomatic combinations of verbs or adjectives and prepositions can be confusing for both native and nonnative speakers of English. A number of these pairings are listed below.

accords *with*
according *to*
accuse *of* a crime
adapt *from* a source
adapt *to* a situation
agree *on* a plan
agree *to* a proposal
agree *with* a person
angry *with*
capable *of*
charge *for* a purchase
charge *with* a crime
concur *in* an opinion
concur *with* a person
contend *for* a principle
contend *with* a person
differ *about* or *over* a question
differ *from* in appearance
differ *with* a person
disappointed *by* or *in* a person
disappointed *in* or *with* a thing

impatient *at* her conduct
impatient *of* restraint
impatient *for* a raise
impatient *with* a person
independent *of*
infer *from*
inferior *to*
occupied *by* a person
occupied *in* study
occupied *with* a thing
part *from* a person
part *with* a possession
prior *to*
rewarded *by* the judge
rewarded *for* something done
rewarded *with* a gift
similar *to*
superior *to*
wait *at* a place
wait *for* a train, a person
wait *on* a customer

NOTE ESL Those learning English as a second language are justified in stumbling over its prepositions. For instance, *at, in,* and *on* have distinctive uses in expressions of time. *At* precedes actual clock time: *She was born at 8:30. In* precedes a month, year, or century: *She was born in 1975. On* precedes a day or date: *She was born on August 31.*

These and other uses of prepositions, such as in two-word

verbs (see p. 110), must be memorized. The best source for idioms is a good ESL dictionary, such as *Longman Dictionary of Contemporary English* or *Oxford Advanced Learner's Dictionary*.

4. Figurative language

FIGURATIVE LANGUAGE (or a FIGURE OF SPEECH) departs from the literal meanings of words, usually by comparing very different ideas or objects.

> LITERAL   As I try to write, I can think of nothing to say.
>
> FIGURATIVE As I try to write, *my mind is a blank slab of black slate.*

exact

12b

Imaginatively and carefully used, figurative language can capture meaning more precisely and feelingly than literal language.

The two most common figures of speech are the simile and the metaphor. Both compare two things of different classes, often one abstract and the other concrete. A SIMILE makes the comparison explicit and usually begins with *like* or *as*.

> Whenever we grow, we tend to feel it, *as* a young seed must feel the weight and inertia of the earth when it seeks to break out of its shell on its way to becoming a plant.   —ALICE WALKER

A METAPHOR claims that the two things are identical, omitting such words as *like* and *as.*

> A school is a hopper into which children are heaved while they are young and tender; therein they are pressed into certain standard shapes and covered from head to heels with official rubber stamps.
> —H. L. MENCKEN

To be successful, figurative language must be fresh and unstrained, calling attention not to itself but to the writer's meaning. Be especially wary of mixed metaphors, which combine two or more incompatible figures.

> MIXED   Various thorny problems that we try to sweep under the rug continue to bob up all the same.
>
> IMPROVED   Various thorny problems that we try to weed out continue to thrive all the same.

5. Trite expressions

TRITE EXPRESSIONS, or CLICHÉS, are phrases so old and so often repeated that they have become stale. They include the following:

add insult to injury   cool, calm, and collected
better late than never   crushing blow

easier said that done	pride and joy
face the music	ripe old age
few and far between	rude awakening
green with envy	sadder but wiser
hard as a rock	shoulder the burden
heavy as lead	shoulder to cry on
hit the nail on the head	sneaking suspicion
hour of need	stand in awe
ladder of success	strong as an ox
moving experience	thin as a rail
a needle in a haystack	tried and true
point with pride	wise as an owl

To prevent clichés from sliding into your writing, be wary of any expression you have heard or used before. Substitute fresh words of your own, or restate the idea in plain language.

13 Completeness

The most serious kind of incomplete sentence is the grammatical fragment (see Chapter 30). But sentences are also incomplete when they omit one or more words needed for clarity.

13a Writing complete compounds

You may omit words from a compound construction when the omission will not confuse readers.

> Environmentalists have hopes for alternative fuels and (for) public transportation.
>
> Some cars will run on electricity; some (will run) on methane.

Such omissions are possible only when the words omitted are common to all the parts of a compound construction. When the parts differ in any way, all words must be included in all parts.

KEY TERM

COMPOUND CONSTRUCTION   Two or more elements (words, phrases, clauses) that are equal in importance and that function as a unit: *dogs and cats* (words); *Rain fell; streams overflowed* (clauses).

One new car *gets* eighty miles per gallon; some old cars *get* as little as five miles per gallon. [One verb is singular, the other plural.]

Environmentalists believe *in* and work *for* fuel conservation. [Idiom requires different prepositions with *believe* and *work*.]

13b Adding needed words

In haste or carelessness, do not omit small words that are needed for clarity.

> **INCOMPLETE** Regular payroll deductions are a type painless savings. You hardly notice missing amounts, and after period of years the contributions can add a large total.
>
> **REVISED** Regular payroll deductions are a type *of* painless savings. You hardly notice *the* missing amounts, and after *a* period of years the contributions can add *up to* a large total.

Attentive proofreading is the only insurance against this kind of omission. *Proofread all your papers carefully.* See page 23 for tips.

NOTE **ESL** Writers whose first language is not English often omit the articles *a, an,* and *the* because their native language uses such words differently or not at all. For guidelines on when to use articles, see pages 127–30.

---

14 Conciseness

Writing concisely means making every word count toward your meaning. Conciseness is not the same as mere brevity: detail and originality should not be cut with needless words. Rather, the length of an expression should be appropriate to the thought.

14a Cutting or shortening empty words and phrases

Empty words and phrases walk in place, gaining little or nothing in meaning. Many can be cut entirely. The following are just a few examples.

con
14a

Ways to achieve conciseness

WORDY (87 words)

The highly pressured [nature] of critical-
care nursing is [due to the fact that] the patients have life-threatening illnesses. Critical-care nurses must [have possession of]
steady nerves to [care for patients who are
critically ill and very sick.] The nurses must
also have possession of interpersonal
skills. They must also have medical skills.

[It is considered by most health-care pro-
fessionals] that these nurses are essential if
[there is to be improvement of patients]
[who are now in critical care from that
status to the status of intermediate care.]

Cut or shorten empty words and phrases (14a).

Use strong verbs (14e).

Cut unneeded repetition (14b).

Combine sentences (14c).

Rewrite passive sentences as active (14f).

Eliminate expletive constructions (14g).

Cut unneeded repetition (14b), and reduce clauses and phrases (14d).

CONCISE (37 words)

Critical-care nursing is highly pressured because the patients have life-threatening illnesses. Critical-care nurses must possess steady nerves and interpersonal and medical skills. Most health-care professionals consider these nurses essential if patients are to improve to intermediate care.

all things considered	in a manner of speaking
as far as I'm concerned	in my opinion
for all intents and purposes	last but not least
for the most part	more or less

Other empty words can also be cut, usually along with some of the words around them:

area	element	kind	situation
aspect	factor	manner	thing
case	field	nature	type

Still others can be reduced from several words to a single word:

FOR	SUBSTITUTE
at all times	always
at the present time	now
because of the fact that	because
by virtue of the fact that	because
due to the fact that	because
for the purpose of	for
in the final analysis	finally

Cutting or reducing such words and phrases will make your writing move faster and work harder.

con

14c

> **WORDY** As far as I am concerned, because of the fact that a situation of discrimination continues to exist in the field of medicine, women have not at the present time achieved equality with men.
>
> **CONCISE** Because of continuing discrimination in medicine, women have not yet achieved equality with men.

14b Cutting unneeded repetition

Unnecessary repetition weakens sentences.

> **WORDY** Many unskilled workers *without training in a particular job* are unemployed *and do not have any work.*
>
> **CONCISE** Many unskilled workers are unemployed.

Be especially alert to phrases that say the same thing twice. In the examples below, the unneeded words are italicized.

circle *around*	*important* (*basic*) essentials
consensus of *opinion*	puzzling *in nature*
cooperate *together*	repeat *again*
final completion	return *again*
frank and honest exchange	square (round) *in shape*
the future *to come*	*surrounding* circumstances

NOTE **ESL** Phrases like those above are redundant because the main word already implies the italicized word or words. A dictionary will tell you what meanings a word implies. *Assassinate,* for instance, means "murder someone well known," so the following sentence is redundant: *Julius Caesar was assassinated and killed.*

14c Combining sentences

Often the information in two or more sentences can be combined into one tight sentence.

WORDY	The French and British collaborated on building the Channel Tunnel. The tunnel links France and Britain. The French drilled from Sangatte. The British drilled from Dover.
CONCISE	The French and British collaborated on building the Channel Tunnel between their countries, the French drilling from Sangatte and the British from Dover.

14d Reducing clauses and phrases

Modifiers—subordinate clauses, phrases, and single words—can be expanded or contracted depending on the emphasis you want to achieve. (Generally, the longer a construction, the more emphasis it has.) When editing your sentences, consider whether any modifiers can be reduced without loss of emphasis or clarity.

WORDY	The tunnel, *which was drilled for twenty-three miles*, runs *through a bed of solid chalk that lies under the English Channel.*
CONCISE	The *twenty-three-mile* tunnel runs *through solid chalk under the English Channel.*

14e Using strong verbs

Weak verbs such as *is, has,* and *make* stall sentences. Strong verbs such as *slice, bicker,* and *stroll* energize sentences, moving them along. Weak verbs usually carry extra baggage, too, such as unneeded prepositional phrases and long, abstract nouns or adjectives.

KEY TERMS

MODIFIER A word or word group that limits or qualifies another word: *slippery road.*

PHRASE A word group that lacks a subject or a verb or both. Many phrases serve as modifiers: *road with a slippery surface.*

SUBORDINATE CLAUSE A word group that contains a subject and a verb, begins with a subordinating word such as *because* or *who,* and is not a question. Most subordinate clauses serve as modifiers: *Two accidents occurred on the road, which was unusually slippery.* (See pp. 77 and 137 for fuller lists of subordinating words.)

WORDY	The drillers *made slow advancement,* and costs *were over* $5 million a day. The slow progress *was worrisome for* backers, who *had had expectations of* high profits.
CONCISE	The drillers *advanced slowly,* and costs *topped* $5 million a day. The slow progress *worried* backers, who *had expected* high profits.

14f   Using the active voice

The active voice uses fewer words than the passive voice and is much more direct, because it names the performer of the verb's action up front. Change passive sentences to active by changing the verb and positioning the actor as the subject. (If you need help with this change, see pp. 101–02.)

con
14g

WORDY PASSIVE	As many as *fifteen feet* of chalk an hour *could be chewed through* by the drill.
CONCISE ACTIVE	The *drill could chew through* as many as fifteen feet of chalk an hour.

14g   Eliminating expletive constructions

Expletive constructions are sometimes useful to emphasize a change in direction, but usually they just add needless words.

WORDY	*There are more than half a million shareholders who* have invested in the tunnel. *It is they and the banks that* expect to profit.
CONCISE	*More than half a million shareholders* have invested in the tunnel. *They and the banks* expect to profit.

┌─ KEY TERMS ─────────────────────────────

ACTIVE VOICE   The verb form when the subject names the *performer* of the verb's action: *The drillers* <u>used</u> *huge rotary blades.*

PASSIVE VOICE   The verb form when the subject names the *receiver* of the verb's action: *Huge rotary blades* <u>were used</u> *by the drillers.*

EXPLETIVE CONSTRUCTION   A sentence that begins with *there* or *it* and postpones the sentence subject: *There is a tunnel under the channel.* Compare *A tunnel is under the channel.*

NOTE ESL When you do use an expletive construction, be careful to include *there* or *it*. Only commands and some questions can begin with verbs.

14h Rewriting jargon

JARGON is vague, inflated language that is overcomplicated, even incomprehensible. When it comes from government or business, we call it *bureaucratese*.

You may find yourself writing jargon when you are unsure of your subject or when your thoughts are tangled. It's fine, even necessary, to stumble and grope while drafting. But you should straighten out your ideas and eliminate jargon during revision and editing.

JARGON   The necessity for individuals to become separate entities in their own right may impel children to engage in open rebelliousness against parental authority or against sibling influence, with resultant confusion of those being rebelled against.

TRANSLATION   Children's natural desire to become themselves may make them rebel against bewildered parents or siblings.

III

Sentence Parts and Patterns

III

Sentence Parts and Patterns

❖

Basic Grammar

Grammar describes how language works, and understanding it can help you create clear and accurate sentences. This section explains the kinds of words in sentences (Chapter 15) and how to build basic sentences (16), expand them (17), and classify them (18).

15 Parts of Speech

All English words fall into eight groups, called PARTS OF SPEECH: nouns, pronouns, verbs, adjectives, adverbs, prepositions, conjunctions, and interjections.

NOTE In different sentences a word may serve as different parts of speech. For example:

> The government sent *aid* to the city. [*Aid* is a noun.]
> Governments *aid* citizens. [*Aid* is a verb.]

The *function* of a word in a sentence always determines its part of speech in that sentence.

15a Recognizing nouns

Nouns name. They may name a person (*Lily Tomlin, Jesse Jackson, astronaut*), a thing (*chair, book, Mt. Rainier*), a quality (*pain, mystery, simplicity*), a place (*city, Washington, ocean, Red Sea*), or an idea (*reality, peace, success*).

The forms of nouns depend partly on where they fit in certain groups. As the examples indicate, the same noun may appear in more than one group.

- ❖ COMMON NOUNS name general classes of things and do not begin with capital letters: *earthquake, citizen, earth, fortitude, army.*
- ❖ PROPER NOUNS name specific people, places, and things and begin with capital letters: *Helen Hunt, Washington Monument, El Paso, U.S. Congress.*

❖ COUNT NOUNS name things considered countable in English. Most add *-s* or *-es* to distinguish between singular (one) and plural (more than one): *citizen, citizens; city, cities.* Some count nouns form irregular plurals: *woman, women; child, children.*

❖ NONCOUNT NOUNS name things that aren't considered countable in English (*earth, sugar*), or they name qualities (*chaos, fortitude*). Noncount nouns do not form plurals.

❖ COLLECTIVE NOUNS are singular in form but name groups: *army, family, herd, U.S. Congress.*

In addition, most nouns form the POSSESSIVE by adding *-'s* to show ownership (*Nadia's books, citizen's rights*), source (*Auden's poems*), and some other relationships.

15b Recognizing pronouns

Most PRONOUNS substitute for nouns and function in sentences as nouns do: *Susanne Ling enlisted in the Air Force when <u>she</u> graduated.*

Pronouns fall into several subclasses depending on their form or function.

gr

15b

❖ PERSONAL PRONOUNS refer to a specific individual or to individuals: *I, you, he, she, it, we,* and *they.*

❖ INDEFINITE PRONOUNS, such as *everybody* and *some,* do not substitute for any specific nouns, though they function as nouns (<u>*Everybody*</u> *speaks*).

❖ RELATIVE PRONOUNS—*who, whoever, which, that*—relate groups of words to nouns or other pronouns (*The book <u>that</u> won is a novel*).

❖ INTERROGATIVE PRONOUNS, such as *who, which,* and *what,* introduce questions (<u>*Who*</u> *will contribute?*).

❖ DEMONSTRATIVE PRONOUNS, including *this, that,* and *such,* identify or point to nouns (<u>*This*</u> *is the problem*).

❖ INTENSIVE PRONOUNS—a personal pronoun plus *-self* or *-selves* (*himself, ourselves*)—emphasize a noun or other pronoun (*He <u>himself</u> asked that question*).

❖ REFLEXIVE PRONOUNS have the same form as intensive pronouns but indicate that the sentence subject also receives the action of the verb (*They injured <u>themselves</u>*).

The personal pronouns *I, he, she, we,* and *they* and the relative pronouns *who* and *whoever* change form depending on their function in the sentence. (See Chapter 25.)

15c Recognizing verbs

Verbs express an action (*bring, change, grow, consider*), an occurrence (*become, happen, occur*), or a state of being (*be, seem, remain*).

Verbs have five distinctive forms. If the form can change as described here, the word is a verb.

❖ The PLAIN FORM is the dictionary form of the verb. When the subject is a plural noun or the pronoun *I, we, you,* or *they,* the plain form indicates action that occurs in the present, occurs habitually, or is generally true.

A few artists *live* in town today.
They *hold* classes downtown.

❖ The *-s* FORM ends in *-s* or *-es.* When the subject is a singular noun, a pronoun such as *everyone,* or the personal pronoun *he, she,* or *it,* the *-s* form indicates action that occurs in the present, occurs habitually, or is generally true.

The artist *lives* in town today.
She *holds* classes downtown.

❖ The PAST-TENSE FORM indicates that the action of the verb occurred before now. It usually adds *-d* or *-ed* to the plain form, although most irregular verbs create it in different ways (see pp. 86–88).

Many artists *lived* in town before this year.
They *held* classes downtown. [Irregular verb.]

❖ The PAST PARTICIPLE is usually the same as the past-tense form, except in most irregular verbs. It combines with forms of *have* or *be* (*has climbed, was created*), or by itself it modifies nouns and pronouns (*the sliced apples*).

Artists have *lived* in town for decades.
They have *held* classes downtown. [Irregular verb.]

❖ The PRESENT PARTICIPLE adds *-ing* to the verb's plain form. It combines with forms of *be* (*is buying*), modifies nouns and pronouns (*the boiling water*), or functions as a noun (*Running exhausts me*).

A few artists are *living* in town today.
They are *holding* classes downtown.

NOTE ESL For verbs expressing feeling, the present and past participles have different meanings: *It was a boring lecture. The bored students slept.* (See p. 127.)

The verb *be* has eight forms rather than the five forms of most other verbs.

Plain form	be		
Present participle	being		
Past participle	been		

	I	*he, she, it*	*we, you, they*
Present tense	am	is	are
Past tense	was	was	were

Some verb forms combine with HELPING VERBS to indicate time and other kinds of meaning.

> *Having been trained* to draw, some artists *can train* others.
> The techniques *have changed* little.

These are the helping verbs:

can	may	must	shall	will
could	might	ought	should	would

Forms of *be:* be, am, is, are, was, were, been, being
Forms of *have:* have, has, had, having
Forms of *do:* do, does, did

See Chapters 19–24 for more on verbs.

gr

15d

15d Recognizing adjectives and adverbs

ADJECTIVES describe or modify nouns and pronouns. They specify which one, what quality, or how many.

old   city
adjective noun

generous one
adjective pronoun

two pears
adjective noun

ADVERBS describe or modify verbs, adjectives, other adverbs, and whole groups of words. They specify when, where, how, and to what extent.

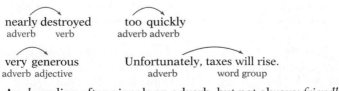

nearly destroyed
adverb   verb

too quickly
adverb adverb

very generous
adverb adjective

Unfortunately, taxes will rise.
adverb   word group

An *-ly* ending often signals an adverb, but not always: *friendly* is an adjective; *never, not,* and *always* are adverbs. The only way to tell whether a word is an adjective or an adverb is to determine what it modifies.

Adjectives and adverbs appear in three forms: POSITIVE (*green, angrily*), COMPARATIVE (*greener, more angrily*), and SUPERLATIVE (*greenest, most angrily*).

See Chapter 28 for more on adjectives and adverbs.

15e   Recognizing connecting words: prepositions and conjunctions

gr

15e

Connecting words are mostly small words that link parts of sentences. They never change form.

1. Prepositions

PREPOSITIONS form nouns or pronouns (plus any modifiers) into word groups called PREPOSITIONAL PHRASES: <u>*about*</u> *love,* <u>*down*</u> *the steep stairs.* These phrases usually serve as modifiers in sentences, as in *The plants trailed <u>down the steep stairs.</u>* (See p. 81 for more on prepositional phrases.)

Common prepositions

about	before	except for	of	throughout
above	behind	excepting	off	till
according to	below	for	on	to
across	beneath	from	onto	toward
after	beside	in	out	under
against	between	in addition to	out of	underneath
along	beyond	inside	outside	unlike
along with	by	in spite of	over	until
among	concerning	instead of	past	up
around	despite	into	regarding	upon
as	down	like	round	with
at	during	near	since	within
because of	except	next to	through	without

NOTE   ESL   The meanings and uses of English prepositions can be difficult to master. See pages 60–61 for a discussion of prepositions in idioms. See pages 110–11 for uses of prepositions in two-word verbs such as *look after* or *look up.*

2. Subordinating conjunctions

SUBORDINATING CONJUNCTIONS form sentences into word groups called SUBORDINATE CLAUSES, such as *when the meeting ended*. These clauses serve as parts of sentences: *Everyone was relieved when the meeting ended*. (See p. 83 for more information on subordinate clauses.)

Common subordinating conjunctions

after	even if	since	until
although	even though	so that	when
as	if	than	whenever
as if	if only	that	where
as long as	in order that	though	whereas
as though	now that	till	wherever
because	once	unless	while
before	rather than		

---

3. Coordinating and correlative conjunctions

Coordinating and correlative conjunctions connect words or word groups of the same kind, such as nouns, adjectives, or sentences.

COORDINATING CONJUNCTIONS consist of a single word.

Coordinating conjunctions

and	nor	for	yet
but	or	so	

Biofeedback *or* simple relaxation can relieve headaches.
Relaxation works well, *and* it is inexpensive.

CORRELATIVE CONJUNCTIONS are combinations of coordinating conjunctions and other words.

Common correlative conjunctions

both . . . and	neither . . . nor
not only . . . but also	whether . . . or
not . . . but	as . . . as
either . . . or	

---

gr

15e

Both biofeedback *and* relaxation can relieve headaches.

The headache sufferer learns *not only* to recognize the causes of headaches *but also* to control those causes.

15f Recognizing interjections

INTERJECTIONS express feeling or command attention. They are rarely used in academic or business writing.

Oh, the meeting went fine.
They won seven thousand dollars! *Wow!*

16 The Sentence

The SENTENCE is the basic unit of expression. It is grammatically complete and independent: it does not serve as an adjective, adverb, or other single part of speech.

16a Recognizing subjects and predicates

Most sentences make statements. First the SUBJECT names something; then the PREDICATE makes an assertion about the subject or describes an action by the subject.

SUBJECT	PREDICATE
Art	*can be* controversial.
It	*has caused* disputes in Congress and in artists' studios.
Its *meaning and value* to society	*are* often the focus of dispute.

The SIMPLE SUBJECT is usually one or more nouns or pronouns (italicized in the sentences above). The COMPLETE SUBJECT is the simple subject plus any modifiers. The SIMPLE PREDICATE is the verb (italicized in the sentences above). The COMPLETE PREDICATE adds any words needed to complete the meaning of the verb, plus any modifiers.

16b Recognizing predicate patterns

All English sentences are based on five patterns, each differing in the complete predicate (the verb and any words following it).

Pattern 1: The earth trembled.

In the simplest pattern the predicate consists only of an INTRANSITIVE VERB, a verb that does not require a following word to complete its meaning.

SUBJECT	PREDICATE
	Intransitive verb
The earth	trembled.
The hospital	may close.

Pattern 2: The earthquake destroyed the city.

In pattern 2 the verb is followed by a DIRECT OBJECT, a noun or pronoun that identifies who or what receives the action of the verb. A verb that requires a direct object to complete its meaning is called TRANSITIVE.

SUBJECT	PREDICATE	
	Transitive verb	*Direct object*
The earthquake	destroyed	the city.
Education	opens	doors.

gr

16b

NOTE ESL The distinction between transitive verbs and intransitive verbs like those in pattern 1 is important because only transitive verbs can be used in the passive voice (*The city was destroyed*). (See p. 101.) Your dictionary will indicate whether a verb is transitive or intransitive. For some verbs (*begin, learn, read, write,* and others), it will indicate both uses.

Pattern 3: The result was chaos.

In pattern 3 the verb is followed by a SUBJECT COMPLEMENT, a word that renames or describes the subject. A verb in this pattern is called a LINKING VERB because it links its subject to the description following. The linking verbs include *be, seem, appear, become, grow, remain, stay, prove, feel, look, smell, sound,* and *taste*. Subject complements are usually nouns or adjectives.

Subject	Predicate	
	Linking verb	*Subject complement*
The result	was	chaos.
The man	became	an accountant.

Pattern 4: *The government sent the city aid.*

In pattern 4 the verb is followed by a direct object and an IN-DIRECT OBJECT, a word identifying to or for whom the action of the verb is performed. The direct object and indirect object refer to different things, people, or places.

Subject	Predicate		
	Transitive verb	*Indirect object*	*Direct object*
The government	sent	the city	aid.
One company	offered	its employees	bonuses.

A number of verbs can take indirect objects, including those above and *allow, bring, buy, deny, find, get, give, leave, make, pay, read, sell, show, teach,* and *write.*

NOTE ESL Some verbs expressing action done to or for someone must be followed by *to* or *for.* These verbs include *admit, announce, demonstrate, explain, introduce, mention, prove, recommend, say,* and *suggest: The manual explains the new procedure to workers.*

Pattern 5: *The citizens considered the earthquake a disaster.*

In pattern 5 the verb is followed by a direct object and an OB-JECT COMPLEMENT, a word that renames or describes the direct object. Object complements may be nouns or adjectives.

Subject	Predicate		
	Transitive verb	*Direct object*	*Object complement*
The citizens	considered	the earthquake	a disaster.
Success	makes	some people	nervous.

17 Phrases and Subordinate Clauses

Most sentences contain word groups that serve as adjectives, adverbs, or nouns and thus cannot stand alone as sentences.

❖ A PHRASE lacks either a subject or a predicate or both: *fearing an accident; in a panic.*

❖ A SUBORDINATE CLAUSE contains a subject and a predicate (like a sentence) but begins with a subordinating word: *when prices rise; whoever laughs.*

17a Recognizing phrases

1. Prepositional phrases

A PREPOSITIONAL PHRASE consists of a preposition plus a noun, a pronoun, or a word group serving as a noun, called the OBJECT OF THE PREPOSITION. A list of prepositions appears on page 76.

PREPOSITION	OBJECT
of	spaghetti
on	the surface
with	great satisfaction
upon	entering the room
from	where you are standing

Prepositional phrases usually function as adjectives or adverbs.

Life *on a raft* was an opportunity *for adventure.*
　adjective phrase　　　　　　　　　adjective phrase

Huck Finn rode the raft *by choice.*
　　　　　　　　　　adverb phrase

gr

17a

2. Verbal phrases

Certain forms of verbs, called VERBALS, can serve as modifiers or nouns. Often these verbals appear with their own modifiers and objects in VERBAL PHRASES.

NOTE Verbals cannot serve as verbs in sentences. *The sun rises over the dump* is a sentence; *The sun rising over the dump* is a sentence fragment. (See p. 136.)

Participial phrases

Phrases made from present participles (ending in *-ing*) or past participles (usually ending in *-d* or *-ed*) serve as adjectives.

Strolling shoppers fill the malls.
adjective

They make selections *determined by personal taste.*
　　　　　　　　　　adjective phrase

NOTE With irregular verbs, the past participle may have a different ending—for instance, *hidden funds.* (See p. 86.)

Gerund phrases

A GERUND is the *-ing* form of a verb when it serves as a noun. Gerunds and gerund phrases can do whatever nouns can do.

sentence
subject
Shopping satisfies personal needs.
noun

                               object of preposition
Malls are good at *creating such needs.*
                               noun phrase

Infinitive phrases

An INFINITIVE is the plain form of a verb plus *to: to hide.* Infinitives and infinitive phrases serve as adjectives, adverbs, or nouns.

sentence subject   ┌──────subject complement──────┐
To design a mall is *to create an artificial environment.*
    noun phrase   noun phrase

Malls are designed *to make shoppers feel safe.*
                        adverb phrase

The environment supports the impulse *to shop.*
                                          adjective

NOTE ESL Infinitives and gerunds may follow some verbs and not others and may differ in meaning after a verb: *The singer stopped to sing. The singer stopped singing.* (See pp. 108–09.)

3. Absolute phrases

An ABSOLUTE PHRASE consists of a noun or pronoun and a participle, plus any modifiers. It modifies the entire rest of the sentence it appears in.

┌────── absolute phrase ──────┐
Their own place established, many ethnic groups are making way for new arrivals.

Unlike a participial phrase (previous page), an absolute phrase always contains a noun that serves as a subject:

┌participial phrase┐
Learning English, many immigrants discover American culture.

┌────── absolute phrase ──────┐
The immigrants having learned English, their opportunities widen.

gr

17a

4. Appositive phrases

An APPOSITIVE is usually a noun that renames another noun. An appositive phrase includes modifiers as well.

> appositive phrase
> Bizen ware, *a dark stoneware,* is produced in Japan.

Appositives and appositive phrases sometimes begin with *that is, such as, for example,* or *in other words.*

> Bizen ware is used in the Japanese tea ceremony, *that is, the Zen*
> ———————— appositive phrase ————————
> *Buddhist observance that links meditation and art.*

17b Recognizing subordinate clauses

A CLAUSE is any group of words that contains both a subject and a predicate. There are two kinds of clauses, and the distinction between them is important.

- ◆ A MAIN CLAUSE makes a complete statement and can stand alone as a sentence: *The sky darkened.*
- ◆ A SUBORDINATE CLAUSE is just like a main clause *except* that it begins with a subordinating word: *when the sky darkened; whoever calls.* The subordinating word reduces the clause to a single part of speech: an adjective, adverb, or noun.

NOTE A subordinate clause punctuated as a sentence is a sentence fragment. (See pp. 136–37.)

Adjective clauses

An ADJECTIVE CLAUSE modifies a noun or pronoun. It usually begins with the relative pronoun *who, whom, whose, which,* or *that.* The relative pronoun is the subject or object of the clause it begins. The clause ordinarily falls immediately after the word it modifies.

> adjective clause
> Parents *who are illiterate* may have bad memories of school.

> adjective clause
> One school, *which is open year-round,* helps parents learn to read.

Adverb clauses

An ADVERB CLAUSE modifies a verb, an adjective, another adverb, or a whole word group. It always begins with a subordinating

gr

17b

conjunction, such as *although, because, if,* or *when* (see p. 77 for a list).

—— adverb clause ——
The school began teaching parents *when adult illiteracy gained national attention.*

—— adverb clause —— main clause
Because it was directed at people who could not read, advertising had to be inventive.

Noun clauses

A NOUN CLAUSE replaces a noun in a sentence and serves as a subject, object, or complement. It begins with *that, what, whatever, who, whom, whoever, whomever, when, where, whether, why,* or *how.*

—— sentence subject ——
Whether the program would succeed depended on door-to-door advertising.
noun clause

—— direct object ——
Teachers explained in person *how the program would work.*
noun clause

18 Sentence Types

The four basic sentence structures vary in the number of main and coordinate clauses.

18a Recognizing simple sentences

A SIMPLE SENTENCE consists of a single main clause and no subordinate clause.

—— main clause ——
Last summer was unusually hot.

—— main clause ——
The summer made many farmers leave the area for good or reduced them to bare existence.

18b Recognizing compound sentences

A COMPOUND SENTENCE consists of two or more main clauses and no subordinate clause.

┌────main clause────┐ ┌──────main clause──────┐
Last July was hot, but August was even hotter.

┌──────────main clause──────────┐ ┌──────────main clause──────────
The hot sun scorched the earth, and the lack of rain killed many
────┐
crops.

18c Recognizing complex sentences

A COMPLEX SENTENCE consists of one main clause and one or more subordinate clauses.

┌────main clause────┐ ┌────────────subordinate clause────────────┐
Rain finally came, although many had left the area by then.

┌────────────────main clause────────────────┐ ┌─subordinate clause──
Those who remained were able to start anew because the govern-
    subordinate clause
─────────────────────┐
ment came to their aid.

18d Recognizing compound-complex sentences

A COMPOUND-COMPLEX SENTENCE has the characteristics of both the compound sentence (two or more main clauses) and the complex sentence (at least one subordinate clause).

┌──────────────subordinate clause──────────────┐ ┌───main clause──────
Even though government aid finally came, many people had al-
──────────────────────────────────┐ ┌────────main clause─────────
ready been reduced to poverty, and others had been forced to
────┐
move.

gr
18d

Verbs

VERBS express actions, conditions, and states of being. The basic uses and forms of verbs are described on pages 74–75. This section explains and solves the most common problems with verbs' forms (Chapter 19), tenses (20), mood (21), and voice (22). It shows how to make verbs match their subjects (23). And it treats some special challenges of English verbs for nonnative speakers (24).

19 Verb Forms

Verb forms may give you trouble when the verb is irregular, when you omit certain endings, or when you stumble over helping verbs.

vb
19a

19a Use the correct forms of *sing/sang/sung* and other irregular verbs.

Most verbs are REGULAR: they form their past tense and past participle by adding -*d* or -*ed* to the plain form.

PLAIN FORM	PAST TENSE	PAST PARTICIPLE
live	lived	lived
act	acted	acted

About two hundred English verbs are IRREGULAR: they form their past tense and past participle in some irregular way. Check a dictionary under the verb's plain form if you have any doubt about its other forms. If the verb is irregular, the dictionary will list the plain form, the past tense, and the past participle in that order (*go*,

---

KEY TERMS

PLAIN FORM   The dictionary form of the verb: *I walk. You forget.*

PAST-TENSE FORM   The verb form indicating action that occurred in the past: *I walked. You forgot.*

PAST PARTICIPLE   The verb form used with *have, has,* or *had: I have walked.* It may also serve as a modifier: *This is a forgotten book.*

went, gone). If the dictionary gives only two forms (as in *think, thought*), then the past tense and the past participle are the same.

The following list includes the most common irregular verbs. (When two forms are possible, as in *dove* and *dived*, both are included.)

PLAIN FORM	PAST TENSE	PAST PARTICIPLE
arise	arose	arisen
become	became	become
begin	began	begun
bid	bid	bid
bite	bit	bitten, bit
blow	blew	blown
break	broke	broken
bring	brought	brought
burst	burst	burst
buy	bought	bought
catch	caught	caught
choose	chose	chosen
come	came	come
cut	cut	cut
dive	dived, dove	dived
do	did	done
draw	drew	drawn
dream	dreamed, dreamt	dreamed, dreamt
drink	drank	drunk
drive	drove	driven
eat	ate	eaten
fall	fell	fallen
find	found	found
flee	fled	fled
fly	flew	flown
forget	forgot	forgotten, forgot
freeze	froze	frozen
get	got	got, gotten
give	gave	given
go	went	gone
grow	grew	grown
hang (suspend)	hung	hung
hang (execute)	hanged	hanged
hear	heard	heard
hide	hid	hidden
hold	held	held
keep	kept	kept
know	knew	known
lay	laid	laid
lead	led	led

vb

19a

PLAIN FORM	PAST TENSE	PAST PARTICIPLE
leave	left	left
lend	lent	lent
let	let	let
lie	lay	lain
lose	lost	lost
pay	paid	paid
prove	proved	proved, proven
ride	rode	ridden
ring	rang	rung
rise	rose	risen
run	ran	run
say	said	said
see	saw	seen
set	set	set
shake	shook	shaken
shrink	shrank, shrunk	shrunk, shrunken
sing	sang, sung	sung
sink	sank, sunk	sunk
sit	sat	sat
slide	slid	slid
speak	spoke	spoken
spring	sprang, sprung	sprung
stand	stood	stood
steal	stole	stolen
swim	swam	swum
take	took	taken
tear	tore	torn
throw	threw	thrown
wear	wore	worn
write	wrote	written

vb
19b

19b Distinguish between *sit* and *set, lie* and *lay,* and *rise* and *raise.*

The forms of *sit* and *set, lie* and *lay,* and *rise* and *raise* are easy to confuse.

PLAIN FORM	PAST TENSE	PAST PARTICIPLE
sit	sat	sat
set	set	set
lie	lay	lain
lay	laid	laid
rise	rose	risen
raise	raised	raised

In each of these confusing pairs, one verb is intransitive (it does not take an object) and one is transitive (it does take an object). (See p. 79 for more on this distinction.)

INTRANSITIVE

The patients *lie* in their beds. [*Lie* means "recline" and takes no object.]

Visitors *sit* with them. [*Sit* means "be seated" or "be located" and takes no object.]

Patients' temperatures *rise*. [*Rise* means "increase" or "get up" and takes no object.]

TRANSITIVE

Orderlies *lay* the dinner trays on tables. [*Lay* means "place" and takes an object, here *trays*.]

Orderlies *set* the trays down. [*Set* means "place" and takes an object, here *trays*.]

Nursing aides *raise* the shades. [*Raise* means "lift" or "bring up" and takes an object, here *shades*.]

19c Use the -s and -ed forms of the verb when they are required.

vb
19c

Speakers of some English dialects and nonnative speakers of English sometimes omit verb endings required by standard English. One is the *-s* ending of the verb when the subject is *he, she, it,* or a singular noun and the verb's action occurs in the present. (The correct form below is in parentheses.)

The roof *leak* (*leaks*).   Nobody *have* (*has*) a car.
Harry *live* (*lives*) in town.   She *be* (*is*) happy.
He *don't* (*doesn't*) care.

A second omitted ending is the *-ed* or *-d* when (1) the verb's action occurred in the past (*we bagged*), (2) the verb form functions as a modifier (*used cars*), or (3) the verb form combines with a form of

---

KEY TERMS

INTRANSITIVE VERB   A verb that does not require a direct object to complete its meaning (see p. 79).

TRANSITIVE VERB   A verb that does require a direct object to complete its meaning (see p. 79).

be or *have* (*was supposed*, *has asked*). (The correct form below is in parentheses.)

> We *bag* (*bagged*) groceries.   I bought a *use* (*used*) book.
> He was *suppose* (*supposed*) to   Sue has *ask* (*asked*) for help.
> call.

19d Use helping verbs with main verbs appropriately.

HELPING VERBS combine with some verb forms to indicate time, obligation, and other meanings: *The line should have been cut.*

1. Required helping verbs

Some English dialects omit helping verbs required by standard English. In the sentences below, the underlined helping verbs are essential.

> The owl *is hooting*.   Sara *has been* at home.
> I *have taken* French.   That *would* be awful.

The omission of a helping verb may create an incomplete sentence, or SENTENCE FRAGMENT, because a present participle (*hooting*) or an irregular past participle (*taken, been*) cannot stand alone as the only verb in a sentence (see pp. 135–36).

> **FRAGMENTS**   Some people *smoking.* The sign *broken.*
>
> **REVISED**   Some people *were smoking.* The sign *was broken.*

2. Combination of helping verb + main verb ESL

Form of be *+ present participle*

The PROGRESSIVE TENSES indicate action in progress. Create them with *be, am, is, are, was, were,* or *been* followed by the main verb's present participle.

┌─ KEY TERMS ───

PRESENT PARTICIPLE   The *ing* form of the verb: *flying, writing.*

PAST PARTICIPLE   The *-d* or *-ed* form of a regular verb: *hedged, walked.* Most irregular verbs have distinctive past participles: *eaten, swum.*

PROGRESSIVE TENSES   Verb tenses expressing action in progress—for instance, *I am flying* (present progressive), *I was flying* (past progressive), *I will be flying* (future progressive). (See p. 95)

└──

vb
19d

She *is working* on a new book.

Be and *been* require additional helping verbs to form progressive tenses.

can	might	should			have	
could	must	will	} *be* working		has	} *been* working
may	shall	would			had	

When forming the progressive tenses, be sure to use the *-ing* form of the main verb.

> **FAULTY** Her ideas are *grow* more complex. She is *developed* a new approach to ethics.

> **REVISED** Her ideas are *growing* more complex. She is *developing* a new approach to ethics.

Form of **be** + *past participle*

The PASSIVE VOICE of the verb indicates that the subject *receives* the action of the verb. Create the passive voice with *be, am, is, are, was, were, being,* or *been* followed by the main verb's past participle.

Her latest book *was completed* in four months.

Be, being, and *been* require additional helping verbs to form the passive voice.

have			am	was	
has	} *been* completed		is	were	} *being* completed
had			are		

will *be* completed

Be sure to use the main verb's past participle for the passive voice.

> **FAULTY** Her next book will be *publish* soon.

> **REVISED** Her next book will be *published* soon.

NOTE Use only transitive verbs to form the passive voice, as in the following revision.

> **vb**
> **19d**

⌐ KEY TERMS ────────────────────

PASSIVE VOICE   The verb form when the subject names the receiver of the verb's action: *An essay was written by every student.*

TRANSITIVE VERB   A verb that requires an object to complete its meaning: *Every student completed an essay* (*essay* is the object of *completed*).

FAULTY A philosophy conference *will be occurred* in the same week. [*Occur* is not a transitive verb.]

REVISED A philosophy conference *will occur* in the same week.

See pages 101–02 for advice on when to use and when to avoid the passive voice.

Forms of **have**

Four forms of *have* serve as helping verbs: *have, has, had, having.* One of these forms plus the main verb's past participle creates one of the perfect tenses, those expressing action completed before another specific time or action.

Some students *have complained* about the laboratory.
Others *had complained* before.

Will and other helping verbs sometimes accompany forms of *have* in the perfect tenses.

Several more students *will have complained* by the end of the week.

Forms of **do**

Always with the plain form of the main verb, three forms of *do* serve as helping verbs: *do, does, did. Do* has three uses:

❖ To pose a question: *Whom did the officers arrest?*
❖ To emphasize the main verb: *They did arrest someone.*
❖ To negate the main verb, along with *not* or *never: The suspect did not escape.*

Be sure to use the main verb's plain form with any form of *do.*

FAULTY They did *captured* someone.

REVISED They did *capture* someone.

Modals

The modals and their main uses are illustrated below:

❖ *Can* and *could:*

Yuen *can* speak English well. [Ability.]
No one *could* smoke at the meeting. [Permission.]
Could you help us? [Polite request.]

KEY TERM

PERFECT TENSES Verb tenses expressing an action completed before another specific time or action: *We have eaten* (present perfect), *We had eaten* (past perfect), *We will have eaten* (future perfect).

❖ *May* and *might:*

   May Hector come? [Permission.]
   Hector *might* come if you ask. [Possibility.]

❖ *Must:*

   You *must* hurry. [Necessity or obligation.]
   The doors *must* have closed. [Probability.]

❖ *Should* and *ought to:*

   It *should* rain soon. [Expectation.]
   We *ought to* bring umbrellas. [Advisability.]

❖ *Will* and *would:*

   All the guests *will* come. [Promise or agreement.]
   Would you like to come? [Polite request.]

20 | Verb Tenses

TENSE shows the time of a verb's action. The following table illustrates the tense forms for a regular verb. (Irregular verbs have different past-tense and past-participle forms. See pp. 86–88.)

PRESENT Action that is occurring now, occurs habitually, or is generally true

SIMPLE PRESENT Plain form or -s form	PRESENT PROGRESSIVE *Am, is,* or *are* plus *-ing* form
I *walk.*	I *am walking.*
You/we/they *walk.*	You/we/they *are walking.*
He/she/it *walks.*	He/she/it *is walking.*

PAST Action that occurred before now

SIMPLE PAST Past-tense form (*-d* or *-ed*)	PAST PROGRESSIVE *Was* or *were* plus *-ing* form
I/he/she/it *walked.*	I/he/she/it *was walking.*
You/we/they *walked.*	You/we/they *were walking.*

FUTURE Action that will occur in the future

SIMPLE FUTURE Plain form plus *will*	FUTURE PROGRESSIVE *Will be* plus *-ing* form
I/you/he/she/it/we/they *will walk.*	I/you/he/she/it/we/they *will be walking.*

PRESENT PERFECT Action that began in the past and is linked to the present

PRESENT PERFECT *Have* or *has* plus past participle (-*d* or -*ed*)	**PRESENT PERFECT PROGRESSIVE** *Have been* or *has been* plus -*ing* form
I/you/we/they *have walked.*	I/you/we/they *have been walking.*
He/she/it *has walked.*	He/she/it *has been walking.*

PAST PERFECT Action that was completed before another action in the past

PAST PERFECT *Had* plus past participle (-*d* or -*ed*)	**PAST PERFECT PROGRESSIVE** *Had been* plus -*ing* form
I/you/he/she/it/we/they *had walked.*	I/you/he/she/it/we/they *had been walking.*

FUTURE PERFECT Action that will be completed before another future action

FUTURE PERFECT *Will have* plus past participle (-*d* or -*ed*)	**FUTURE PERFECT PROGRESSIVE** *Will have been* plus -*ing* form
I/you/he/she/it/we/they *will have walked.*	I/you/he/she/it/we/they *will have been walking.*

20a Observe the special uses of the present tense (*sing*).

The present tense has several uses.

TO INDICATE ACTION OCCURRING NOW
She *understands* what you mean.

TO INDICATE HABITUAL OR RECURRING ACTION
The store *opens* at ten o'clock.

TO STATE A GENERAL TRUTH
The earth *is* round.

TO DISCUSS THE CONTENT OF LITERATURE, FILM, AND SO ON
Huckleberry Finn *has* adventures we all envy.

TO INDICATE FUTURE TIME
The theater *closes* in a month.

20b Observe the uses of the perfect tenses (*have/had/will have sung*).

The perfect tenses consist of a form of *have* plus the verb's past participle (*closed, hidden*). They indicate an action completed before another specific time or action. The present perfect tense also indicates action begun in the past and continued into the present.

present perfect
The dancer *has performed* here only once. [The action is completed at the time of the statement.]

present perfect
Critics *have written* about the performance ever since. [The action began in the past and continues now.]

past perfect
The dancer *had trained* in Asia before his performance. [The action was completed before another past action.]

future perfect
He *will have performed* here again by next month. [The action begins now or in the future and will be completed by a specified time in the future.]

20c Observe the uses of the progressive tenses (*is/was/will be singing*). ESL

The progressive tenses indicate continuing (therefore progressive) action. They consist of a form of *be* plus the verb's *-ing* form (present participle). (The words *be* and *been* must be combined with other helping verbs. See p. 91.)

present progressive
The economy *is improving*,

past progressive
Last year the economy *was stagnating*.

future progressive
Economists *will be watching* for signs of growth.

present perfect progressive
The government *has been expecting* an upturn.

past perfect progressive
Various indicators *had been suggesting* improvement.

future perfect progressive
By the end of this year, investors *will have been watching* the markets nervously for nearly a decade.

NOTE Verbs that express mental states or activities rather than physical actions do not usually appear in the progressive tenses.

These verbs include *adore, appear, believe, belong, care, hate, have, hear, know, like, love, need, prefer, remember, see, taste, think, understand,* and *want.*

> **FAULTY**   She *is wanting* to study ethics.
>
> **REVISED**   She *wants* to study ethics.

20d   Keep tenses consistent.

Within a sentence, the tenses of verbs and verb forms need not be identical as long as they reflect actual changes in time: *Ramon will graduate from college twenty years after his father arrived in America.* But needless shifts in tense will confuse or distract readers.

> **INCONSISTENT**   Immediately after Booth *shot* Lincoln, Major Rathbone *threw* himself upon the assassin. But Booth *pulls* a knife and *plunges* it into the major's arm.
>
> **REVISED**   Immediately after Booth *shot* Lincoln, Major Rathbone *threw* himself upon the assassin. But Booth *pulled* a knife and *plunged* it into the major's arm.
>
> **INCONSISTENT**   The main character in the novel *suffers* psychologically because he *has* a clubfoot, but he eventually *triumphed* over his handicap.
>
> **REVISED**   The main character in the novel *suffers* psychologically because he *has* a clubfoot, but he eventually *triumphs* over his handicap. [Use the present tense when discussing the content of literature, film, and so on.]

t seq

20e

20e   Use the appropriate sequence of verb tenses.

The SEQUENCE OF TENSES is the relation between the verb tense in a main clause and the verb tense in a subordinate clause. The tenses are often different, as in *He will leave before I arrive.*

KEY TERMS

MAIN CLAUSE   A word group that contains a subject and a verb and does not begin with a subordinating word: *Books are valuable.*

SUBORDINATE CLAUSE   A word group that contains a subject and a verb, begins with a subordinating word such as *because* or *who,* and is not a question: *Books are valuable when they enlighten.*

English tense sequence can be tricky for native speakers and especially challenging for nonnative speakers. The main difficulties are discussed below.

1. Past or past perfect tense in main clause

When the verb in the main clause is in the past or past perfect tense, the verb in the subordinate clause must also be past or past perfect.

>   past   past
> The researchers *discovered* that people *varied* widely in their knowledge of public events.

>   past   past perfect
> The variation *occurred* because respondents *had been born* in different decades.

>   past perfect   past
> None of them *had been born* when Warren G. Harding *was* President.

EXCEPTION Always use the present tense for a general truth, such as *The earth is round.*

>   past   present
> Few *understood* that popular Presidents *are* not necessarily good Presidents.

t seq

20e

2. Conditional sentences ESL

A CONDITIONAL SENTENCE states a factual relation between cause and effect, makes a prediction, or speculates about what might happen. Such a sentence usually consists of a subordinate clause beginning with *if, when,* or *unless* and a main clause stating the result. The three kinds of conditional sentences use distinctive verbs.

Factual relation

For statements asserting that something always or usually happens whenever something else happens, use the present tense in both clauses.

>   present   present
> When a voter *casts* a ballot, he or she *has* complete privacy.

If the linked events occurred in the past, use the past tense in both clauses.

>   past   past
> When voters *registered* in some states, they *had* to pay a poll tax.

Prediction

For a prediction, generally use the present tense in the subordinate clause and the future tense in the main clause.

> present   future
> Unless citizens *regain* faith in politics, they *will* not *vote*.

Sometimes the verb in the main clause consists of *may, can, should,* or *might* plus the verb's plain form: *If citizens regain faith, they may vote.*

Speculation

Speculations are mainly of two kinds, each with its own verb pattern. For events that are possible in the present but unlikely, use the past tense in the subordinate clause and *would, could,* or *might* plus the verb's plain form in the main clause.

> past   would + verb
> If voters *had* more confidence, they *would vote* more often.

Use *were* instead of *was* when the subject is *I, he, she, it,* or a singular noun. (See p. 100 for more on this distinctive verb form.)

> past   would + verb
> If the voter *were* more confident, he or she *would vote* more often.

For events that are impossible now, that are contrary to fact, use the same forms as above (including the distinctive *were* when applicable).

> past   might + verb
> If Lincoln *were* alive, he *might inspire* confidence.

For events that were impossible in the past, use the past perfect tense in the subordinate clause and *would, could,* or *might* plus the present perfect tense in the main clause.

> past perfect   might + present perfect
> If Lincoln *had lived* past the Civil War, he *might have helped* stabilize the country.

t seq
20e

3. Indirect quotations ESL

An indirect quotation reports what someone said or wrote but not in the exact words and not in quotation marks: *Lincoln said that events had controlled him* (quotation: "Events have controlled me"). Indirect quotations generally appear in subordinate clauses (underlined above), with certain conventions governing verb tense in most cases.

When the verb in the main clause is in the present tense, the verb in the indirect quotation (subordinate clause) is in the same tense as the original quotation.

> present   present
> Haworth *says* that Lincoln *is* our noblest national hero. [Quotation: "Lincoln *is* our noblest national hero."]
>
> present   past
> He *says* that Lincoln *was* a complicated person. [Quotation: "Lincoln *was* a complicated person."]

When the verb in the main clause is in the past tense, the verb in the indirect quotation usually changes tense from the original quotation. Present tense changes to past tense.

> past   past
> An assistant to Lincoln *said* that the President *was* always generous. [Quotation: "The President *is* always generous."]

Past tense and present perfect tense change to past perfect tense. (Past perfect tense does not change.)

> past   past perfect
> Lincoln *said* that events *had controlled* him. [Quotation: "Events *have controlled* me."]

When the direct quotation states a general truth or reports a situation that is still true, use the present tense in the indirect quotation regardless of the verb in the main clause.

> past   present
> Lincoln *said* that right *makes* might. [Quotation: "Right *makes* might."]

NOTE As several of the examples show, an indirect quotation differs in at least two additional ways from the original quotation: (1) the indirect quotation is usually preceded by *that,* and (2) the indirect quotation changes pronouns, especially from forms of *I* or *we* to forms of *he, she,* or *they.*

---

21 Verb Mood

MOOD in grammar is a verb form that indicates the writer's or speaker's attitude toward what he or she is saying. The INDICATIVE MOOD states a fact or opinion or asks a question: *The theater needs help.* The IMPERATIVE MOOD expresses a command or gives a direction. It omits the subject of the sentence, *you: Help the theater.*

vb
21

The SUBJUNCTIVE MOOD is trickier and requires distinctive verb forms described below.

21a   Use the subjunctive verb forms appropriately, as in *I wish he were*.

The subjunctive mood expresses a suggestion, requirement, or desire, or it states a condition that is contrary to fact (that is, imaginary or hypothetical).

❖ Verbs such as *ask, insist, urge, require, recommend,* and *suggest* indicate request or requirement. They often precede a subordinate clause beginning with *that* and containing the substance of the request or requirement. For all subjects, the verb in the *that* clause is the plain form.

> plain
> form
> Rules require that every donation *be* mailed.

❖ Contrary-to-fact clauses state imaginary or hypothetical conditions and usually begin with *if* or *unless* or follow *wish*. For present contrary-to-fact clauses, use the verb's past-tense form (for *be,* use the past-tense form *were*).

> past   past
> If the theater *were* in better shape and *had* more money, its future would be assured.

> past
> The manager wishes that he *were* blameless.

For past contrary-to-fact clauses, use the verb's past-perfect form (*had* + past participle).

> past perfect
> The theater would be better funded if it *had been* better managed.

NOTE Do not use the helping verb *would* or *could* in a contrary-to-fact clause beginning with *if.*

> **NOT**   Many people would have helped if they *would have* known.
>
> **BUT**   Many people would have helped if they *had* known.

See also page 98 for more on verb tenses in conditional sentences like this one.

21b   Keep mood consistent

Shifts in mood within a sentence or among related sentences can be confusing. Such shifts occur most frequently in directions.

vb
21b

INCONSISTENT	*Cook* the mixture slowly, and *you should stir* it until the sugar is dissolved. [Mood shifts from imperative to indicative.]
REVISED	*Cook* the mixture slowly, and *stir* it until the sugar is dissolved. [Consistently imperative.]

22 Verb Voice

The VOICE of a verb tells whether the subject of the sentence performs the action (ACTIVE) or is acted upon (PASSIVE).

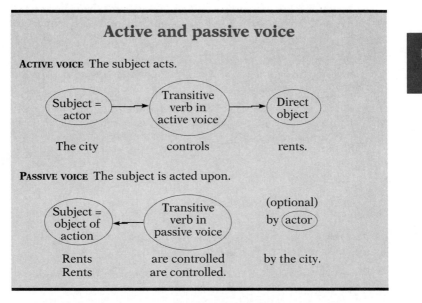

Active and passive voice

ACTIVE VOICE The subject acts.

Subject = actor → Transitive verb in active voice → Direct object

The city   controls   rents.

PASSIVE VOICE The subject is acted upon.

Subject = object of action ← Transitive verb in passive voice   (optional) by (actor)

Rents   are controlled   by the city.
Rents   are controlled.

pass
22

The actor in a passive sentence may be named in a prepositional phrase (as in the first passive example above), or the actor may be omitted (as in the second passive example).

NOTE   ESL   A passive verb always consists of a form of *be* plus the past participle of the main verb: *rents are controlled, people were inspired*. Other helping verbs must also be used with the words *be*, *being*, and *been: rents have been controlled, people would have been inspired.* Only a transitive verb (one that takes an object) may be used in the passive voice. (See pp. 91–92.)

22a Generally, prefer the active voice. Use the passive voice when the actor is unknown or unimportant.

The active voice is usually clearer, more concise, and more forthright than the passive voice.

WEAK PASSIVE   The exam was thought by us to be unfair because we were tested on material that was not covered in the course.

STRONG ACTIVE   We thought the exam unfair because it tested us on material the course did not cover.

The passive voice is useful in two situations: when the actor is unknown and when the actor is unimportant or is less important than the object of the action.

Ray Appleton *was murdered* after he returned home. [The murderer may be unknown, and in any event Ray Appleton's death is the point of the sentence.]

In the first experiment acid *was added* to the solution. [The person who added the acid, perhaps the writer, is less important than the fact that acid was added. Passive sentences are common in scientific writing.]

22b Keep voice consistent.

Shifts in voice that involve shifts in subject are usually unnecessary and confusing.

INCONSISTENT   In the morning the *children rode* their bicycles; in the afternoon *their skateboards were given* a good workout.

REVISED   In the morning the *children rode* their bicycles; in the afternoon *they gave* their skateboards a good workout.

A shift in voice is appropriate when it helps focus the reader's attention on a single subject, as in *The candidate campaigned vigorously and was nominated on the first ballot.*

23 Agreement of Subject and Verb

A subject and its verb should agree in number and person.

More *Japanese-Americans live* in Hawaii and California than elsewhere.   subject   verb

Daniel Inouye was the first Japanese-American in Congress.
subject   verb

Most problems of subject-verb agreement arise when endings are omitted from subjects or verbs or when the relation between sentence parts is uncertain.

23a   Subject and verb should agree even when other words come between them.

A catalog of courses and requirements often *baffles* (not *baffle*) students.

The requirements stated in the catalog *are* (not *is*) unclear.

NOTE Phrases beginning with *as well as, together with, along with,* and *in addition to* do not change the number of the subject.

The president, as well as the deans, *has* (not *have*) agreed to revise the catalog.

23b   Subjects joined by *and* usually take plural verbs.

Frost and Roethke *were* contemporaries.

vb agr

23b

┌ **KEY TERMS** ─────────────────────────────

	NUMBER	
PERSON	SINGULAR	PLURAL
FIRST	I eat.	We eat.
SECOND	You eat.	You eat.
THIRD	He/she/it eats.	They eat.
	The bird eats.	Birds eat.

EXCEPTIONS When the parts of the subject form a single idea or refer to a single person or thing, they take a singular verb.

Avocado and bean sprouts *is* a California sandwich.

When a compound subject is preceded by the adjective *each* or *every,* the verb is usually singular.

Each man, woman, and child *has* a right to be heard.

23c When parts of a subject are joined by *or* or *nor,* the verb agrees with the nearer part.

Either the painter or the carpenter *knows* the cost.

The cabinets or the bookcases *are* too costly.

When one part of the subject is singular and the other plural, avoid awkwardness by placing the plural part closer to the verb so that the verb is plural.

vb agr
23d

AWKWARD Neither the owners nor the contractor *agrees.*

REVISED Neither the contractor nor the owners *agree.*

23d Generally, use singular verbs with *everyone* and other indefinite pronouns.

Most indefinite pronouns are singular in meaning (they refer to a single unspecified person or thing), and they take singular verbs.

Something *smells.*   Neither *is* right.

A few indefinite pronouns such as *all, any, none,* and *some* may take a singular or plural verb depending on meaning.

┌─ KEY TERM ───

INDEFINITE PRONOUN   A pronoun that does not refer to a specific person or thing:

all	each	neither	one
any	either	nobody	some
anybody	everybody	none	somebody
anyone	everyone	no one	someone
anything	everything	nothing	something

All of the money *is* reserved for emergencies. [*All* refers to the singular noun *money,* so the verb is singular.]

All of the funds *are* reserved for emergencies. [*All* refers to the plural noun *funds,* so the verb is plural.]

23e Collective nouns such as *team* take singular or plural verbs depending on meaning.

Use a singular verb with a collective noun when the group acts as a unit.

The group *agrees* that action is necessary.

But when the group's members act separately, use a plural verb.

The old group *have* gone their separate ways.

The collective noun *number* may be singular or plural. Preceded by *a,* it is plural; preceded by *the,* it is singular.

A number of people *are* in debt.

The number of people in debt *is* very large.

NOTE **ESL** Certain collective nouns are always considered plural: *clergy, military, people, police.* If you mean one representative of the group, use a singular noun such as *police officer.*

23f *Who, which,* and *that* take verbs that agree with their antecedents.

vb agr
23f

When used as subjects, *who, which,* and *that* refer to another word in the sentence, called the ANTECEDENT. The verb agrees with the antecedent.

Mayor Garber ought to listen to the people who *work* for her.

Bardini is the only aide who *has* her ear.

┌─ KEY TERM ───
│ COLLECTIVE NOUN   A noun with singular form that names a group of
│ individuals or things—for instance, *army, audience, committee,*
│ *crowd, family, group, team.*
└──

Agreement problems often occur with relative pronouns when the sentence includes *one of the* or *the only one of the.*

Bardini is one of the aides who *work* unpaid. [Of the aides who work unpaid, Bardini is one.]

Bardini is the only one of the aides who *knows* the community. [Of the aides, only one, Bardini, knows the community.]

NOTE ESL In phrases like those above beginning with *one of the,* be sure the noun is plural: *Bardini is one of the aides* (not *aide*) *who work unpaid.*

23g *News* and other singular nouns ending in *-s* take singular verbs.

Singular nouns ending in *-s* include *athletics, economics, linguistics, mathematics, measles, mumps, news, physics, politics,* and *statistics,* as well as place names such as *Athens, Wales,* and *United States.*

After so long a wait, the news *has* to be good.

Statistics *is* required of psychology majors.

Measurements and figures ending in *-s* may also be singular when the quantity they refer to is a unit.

Three years *is* a long time to wait.

Three-fourths of the library *consists* of reference books.

NOTE These words take plural verbs when they describe individual items rather than whole bodies of activity or knowledge.

The statistics *prove* him wrong.

23h The verb agrees with the subject even when the normal word order is inverted.

Inverted subject-verb order occurs mainly in questions and in constructions beginning with *there* or *it* and a form of *be.*

Is voting a right or a privilege?

vb agr

23h

Are a right and a privilege the same thing?

There *are* differences between them.

23i   *Is, are,* and other linking verbs agree with their subjects, not subject complements.

Make a linking verb agree with its subject, usually the first element in the sentence, not with the noun or pronoun serving as a subject complement.

Henry's sole support *is* his mother and father.

Henry's mother and father *are* his sole support.

23j   Use singular verbs with titles and with words being described or defined.

Hakada Associates *is* a new firm.

Dream Days *remains* a favorite book.

Folks *is* a down-home word for people.

vb
24

---

24   Other Complications with Verbs   ESL

If your native language is not English, you may have difficulty with combinations of verbs and other words: gerunds and infinitives (24a) and prepositions and adverbs (24b).

> KEY TERMS
>
> LINKING VERB   A verb that connects or equates the subject and subject complement: for example, *seem, become,* and forms of *be.*
>
> SUBJECT COMPLEMENT   A word that describes or renames the subject: *They became chemists.*

24a Use a gerund or an infinitive after a verb as appropriate. ESL

Gerunds and infinitives may follow certain verbs but not others. And sometimes the use of a gerund or infinitive with the same verb changes the meaning of the verb.

1. Either gerund or infinitive

A gerund or an infinitive may follow these verbs with no significant difference in meaning:

begin	hate	love
can't bear	hesitate	prefer
can't stand	intend	pretend
continue	like	start

The pump began *working*. The pump began *to work*.

2. Meaning change with gerund or infinitive

With four verbs, a gerund has quite a different meaning from an infinitive.

forget	remember	stop	try

The engineer stopped *eating*. [He no longer ate.]
The engineer stopped *to eat*. [He stopped in order to eat.]

3. Gerund, not infinitive

Do not use an infinitive after these verbs:

admit	dislike	miss	resent
adore	enjoy	postpone	resist
appreciate	escape	practice	risk
avoid	finish	put off	suggest
deny	imagine	quit	tolerate
detest	keep	recall	understand
discuss	mind	recollect	

vb
24a

KEY TERMS

GERUND   The *-ing* form of the verb used as a noun: <u>*Smoking*</u> *is unhealthful.*

INFINITIVE   The plain form of the verb usually preceded by *to: to smoke.* An infinitive may serve as an adjective, adverb, or noun.

FAULTY   He finished *to eat* lunch.
REVISED   He finished *eating* lunch.

4. Infinitive, not gerund

Do not use a gerund after these verbs:

agree	decide	mean	refuse
ask	expect	offer	say
assent	have	plan	wait
beg	hope	pretend	want
claim	manage	promise	wish

FAULTY   He decided *checking* the pump.
REVISED   He decided *to check* the pump.

5. Noun or pronoun + infinitive

Some verbs may be followed by an infinitive alone or by a noun or pronoun and an infinitive. The presence of a noun or pronoun changes the meaning.

ask	need	would like
expect	want	

He expected *to watch.*
He expected *his workers to watch.*

Some verbs *must* be followed by a noun or pronoun before an infinitive:

admonish	dare	oblige	require
advise	encourage	order	teach
allow	forbid	permit	tell
cause	force	persuade	train
challenge	hire	remind	urge
command	instruct	request	warn
convince	invite		

He instructed *his workers to watch.*

Do not use *to* before the infinitive when it follows one of these verbs and a noun or pronoun:

feel	make ("force")
have	see
hear	watch
let	

He let his workers *learn* by observation.

24b   Use the appropriate particles with two-word verbs.   ESL

Some verbs consist of two words: the verb itself and a PARTICLE, a preposition or adverb that affects the meaning of the verb. For example:

Look up the answer. [Research the answer.]
Look over the answer. [Examine the answer.]

The meanings of these two-word verbs are often quite different from the meanings of the individual words that make them up. (There are some three-word verbs, too, such as *put up with* and *run out of.*) A good ESL dictionary, such as one of those mentioned on page 61, will define two-word verbs for you. It will also tell you whether the verbs may be separated in a sentence, as explained below.

NOTE Many of these two-word verbs are more common in speech than in more formal academic or business writing. For formal writing, consider using *research* instead of *look up, examine* or *inspect* instead of *look over.*

1. Inseparable two-word verbs

Verbs and particles that may not be separated by any other words include the following:

catch on	go over	play around	stay away
come across	grow up	run into	stay up
get along	keep on	run out of	take care of
give in	look into	speak up	turn up at

FAULTY   Children *grow* quickly *up.*
REVISED   Children *grow up* quickly.

2. Separable two-word verbs

Most two-word verbs that take direct objects may be separated by the object.

KEY TERMS

PREPOSITION   A word such as *about, for,* or *to* that takes a noun or pronoun as its object: *at the house, in the woods.* See page 76 for a list of prepositions.

ADVERB   A word that modifies a verb (*went down*), adjective (*very pretty*), another adverb (*too sweetly*), or a whole word group (*Eventually, the fire died*). Adverbs tell when, where, how, and to what extent.

Parents *help out* their children.
Parents *help* their children *out*.

If the direct object is a pronoun, the pronoun *must* separate the verb from the particle.

FAULTY   Parents *help out* them.

REVISED   Parents *help* them *out*.

The separable two-word verbs include the following:

bring up	give back	make up	throw out
call off	hand in	point out	try on
call up	hand out	put away	try out
drop off	help out	put back	turn down
fill out	leave out	put off	turn on
fill up	look over	take out	turn up
give away	look up	take over	wrap up

vb

24b

Pronouns

PRONOUNS—words such as *she* and *who* that refer to nouns—merit special care because all their meaning comes from the other words they refer to. This section discusses pronoun forms (Chapter 25), matching pronouns and the words they refer to (26), and making sure pronouns refer to the right nouns (27).

25 Pronoun Case

CASE is the form of a noun or pronoun that shows the reader how it functions in a sentence.

- ❖ The SUBJECTIVE CASE indicates that the word is a subject or subject complement.
- ❖ The OBJECTIVE CASE indicates that the word is an object of a verb or preposition.
- ❖ The POSSESSIVE CASE indicates that the word owns or is the source of a noun in the sentence.

case

25a

Nouns change form only to show possession: *teacher's* (see pp. 163–65). The following pronouns change much more frequently.

SUBJECTIVE	OBJECTIVE	POSSESSIVE
I	me	my, mine
you	you	your, yours
he	him	his
she	her	her, hers
it	it	its
we	us	our, ours
you	you	your, yours
they	them	their, theirs
who	whom	whose
whoever	whomever	—

25a **Distinguish between compound subjects and compound objects: *she and I* vs. *her and me*.**

Compound subjects or objects—those consisting of two or more nouns or pronouns—have the same case forms as they would if one noun or pronoun stood alone.

compound subject
She and Novick discussed the proposal.
         compound object
The proposal disappointed *her and him.*

If you are in doubt about the correct form, try the test below.

❖ Identify a compound construction (one connected by *and, but, or,* or *nor*).

(*He, Him*) and (*I, me*) won the prize.
The prize went to (*he, him*) and (*I, me*).

❖ Write a separate sentence for each part of the compound.

(*He, Him*) won the prize. (*I, Me*) won the prize.
The prize went to (*he, him*). The prize went to (*I, me*).

❖ Choose the pronouns that sound correct.

He won the prize. *I* won the prize. [Subjective.]
The prize went to *him.* The prize went to *me.* [Objective.]

❖ Put the separate sentences back together.

He and *I* won the prize.
The prize went to *him* and *me.*

<table>
<tr><td>**25b**</td><td>**Use the subjective case for subject complements:** *It was she.*</td></tr>
</table>

case

25b

After a linking verb, a pronoun renaming the subject (a subject complement) should be in the subjective case.

┌─ KEY TERMS ────────────────────────────────

SUBJECT   Who or what a sentence is about: *Biologists study animals. They often work in laboratories.*

OBJECT OF VERB   The receiver of the verb's action (DIRECT OBJECT): *Biologists study animals. The animals teach them.* Or the person or thing the action is performed for (INDIRECT OBJECT): *Some biologists give animals homes. The animals give them pleasure.*

OBJECT OF PREPOSITION   The word linked by *with, for,* or another preposition to the rest of the sentence: *Many biologists work in a laboratory. For them the lab provides a second home.*

SUBJECT COMPLEMENT   A word that renames or describes the sentence subject: *Biologists are scientists. The best biologists are she and Scoggins.*

LINKING VERB   A verb, such as a form of *be,* that connects a subject and a word that renames or describes the subject (subject complement): *They are biologists.* (See also pp. 79–80.)

subject complement
The ones who care most are *she and Novick.*

subject
complement
It was *they* whom the mayor appointed.

If this construction sounds stilted to you, use the more natural order: *She and Novick are the ones who care most. The mayor appointed them.*

25c The use of *who* vs. *whom* depends on the pronoun's function in its clause.

1. Questions

At the beginning of a question use *who* for a subject and *whom* for an object.

subject ⟶
Who wrote the policy? *Whom* does it affect? object ⟵⟶

To find the correct case of *who* in a question, try the test below.

❖ Pose the question.

(*Who, Whom*) makes that decision?
(*Who, Whom*) does one ask?

❖ Answer the question, using a personal pronoun. Choose the pronoun that sounds correct, and note its case.

(*She, Her*) makes that decision. *She* makes that decision. [Subjective.]

One asks (*she, her*). One asks *her.* [Objective.]

❖ Use the same case (*who* or *whom*) in the question.

Who makes that decision? [Subjective.]
Whom does one ask? [Objective.]

2. Subordinate clauses

In subordinate clauses use *who* and *whoever* for all subjects, *whom* and *whomever* for all objects.

┌─ KEY TERM ─────────────────────────────────────
│ SUBORDINATE CLAUSE A word group that contains a subject and a
│ verb and also begins with a subordinating word, such as *who,*
│ *whom,* or *because.*
└──

subject ⟍
Give old clothes to *whoever* needs them.

object ⟵──────────
I don't know *whom* the mayor appointed.

To determine which form to use, try the test below.

❖ Locate the subordinate clause.

Few people know (*who, whom*) they should ask.
They are unsure (*who, whom*) makes the decision.

❖ Rewrite the subordinate clause as a separate sentence, substituting a personal pronoun for *who, whom*. Choose the pronoun that sounds correct, and note its case.

They should ask (*she, her*). They should ask *her*. [Objective.]
(*She, her*) usually makes the decision. *She* usually makes the decision. [Subjective.]

❖ Use the same case (*who* or *whom*) in the subordinate clause.

Few people know *whom* they should ask. [Objective.]
They are unsure *who* makes the decision. [Subjective.]

NOTE Don't let expressions such as *I think* and *she says* mislead you into using *whom* rather than *who* for the subject of a clause.

subject ──────⟍
He is the one *who* I think is best qualified.

To choose between *who* and *whom* in such constructions, delete the interrupting phrase so that you can see the true relation between parts: *He is the one who is best qualified.*

case

25d

25d **Use the appropriate case in other constructions.**

1. *We* or *us* with a noun

The choice of *we* or *us* before a noun depends on the use of the noun.

object of
preposition
Freezing weather is welcomed by *us* skaters.

subject ──────⟍
We skaters welcome freezing weather.

2. Pronoun in an appositive

In an appositive the case of a pronoun depends on the function of the word the appositive describes or identifies.

object of verb

The class elected two representatives, DeShawn and *me*.

subject

Two representatives, DeShawn and *I*, were elected.

3. Pronoun after *than* or *as*

When a pronoun follows *than* or *as* in a comparison, the case of the pronoun indicates what words may have been omitted. A subjective pronoun must be the subject of the omitted verb:

subject

Some critics like Glass more than *he* (does).

An objective pronoun must be the object of the omitted verb:

object

Some critics like Glass more than (they like) *him*.

4. Subject and object of infinitive

Both the object *and* the subject of an infinitive are in the objective case.

subject of
infinitive

The school asked *him* to speak.

object of
infinitive

Students chose to invite *him*.

5. Case before a gerund

Ordinarily, use the possessive form of a pronoun or noun immediately before a gerund.

The coach disapproved of *their* lifting weights.

The *coach's* disapproving was a surprise.

KEY TERMS

APPOSITIVE   A noun or noun substitute that renames another noun immediately before it.

INFINITIVE   The plain form of the verb plus *to: to run.*

GERUND   The *-ing* form of a verb used as a noun: *Running is fun.*

---

case

25d

26 Agreement of Pronoun and Antecedent

The ANTECEDENT of a pronoun is the noun or other pronoun it refers to.

Home *owners* fret over *their* tax bills.
antecedent   pronoun

Its constant increases make the tax *bill* a dreaded document.
pronoun   antecedent

For clarity, a pronoun should agree with its anteccdent in person, number, and gender.

NOTE ESL The gender of a pronoun should match its antecedent, not a noun the pronoun may modify: *President Clinton appointed his* (not *her*) *wife to redesign health care.* Also, nouns in English have only neuter gender unless they specifically refer to males or females. Thus nouns such as *book, table, sun,* and *earth* take the pronoun *it.*

26a Antecedents joined by *and* usually take plural pronouns.

pn agr

26a

Mr. Bartos and I cannot settle *our* dispute.

The dean and my adviser have offered *their* help.

EXCEPTIONS When the compound antecedent refers to a single idea, person, or thing, then the pronoun is singular.

KEY TERMS

PERSON	NUMBER	
	SINGULAR	PLURAL
FIRST	*I*	*we*
SECOND	*you*	*you*
THIRD	*he, she, it,*	*they,*
	indefinite pronouns,	plural nouns
	singular nouns	
GENDER		
MASCULINE	*he,* nouns naming males	
FEMININE	*she,* nouns naming females	
NEUTER	*it,* all other nouns	

My friend and adviser offered *her* help.

When the compound antecedent follows *each* or *every,* the pronoun is singular.

Every girl and woman took *her* seat.

26b   When parts of an antecedent are joined by *or* or *nor,* the pronoun agrees with the nearer part.

Tenants or owners must present *their* grievances.

Either the tenant or the owner will have *her* way.

When one subject is plural and the other singular, the sentence will be awkward unless you put the plural subject second.

AWKWARD   Neither the tenants nor the owner has yet made *her* case.

REVISED   Neither the owner nor the tenants have yet made *their* case.

26c   Generally, use a singular pronoun with *everyone* and other indefinite pronouns.

Most indefinite pronouns are singular in meaning. When they serve as antecedents to other pronouns, the other pronouns are singular.

Everyone on the team had *her* own locker.

Each of the boys likes *his* teacher.

In speech we commonly use a plural pronoun when the indefi-

┌─ KEY TERM ─────────────────────────────────

INDEFINITE PRONOUN   A pronoun that does not refer to a specific person or thing:

all	each	neither	one
any	either	nobody	some
anybody	everybody	none	somebody
anyone	everyone	no one	someone
anything	everything	nothing	something

nite pronoun means "many" or "all" rather than "one." In writing, however, you should revise sentences to avoid the misuse.

FAULTY   Everyone feared for *their* lives.

REVISED   *All the riders* feared for *their* lives.

The generic he

The meaning of an indefinite pronoun often includes both masculine and feminine genders, not one or the other. The same is true of other indefinite words such as *child, adult, individual,* and *person.* In such cases tradition has called for *he (him, his)* to refer to the antecedent. But this so-called GENERIC *HE* (or generalized *he*) appears to exclude females. To avoid it, try one of the techniques below:

GENERIC *HE*   None of the students had the credits *he* needed.

❖ Substitute *he or she.*

REVISED   None of the students had the credits *he or she* needed.

To avoid awkwardness, don't use *he or she* more than once in several sentences.

❖ Recast the sentence using a plural antecedent and pronoun.

REVISED   *All the students* in the class lacked the credits *they* needed.

❖ Rewrite the sentence to avoid the pronoun.

REVISED   None of the students had the *needed credits.*

For more on avoiding sexist and other biased language, see pages 57–58.

pn agr

26d

26d Collective nouns such as *team* take singular or plural pronouns depending on meaning.

Use a singular pronoun with a collective noun when referring to the group as a unit.

The committee voted to disband *itself.*

┌ KEY TERM ──────────────────────────────

COLLECTIVE NOUN   A noun with singular form that names a group of individuals or things—for instance, *army, audience, committee, crowd, family, group, team.*

When referring to the individual members of the group, use a plural pronoun.

The old group have gone *their* separate ways.

27 Reference of Pronoun to Antecedent

A pronoun should refer clearly to its ANTECEDENT, the noun it substitutes for. Otherwise, readers will have difficulty grasping the pronoun's meaning.

27a Make a pronoun refer clearly to one antecedent.

When either of two nouns can be a pronoun's antecedent, the reference will not be clear.

> **CONFUSING**   The workers removed all the furniture from the room and cleaned *it*.

Revise such a sentence in one of two ways:

❖ Replace the pronoun with the appropriate noun.

> **CLEAR**   The workers removed all the furniture from the room and cleaned *the room* (or *the furniture*).

❖ Avoid repetition by rewriting the sentence with the pronoun but with only one possible antecedent.

> **CLEAR**   After removing all the furniture from *it*, the workers cleaned the room.
>
> **CLEAR**   The workers cleaned all the furniture after removing *it* from the room.

27b Place a pronoun close enough to its antecedent to ensure clarity.

A clause beginning *who, which,* or *that* should generally fall immediately after the word it refers to.

CONFUSING   Jody found a dress in the attic *that* her aunt had worn.

CLEAR   In the attic Jody found a dress *that* her aunt had worn.

27c Make a pronoun refer to a specific antecedent, not an implied one.

A pronoun should refer to a specific noun or other pronoun. When the antecedent is not specifically stated but is implied by the context, the reference can only be inferred by the reader.

1. Vague *this, that, which,* or *it*

This, that, which, or *it* should refer to a specific noun, not to a whole word group expressing an idea or situation.

CONFUSING   The faculty agreed on a change in the requirements, but *it* took time.

CLEAR   The faculty agreed on a change in the requirements, but *agreeing* took time.

CLEAR   The faculty agreed on a change in the requirements, but *the change* took time.

CONFUSING   The British knew little of the American countryside and had no experience with the colonists' guerrilla tactics. *This* gave the colonists an advantage.

CLEAR   The British knew little of the American countryside and had no experience with the colonists' guerrilla tactics. This *ignorance and inexperience* gave the colonists an advantage.

2. Implied nouns

A noun may be implied in some other word or phrase: *happiness* is implied in *happy*, *news* in *newspaper*. But a pronoun cannot refer clearly to such an implied noun; it must refer to a specific, stated antecedent.

CONFUSING   In Joan Cohen's advice *she* was not concrete enough.

CLEAR   *Joan Cohen's advice* was not concrete enough.

ref

27c

CONFUSING	She spoke once before, but *it* was sparsely attended.
CLEAR	She spoke once before, but *the speech* was sparsely attended.

3. Indefinite *it, they,* or *you*

It, they, and *you* should have definite antecedents—nouns for *it* and *they,* an actual reader being addressed for *you.* Rewrite the sentence if the antecedent is missing.

CONFUSING	In Chapter 4 of this book *it* describes the early flights of the Wright brothers.
CLEAR	*Chapter 4* of this book describes the early flights of the Wright brothers.
CONFUSING	In the average television drama *they* present a false picture of life.
CLEAR	The average television *drama* presents a false picture of life.

In all but very formal writing, *you* is acceptable when the meaning is clearly "you, the reader." But the context must be appropriate for such a meaning.

INAPPROPRIATE	In the fourteenth century *you* had to struggle simply to survive.
REVISED	In the fourteenth century *one* (or *a person*) had to struggle simply to survive.

shift

27d

27d   Keep pronouns consistent.

Within a sentence or a group of related sentences, pronouns should be consistent. Partly, consistency comes from making pronouns and their antecedents agree (see Chapter 26). In addition, the pronouns within a passage should match each other.

INCONSISTENT	*One* finds when reading that *your* concentration improves with practice, so that *I* now comprehend more in less time.
REVISED	*I* find when reading that *my* concentration improves with practice, so that I now comprehend more in less time.

Modifiers

MODIFIERS describe or limit other words in a sentence. They are adjectives, adverbs, or word groups serving as adjectives or adverbs. This section identifies and solves problems in the forms of modifiers (Chapter 28) and in their relation to the rest of the sentence (29).

28 Adjectives and Adverbs

ADJECTIVES modify nouns (*happy* child) and pronouns (*special* someone). ADVERBS modify verbs (*almost* see), adjectives (*very* happy), other adverbs (*not* very), and whole word groups (*Otherwise, the room was empty*). The only way to tell if a modifier should be an adjective or an adverb is to determine its function in the sentence.

ad

28b

28a Use adjectives only to modify nouns and pronouns.

Using adjectives instead of adverbs to modify verbs, adverbs, or other adjectives is nonstandard.

NONSTANDARD Educating children *good* is everyone's focus.

STANDARD Educating children *well* is everyone's focus.

NONSTANDARD Some children suffer *bad*.

STANDARD Some children suffer *badly*.

28b Use an adjective after a linking verb to modify the subject. Use an adverb to modify a verb.

Some verbs may or may not be linking verbs, depending on their meaning in the sentence. When the word after the verb modifies the subject, the verb is linking and the word should be an adjective. When the word modifies the verb, however, it should be an adverb.

Two word pairs are especially troublesome in this context. One is *bad* and *badly.*

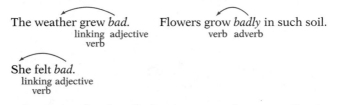

The weather grew *bad.*
            linking adjective
               verb

Flowers grow *badly* in such soil.
            verb adverb

She felt *bad.*
   linking adjective
     verb

The other is *good* and *well. Good* serves only as an adjective. *Well* may serve as an adverb with a host of meanings or as an adjective meaning only "fit" or "healthy."

Decker trained *well.*
    verb   adverb

She felt *well.*
  linking adjective
    verb

Her health was *good.*
    linking adjective
      verb

28c Use the comparative and superlative forms of adjectives and adverbs appropriately.

Adjectives and adverbs can show degrees of quality or amount with the endings *-er* and *-est* or with the words *more* and *most* or *less* and *least.* Most modifiers have three forms:

	ADJECTIVES	**ADVERBS**
POSITIVE The basic form listed in the dictionary	red awful	soon quickly
COMPARATIVE A greater or lesser degree of the quality named	redder more/less awful	sooner more/less quickly
SUPERLATIVE The greatest or least degree of the quality named	reddest most/least awful	soonest most/least quickly

---

KEY TERM

LINKING VERB   A verb that links, or connects, a subject and a word that describes the subject: *They are golfers.* Linking verbs are forms of *be,* the verbs associated with our five senses (*look, sound, smell, feel, taste*), and a few others (*appear, seem, become, grow, turn, prove, remain*).

If sound alone does not tell you whether to use *-er/-est* or *more/most,* consult a dictionary. If the endings can be used, the dictionary will list them. Otherwise, use *more* or *most.*

1. Irregular adjectives and adverbs

The irregular modifiers change the spelling of their positive form to show comparative and superlative degrees.

POSITIVE	COMPARATIVE	SUPERLATIVE
Adjectives		
good	better	best
bad	worse	worst
little	littler, less	littlest, least
many		
some	more	most
much		
Adverbs		
well	better	best
badly	worse	worst

2. Double comparisons

A double comparative or double superlative combines the *-er* or *-est* ending with the word *more* or *most.* It is redundant.

Chang was the *wisest* (not *most wisest*) person in town.
He was *smarter* (not *more smarter*) than anyone else.

3. Logical comparisons

Absolute modifiers

Some adjectives and adverbs cannot logically be compared—for instance, *perfect, unique, dead, impossible, infinite.* These absolute words can be preceded by adverbs like *nearly* or *almost* that mean "approaching," but they cannot logically be modified by *more* or *most* (as in *most perfect*).

NOT   He was the *most unique* teacher we had.

BUT   He was a *unique* teacher.

Completeness

To be logical, a comparison must also be complete in the following ways.

ad

28c

❖ The comparison must state a relation fully enough to ensure clarity.

UNCLEAR   Car makers worry about their industry more than environmentalists.

CLEAR   Car makers worry about their industry more than environmentalists *do*.

CLEAR   Car makers worry about their industry more than *they worry about* environmentalists.

❖ The items being compared should in fact be comparable.

ILLOGICAL   The cost of an electric car is greater than a gasoline-powered car. [Illogically compares a cost and a car.]

REVISED   The cost of an electric car is greater than *the cost of* (or *that of*) a gasoline-powered car.

Any *versus* any other

Use *any other* when comparing something with others in the same group. Use *any* when comparing something with others in a different group.

ILLOGICAL   Los Angeles is larger than *any* city in California. [Since Los Angeles is itself a city in California, the sentence seems to say that Los Angeles is larger than itself.]

REVISED   Los Angeles is larger than *any other* city in California.

ILLOGICAL   Los Angeles is larger than *any other* city in Canada. [The cities in Canada constitute a group to which Los Angeles does not belong.]

REVISED   Los Angeles is larger than *any* city in Canada.

ad

28d

28d Avoid double negatives.

A DOUBLE NEGATIVE is a nonstandard construction in which two negative words such as *no, none, neither, barely, hardly,* or *scarcely* cancel each other out. For instance, *Jenny did not feel nothing* asserts that Jenny felt other than nothing, or something. For the opposite meaning, one of the negatives must be eliminated or changed to a positive: *She felt nothing* or *She did not feel anything.*

FAULTY   We could *not hardly* hear the speaker. *None* of her ideas *never* made it to the back of the room.

REVISED   We could *hardly* hear the speaker. *None* of her ideas made it to the back of the room.

Revised   We could *not* hear the speaker. Her ideas *never* made it to the back of the room.

28e Distinguish between present and past participles as adjectives.   ESL

Both present participles and past participles may serve as adjectives: *a burning bush, a burned bush.* As in the examples, the two participles usually differ in the time they indicate.

But some present and past participles—those derived from verbs expressing feeling—can have altogether different meanings. The present participle refers to something that causes the feeling: *That was a frightening storm.* The past participle refers to something that experiences the feeling: *They quieted the frightened horses.*

The following participles are among those likely to be confused:

amazing/amazed
amusing/amused
annoying/annoyed
astonishing/astonished
boring/bored
confusing/confused
depressing/depressed
embarrassing/embarrassed
exciting/excited
exhausting/exhausted

fascinating/fascinated
frightening/frightened
frustrating/frustrated
interesting/interested
pleasing/pleased
satisfying/satisfied
shocking/shocked
surprising/surprised
tiring/tired
worrying/worried

ad

28f

28f Use *a, an, the,* and other determiners appropriately.   ESL

DETERMINERS are special kinds of adjectives that mark nouns because they always precede nouns. Some common determiners are *a, an,* and *the* (called ARTICLES) and *my, their, whose, this, these, those, one, some,* and *any.*

Native speakers of English can rely on their intuition when using determiners, but nonnative speakers often have difficulty with them because many other languages use them quite differently or not at all. In English the use of determiners depends on the context they appear in and the kind of nouns they precede:

❖ A PROPER NOUN names a particular person, place, or thing and begins with a capital letter: *February, Joe Allen, Red River.*

❖ A COUNT NOUN names something that is countable in English and can form a plural: *girl/girls, apple/apples, child/children.*

❖ A NONCOUNT NOUN names something not usually considered countable in English. A noncount noun does not form a plural. Here is a sample of noncount nouns:

advice	happiness	mail	silver
baggage	health	meat	supervision
cereal	homework	money	traffic
confidence	information	oil	truth
courage	intelligence	police	underwear
equipment	knowledge	pollution	water
evidence	legislation	research	wealth
furniture	lightning	satisfaction	weather
hair	love	scenery	work

An ESL dictionary will tell you whether a noun is a count noun, a noncount noun, or both. (See p. 61 for recommended dictionaries.)

NOTE Many nouns are sometimes count nouns and sometimes noncount nouns.

The library has *a room* for readers. [*Room* is a count noun meaning "walled area."]

The library has *room* for reading. [*Room* is a noncount noun meaning "space."]

ad
28f

1. *A, an,* and *the*

With singular count nouns

A or *an* precedes a singular count noun when the reader does not already know its identity, usually because you have not mentioned it before.

A scientist in our chemistry department developed *a* process to strengthen metals. [*Scientist* and *process* are being introduced for the first time.]

The precedes a singular count noun that has a specific identity for the reader, usually because (1) you have mentioned it before, (2) you identify it immediately before or after you state it, (3) it is unique (the only one in existence), or (4) it refers to an institution or facility that is shared by a community.

A scientist in our chemistry department developed a process to strengthen metals. *The* scientist patented *the* process. [*Scientist* and *process* were identified in the preceding sentence.]

The most productive laboratory is *the* research center in the chemistry department. [*Most productive* identifies *laboratory,* and *in the chemistry department* identifies *research center.*]

The sun rises in *the* east. [*Sun* and *east* are unique.]

Many men and women aspire to *the* Presidency. [*Presidency* is a shared institution.]

The fax machine has changed business communication. [*Fax machine* is a shared facility.]

The is not used before a singular noun that names a general category.

Wordsworth's poetry shows his love of *nature* (not *the nature*).

General Sherman said that *war* is hell. [*War* names a general category.]

The war in Croatia left many dead. [*War* names a specific war.]

With plural count nouns

A or *an* never precedes a plural noun. *The* does not precede a plural noun that names a general category. *The* does precede a plural noun that names specific representatives of a category.

Men and *women* are different. [*Men* and *women* name general categories.]

The women formed a team. [*Women* refers to specific people.]

With noncount nouns

A or *an* never precedes a noncount noun. *The* does precede a noncount noun that names specific representatives of a general category.

Vegetation suffers from drought. [*Vegetation* names a general category.]

The vegetation in the park withered or died. [*Vegetation* refers to specific plants.]

With proper nouns

A or *an* never precedes a proper noun. *The* generally does not precede proper nouns.

Garcia lives in *Boulder.*

There are exceptions, however. For instance, we generally use *the* before the names of ships (*the* Lusitania), oceans (*the* Pacific), mountain ranges (<u>the</u> Alps), regions (<u>the</u> Middle East), rivers (<u>the</u> Mississippi), and some countries (<u>the</u> United States, <u>the</u> Netherlands).

2. Other determiners

The uses of English determiners besides articles also depend on context and kind of noun. The following determiners may be used with each kind of noun.

With singular count nouns

my, our, your, his, her, its, their, possessive nouns (*boy's, boys'*)
whose, which(*ever*)*, what*(*ever*)
this, that
one, any, some, every, each, either, neither, another, the other
the first, the second, etc.; *the last*

Their bank account is overdrawn.
Every dollar was spent.

With plural count nouns

my, our, your, his, her, its, their, possessive nouns (*boy's, boys'*)
whose, which(*ever*)*, what*(*ever*)
these, those
*some, any, both, many, enough, more, most, other, the other, such,
     few, a few, fewer, fewest, several, all, all of the, a lot of*
no; two, three, etc.; *the first, the second,* etc.; *the last*

Those numbers are incorrect.
Some mistakes were made.

NOTE *Few* means "not many" or "not enough." *A few* means "some" or "a small but sufficient quantity."

Few committee members came to the meeting.
A few members can keep the committee going.

Do not use *much* with a plural count noun.

Many (not *much*) members want to help.

With noncount nouns

my, our, your, his, her, its, their, possessive nouns (*boy's, boys'*)
whose, which(*ever*)*, what*(*ever*)
this, that
*some, any, much, more, most, enough, other, the other, such, little, a
     little, less, least, all, all of the, a lot of, a large amount of*
no; the first, the second, etc.; *the last*

That money should be saved.
Would *more* evidence convince you?

NOTE *Little* means "not many" or "not enough." *A little* means "some" or "a small but sufficient quantity."

Little time remains before the conference.
The members need *a little* help from their colleagues.

Do not use *many* with a noncount noun.

Much (not *many*) work remains.

29 Misplaced and Dangling Modifiers

The arrangement of words in a sentence is an important clue to their relationships. Modifiers will be unclear if readers can't connect them to the words they modify.

mm

29a

29a Reposition misplaced modifiers.

A MISPLACED MODIFIER falls in the wrong place in a sentence. It may be awkward, confusing, or even unintentionally funny.

1. Clear placement

Readers tend to link a modifier to the nearest word it could modify. Any other placement can link the modifier to the wrong word.

CONFUSING   He served steak to the men *on paper plates.*

CLEAR   He served the men steak *on paper plates.*

CONFUSING   According to the police, many dogs are killed by automobiles and trucks *roaming unleashed.*

CLEAR   According to the police, many dogs *roaming unleashed* are killed by automobiles and trucks.

2. *Only* and other limiting modifiers

LIMITING MODIFIERS include *almost, even, exactly, hardly, just, merely, nearly, only, scarcely,* and *simply.* For clarity place such a modifier immediately before the word or word group you intend it to limit.

UNCLEAR   They *only* saw each other during meals.

CLEAR   They saw *only* each other during meals.

CLEAR   They saw each other *only* during meals.

3. Infinitives and other grammatical units

Some grammatical units should generally not be split by long modifiers. For example, a long adverb modifier between subject and verb can be awkward and confusing.

AWKWARD   The *wreckers,* soon after they began demolishing the old house, *discovered* a large box of coins.

REVISED   Soon after they began demolishing the old house, the wreckers *discovered* a large box of coins.

A SPLIT INFINITIVE—a modifier placed between *to* and the verb—can be especially awkward and annoys many readers.

AWKWARD   The weather service expected temperatures *to* not *rise.*

REVISED   The weather service expected temperatures not *to rise.*

A split infinitive may sometimes be natural and preferable, though it may still bother some readers.

Several U.S. industries expect *to* more than *triple* their use of robots.

┌─ KEY TERMS ──────────────────────────────

ADVERB   A word that describes a verb, adjective, other adverb, or whole word group, specifying how, when, where, or to what extent: *quickly* see, solid *like a boulder.*

INFINITIVE   A verb form consisting of *to* plus the verb's plain (or dictionary) form: *to produce, to enjoy.*

Here the split infinitive is more economical than the alternatives, such as *Several U.S. industries expect to increase their use of robots by more than three times.*

4. Adverbs of frequency ESL

Adverbs such as *always, seldom, rarely, often, sometimes,* and *never* tell how frequently something happens. These adverbs usually appear before the verb or between a helping verb and the main verb.

> helping main
> verb verb adverb
>
> **AWKWARD**   Robots *have put* sometimes humans out of work.

> helping   main
> verb   adverb   verb
>
> **REVISED**   Robots *have* sometimes *put* humans out of work.

> adverb   verb phrase
>
> **REVISED**   Sometimes robots *have put* humans out of work.

Adverbs of frequency always follow the verb *be.*

> adverb verb
>
> **AWKWARD**   Robots often *are* helpful to workers.

> verb adverb
>
> **REVISED**   Robots *are* often helpful to workers.

5. Order of adjectives ESL

English follows distinctive rules for arranging two or three adjectives before a noun. (A string of more than three adjectives before a noun is rare.) The adjectives follow this order:

DETERMINER	OPINION	SIZE OR SHAPE	AGE	COLOR	ORIGIN	MATERIAL	NOUN USED AS ADJECTIVE	NOUN
many			new				state	laws
	lovely			green	Thai			birds
a		square				wooden		table
all			recent				business	reports
the				blue		litmus		paper

See page 154 on punctuating adjectives before a noun.

KEY TERM

ADJECTIVE A word that describes a noun or pronoun, specifying which one, what quality, or how many: *good* one, *three* cars.

mm

29a

29b Connect dangling modifiers to their sentences.

A DANGLING MODIFIER does not sensibly modify anything in its sentence.

DANGLING *Passing the building,* the vandalism became visible. [The modifying phrase seems to describe *vandalism,* but vandalism does not pass buildings. Who was passing the building? Who saw the vandalism?]

Dangling modifiers usually introduce sentences, contain a verb form, and imply but do not name a subject: in the example above, the implied subject is the someone or something passing the building. Readers assume that this implied subject is the same as the subject of the sentence (*vandalism* in the example). When it is not, the modifier "dangles" unconnected to the rest of the sentence.

Revise dangling modifiers by recasting the sentences they appear in. The choice of method depends on what you want to emphasize in the sentence.

❖ Rewrite the dangling modifier as a complete clause with its own stated subject and verb. Readers can accept that the new subject and the sentence subject are different.

DANGLING *Passing the building,* the vandalism became visible.

REVISED *As we passed* the building, the vandalism became visible.

DANGLING Although intact, graffiti covered every inch of the walls and windows.

REVISED Although *the walls and windows were* intact, graffiti covered every inch of *them.*

❖ Change the subject of the sentence to a word the modifier properly describes.

DANGLING After seeing such a sight, a sense of loss is experienced.

REVISED After seeing such as sight, *one experiences* a sense of loss.

DANGLING *Trying to understand the causes,* vandalism has been extensively studied.

REVISED Trying to understand the causes, *researchers have* extensively *studied* vandalism.

Sentence Faults

A word group punctuated as a sentence will confuse or annoy readers if it lacks needed parts, has too many parts, or has parts that don't fit together.

30 Sentence Fragments

A SENTENCE FRAGMENT is part of a sentence that is set off as if it were a whole sentence by an initial capital letter and a final period or other end punctuation. Although writers occasionally use fragments deliberately and effectively (see 30c), readers perceive most fragments as serious errors.

frag

30a

Complete sentence versus sentence fragment

A COMPLETE SENTENCE or MAIN CLAUSE
1. contains a subject and a verb (*The wind blows*)
2. and is not a subordinate clause (beginning with a word such as *because* or *who*).

A SENTENCE FRAGMENT
1. lacks a verb (*The wind blowing*),
2. or lacks a subject (*And blows*),
3. or is a subordinate clause not attached to a complete sentence (*Because the wind blows*).

NOTE ESL Some languages other than English allow the omission of the subject or verb. Except in commands (*Close the door*), English always requires you to state the subject and verb.

30a Test your sentences for completeness.

A word group punctuated as a sentence should pass *all three* of the following tests. If it does not, it is a fragment and needs to be revised.

Test 1: Find the verb.

Look for a verb in the group of words.

FRAGMENT   The baboon with a stick in his mouth. [Compare a complete sentence: *The baboon held a stick in his mouth.*]

Any verb form you find must be a FINITE VERB, one that changes form as indicated below. A verbal does not change; it cannot serve as a sentence verb without the aid of a helping verb.

	FINITE VERBS IN COMPLETE SENTENCES	VERBALS IN SENTENCE FRAGMENTS
SINGULAR	The baboon *looks.*	The baboon *looking.*
PLURAL	The baboons *look.*	The baboons *looking.*
PRESENT	The baboon *looks.*	
PAST	The baboon *looked.*	The baboon *looking.*
FUTURE	The baboon *will* look.	

Test 2: Find the subject.

The subject of the sentence will usually come before the verb. If there is no subject, the word group is probably a fragment.

FRAGMENT   And eyed the guard nervously. [Compare a complete sentence: *And he eyed the guard nervously.*]

Test 3: Make sure the clause is not subordinate.

A subordinate clause usually begins with a subordinating word, such as one of the following.

frag

30a

┌─ KEY TERMS ───

VERB   The part of a sentence that asserts something about the subject: *Ducks swim.* Also called PREDICATE.

VERBAL   A verb form that can serve as a noun, a modifier, or a part of a sentence verb, but not alone as the only verb of a sentence: *drawing, to draw, drawn.*

HELPING VERB   A verb such as *is, were, have, might,* and *could* that combines with various verb forms to indicate time and other kinds of meaning: for instance, *were drawing, might draw.*

SUBJECT   The part of a sentence that names who or what performs the action or makes the assertion of the verb: *Ducks swim.*

SUBORDINATE CLAUSE   A word group that contains a subject and a verb, begins with a subordinating word such as *because* or *who,* and is not a question: *Ducks can swim when they are young.* A subordinate clause may serve as a modifier or as a noun.

SUBORDINATING CONJUNCTIONS			RELATIVE PRONOUNS	
after	once	until	that	who/whom
although	since	when	which	whoever/whomever
as	than	where		
because	that	whereas		
if	unless	while		

Subordinate clauses serve as parts of sentences (nouns or modifiers), not as whole sentences.

> **FRAGMENT**   When the next cage rattled. [Compare a complete sentence: *The next cage rattled.*]

NOTE Questions beginning with *how* or the *wh-* words (such as *who, which, when*) are not sentence fragments: *Who rattled the cage?*

30b Revise sentence fragments.

Correct sentence fragments in one of two ways depending on the importance of the information in the fragment and thus how much you want to stress it.

- ❖ Rewrite the fragment as a complete sentence. The information in the fragment will then have the same importance as that in other complete sentences.

> **FRAGMENT**   The baboon and his challenger stared at each other. *Poised for combat.*
>
> **REVISED**   The baboon and his challenger stared at each other. *They were* poised for combat.

> **FRAGMENT**   The animals acted out a rivalry. *Which mystified their keepers.*
>
> **REVISED**   The animals acted out a rivalry. *It* mystified their keepers.

- ❖ Combine the fragment with the appropriate main clause. The information in the fragment will then be subordinated to that in the main clause.

> **FRAGMENT**   The baboon and his challenger stared at each other. *Poised for combat.*
>
> **REVISED**   The baboon and his challenger stared at each other, poised for combat.
>
> **REVISED**   Poised for combat, the baboon and his challenger stared at each other.

FRAGMENT   Some of the keepers were afraid of the challenger. *A newcomer who was usually fierce.*

REVISED   Some of the keepers were afraid of the challenger, a newcomer who was unusually fierce.

30c Be aware of the acceptable uses of incomplete sentences.

A few word groups lacking the usual subject-predicate combination are incomplete sentences, but they are not fragments because they conform to the expectations of most readers. They include exclamations (*Oh no!*); questions and answers (*Where next? To Kansas.*); and commands (*Move along. Shut the window.*).

Experienced writers sometimes use sentence fragments when they want to achieve a special effect. Such fragments appear more in informal than in formal writing. Unless you are experienced and thoroughly secure in your own writing, you should avoid all fragments and concentrate on writing clear, well-formed sentences.

cs/fs
31

31 Comma Splices and Fused Sentences

Two problems commonly occur in punctuating consecutive main clauses. One is the COMMA SPLICE, in which the clauses are joined (or spliced) *only* with a comma.

COMMA SPLICE   The ship was huge, its mast stood eighty feet high.

The other is the FUSED SENTENCE (or RUN-ON SENTENCE), in which no punctuation or conjunction appears between the clauses.

FUSED SENTENCE   The ship was huge its mast stood eighty feet high.

KEY TERM

MAIN CLAUSE   A word group that contains a subject and a verb and does not begin with a subordinating word: *A dictionary is essential.*

31a **Separate main clauses not joined by *and, but,* or another coordinating conjunction.**

Readers need a signal that one main clause is ending and another is beginning. No punctuation at all or even a comma alone (without *and, but, or, nor, for, so,* or *yet*) fails to provide that signal.

Revision of comma splices and fused sentences

❖ Make the clauses into separate sentences when the ideas expressed are only loosely related.

COMMA SPLICE	Chemistry has contributed much to our understanding of foods, many foods such as wheat and beans can be produced in the laboratory.
REVISED	Chemistry has contributed much to our understanding of foods. Many foods such as wheat and beans can be produced in the laboratory.

❖ Insert a coordinating conjunction in a comma splice when the ideas in the main clauses are closely related and equally important.

COMMA SPLICE	Some laboratory-grown foods taste good, they are nutritious.
REVISED	Some laboratory-grown foods taste good, *and* they are nutritious.

In a fused sentence insert a comma and a coordinating conjunction.

FUSED	Chemists have made much progress they still have a way to go.
REVISED	Chemists have made much progress, *but* they still have a way to go.

❖ Insert a semicolon between clauses if the relation between the ideas is very close and obvious without a conjunction.

COMMA SPLICE	Good taste is rare in laboratory-grown vegetables, they are usually bland.
REVISED	Good taste is rare in laboratory-grown vegetables; they are usually bland.

(continued)

cs/fs

31a

Revision of comma splices and fused sentences
(continued)

❖ Subordinate one clause to the other when one idea is less important than the other.

COMMA SPLICE   The vitamins are adequate, the flavor is deficient.

REVISED   *Even though* the vitamins are adequate, the flavor is deficient.

31b Separate main clauses related by *however, thus,* or another conjunctive adverb.

CONJUNCTIVE ADVERBS are modifiers that describe a relation between two main clauses.

cs/fs
31b

Common conjunctive adverbs

accordingly	furthermore	meanwhile	similarly
anyway	hence	moreover	still
besides	however	namely	then
certainly	incidentally	nevertheless	thereafter
consequently	indeed	nonetheless	therefore
finally	instead	now	thus
further	likewise	otherwise	undoubtedly

When two clauses are related by a conjunctive adverb, they must be separated by a period or by a semicolon. The adverb is also generally set off by a comma or commas.

COMMA SPLICE   Most Americans refuse to give up unhealthful habits, consequently our medical costs are higher than those of many other countries.

REVISED   Most Americans refuse to give up unhealthful habits. *Consequently,* our medical costs are higher than those of many other countries.

REVISED   Most Americans refuse to give up unhealthful habits; *consequently,* our medical costs are higher than those of many other countries.

Unlike coordinating and subordinating conjunctions, conjunctive adverbs do not join two clauses into a grammatical unit but merely describe the way the clauses relate in meaning. To test whether a word is a conjunctive adverb, try moving it around in its clause. Unlike conjunctions, conjunctive adverbs can move.

> Most Americans refuse to give up unhealthful habits; our medical costs, *consequently*, are higher than those of many other countries.

Note that commas set off the conjunctive adverb.

Mixed Sentences

A MIXED SENTENCE contains parts that do not fit together.

32a Match subjects and predicates in meaning.

In a sentence with mixed meaning, the subject is said to do or be something illogical. Such a mixture is sometimes called FAULTY PREDICATION because the predicate conflicts with the subject.

mixed

32a

1. Illogical equation with *be*

When a form of *be* connects a subject and a word that describes the subject (a complement), the subject and complement must be logically related.

> **MIXED**   A *compromise* between the city and the country would be
> the ideal *place* to live.

> **REVISED**   A *community* that offered the best qualities of both city
> and country would be the ideal *place* to live.

2. *Is when, is where*

Definitions require nouns on both sides of *be*. Clauses that

---

KEY TERMS

SUBJECT   The part of a sentence that names who or what performs the action or makes the assertion of the verb: *Geese fly*.

PREDICATE   The part of a sentence containing the verb and asserting something about the subject: *Geese fly*.

define and begin with *when* or *where* are common in speech but should be avoided in writing.

MIXED An *examination* is *when you are tested* on what you know.

REVISED An *examination* is a *test* of what you know.

3. *Reason is because*

The commonly heard construction *The reason is because* . . . is redundant since *because* means "for the reason that."

MIXED The *reason* the temple requests donations *is because* the school needs expansion.

REVISED The *reason* the temple requests donations *is that* the school needs expansion.

REVISED The temple requests donations *because* the school needs expansion.

4. Other mixed meanings

Faulty predications are not confined to sentences with *be*.

MIXED The *use* of emission controls *was created* to reduce air pollution.

REVISED Emission *controls were created* to reduce air pollution.

32b Untangle sentences that are mixed in grammar.

Many mixed sentences start with one grammatical plan or construction but end with a different one.

MIXED *In all her efforts to please others got* her into trouble.

REVISED *All her efforts to please others got* her into trouble.

MIXED *Although he was seen with a convicted thief does not make* him a thief.

REVISED *That he was seen with a convicted thief does not make* him a thief.

32c State parts of sentences, such as subjects, only once. ESL

In some languages other than English, certain parts of sentences may be repeated. These include the subject in any kind of clause or an object or adverb in an adjective clause. In English, however, these parts are stated only once in a clause.

1. Repetition of subject

You may be tempted to restate a subject as a pronoun before the verb. But the subject needs stating only once in its clause.

> **FAULTY**   The *liquid it* reached a temperature of 180°F.
>
> **REVISED**   The *liquid* reached a temperature of 180°F.

> **FAULTY**   *Gases* in the liquid *they* escaped.
>
> **REVISED**   *Gases* in the liquid escaped.

2. Repetition in an adjective clause

Adjective clauses begin with *who, whom, whose, which, that, where,* and *when.* The beginning word replaces another word: the subject (*He is the person who called*), an object of a verb or preposition (*He is the person whom I mentioned*), or a preposition and pronoun (*He knows the office where [in which] the conference will occur*).

Do not state the word being replaced in an adjective clause by *who, whom,* and the like.

> **FAULTY**   The technician *whom* the test depended on *her* was burned. [*Whom* should replace *her.*]
>
> **REVISED**   The technician *whom* the test depended on was burned.

In adjective clauses beginning with *where* or *when,* no adverb such as *there* or *then* is needed.

> **FAULTY**   Gases escaped at a moment *when* the technician was unprepared *then.*
>
> **REVISED**   Gases escaped at a moment *when* the technician was unprepared.

NOTE *Whom, which,* and similar words are sometimes omitted but are still understood by the reader. Thus the word being replaced should not be stated.

mixed

32c

FAULTY   Accidents rarely happen to technicians the lab has trained *them*. [*Whom* is understood: . . . *technicians whom the lab has trained.*]

REVISED   Accidents rarely happen to technicians the lab has trained.

IV

Punctuation

IV

Punctuation

❖

33 End Punctuation

End a sentence with one of three punctuation marks: a period
(.), a question mark (?), or an exclamation point (!).

33a Use a period after most sentences and in many abbreviations.

1. Statements, mild commands, and indirect questions

STATEMENT

The airline went bankrupt.
It no longer flies.

MILD COMMAND

Think of the possibilities.
Please consider others.

INDIRECT QUESTION

An INDIRECT QUESTION reports what someone asked but not in
the exact form or words of the original question.

The judge asked why I had been driving with my lights off.
No one asked how we got home.

2. Abbreviations

p.	B.C.	B.A.	Mr.
M.D.	A.D.	Ph.D.	Mrs.
Dr.	A.M., a.m.	e.g.	Ms.
St.	P.M., p.m.	i.e.	

Omit periods from most abbreviations of three or more words.
These include ACRONYMS, which are pronounceable words, such as
NATO or AIDS, formed from the initial letters of the words in a
name.

IBM	USMC	JFK	VISTA

NOTE When an abbreviation falls at the end of a sentence, use
only one period: *The school offers a B.A.*

.?!

33a

33b Use a question mark after a direct question and sometimes to indicate doubt.

1. Direct questions

Who will follow her**?**
What is the difference between these two people**?**

After indirect questions, use a period: *We wondered who would follow her.* (See the preceding page.)

Questions in a series are each followed by a question mark.

The officer asked how many times the suspect had been arrested. Three times**?** Four times**?** More than that**?**

2. Doubt

A question mark within parentheses can indicate doubt about a number or date.

The Greek philosopher Socrates was born in 470 (**?**) B.C. and died in 399 B.C. from drinking poison. [Socrates's birthdate is not known for sure.]

Use sentence structure and words, not a question mark, to express sarcasm or irony.

NOT   Stern's friendliness (?) bothered Crane.
BUT   Stern's *insincerity* bothered Crane.

33c Use an exclamation point after an emphatic statement, interjection, or command.

. ? !
33c

No**!** We must not lose this election**!**
"Oh**!**" she gasped.
Come here immediately**!**

Follow mild interjections and commands with commas or periods, as appropriate: *Oh, call whenever you can.*

NOTE Use exclamation points sparingly, even in informal writing. Overused, they'll fail to impress readers and they may make you sound overemphatic.

┌─ KEY TERM ──────────────────────────────────────

INTERJECTION   A word that expresses feeling or commands attention, either alone or within a sentence: *Oh! Hey! Wow!*

34 The Comma

The comma (,) is the most common punctuation mark inside sentences. Its main uses are shown in the box below.

Main uses of the comma

❖ To separate main clauses linked by a coordinating conjunction (34a):

The building is finished, *but* it has no tenants.

❖ To set off most introductory elements (34b):

Unfortunately, the only tenant pulled out.

❖ To set off nonrestrictive elements (34c):

The empty building symbolizes a weak local economy, *which affects everyone.*

The main cause, *the decline of local industry,* is not news.

❖ To separate items in series (34e):

The city needs *healthier businesses, new schools, and improved housing.*

❖ To separate two or more adjectives (34f):

A *tall, sleek* skyscraper is not needed.

❖ Other uses of the comma:

To set off other nonessential elements, such as absolute phrases, parenthetical expressions, and phrases expressing contrast (34d).

To separate parts of dates, addresses, long numbers (34g).

To separate quotations from words such as *she said* (34h).

See also 34i for when *not* to use the comma.

34a Use a comma before *and, but,* or another coordinating conjunction linking main clauses.

When a coordinating conjunction links words or phrases, do not use a comma: *Dugain plays and sings Irish and English folk*

┌ KEY TERM ─────────────────────────────────

COORDINATING CONJUNCTIONS *And, but, or, nor,* and sometimes *for, so, yet.*

songs. However, *do* use a comma when a coordinating conjunction joins main clauses.

> Caffeine can keep coffee drinkers alert, *and* it may elevate their mood.

> Caffeine was once thought to be safe, *but* now researchers warn of harmful effects.

> Coffee drinkers may suffer sleeplessness, *for* the drug acts as a stimulant to the nervous system.

EXCEPTION When main clauses are very short and closely related in meaning, you may omit the comma between them as long as the resulting sentence is clear: *Caffeine helps but it also hurts.* If you are in doubt about whether to use the comma in such a sentence, use it. It will always be correct.

34b Use a comma to set off most introductory elements.

An INTRODUCTORY ELEMENT begins a sentence and modifies a word or words in the main clause that follows. It is usually followed by a comma.

SUBORDINATE CLAUSE

Even when identical twins are raised apart, they grow up very like each other.

VERBAL OR VERBAL PHRASE

Explaining the similarity, some researchers claim that one's genes are one's destiny.

Concerned, other researchers deny the claim.

KEY TERMS

MAIN CLAUSE A word group that contains a subject and a verb and does not begin with a subordinating word: *Water freezes at temperatures below 32°F.*

SUBORDINATE CLAUSE A word group that contains a subject and a verb, begins with a subordinating word such as *because* or *who,* and is not a question: *When water freezes, crystals form.*

VERBAL A verb form used as an adjective, adverb, or noun. A verbal plus any object or modifier is a VERBAL PHRASE: *frozen water, ready to freeze, rapid freezing.*

PREPOSITIONAL PHRASE

In a debate that has lasted centuries, scientists use identical twins to argue for or against genetic destiny.

SENTENCE MODIFIER

Of course, scientists can now look directly at the genes themselves.

You may omit the comma after a short subordinate clause or prepositional phrase if its omission does not create confusion: *When snow falls* the city collapses. *By the year 2000* the world population will top 6 billion. But the comma is never wrong.

NOTE Take care to distinguish verbals used as modifiers from verbals used as subjects. The former almost always take a comma; the latter never do.

VERBAL AS MODIFIER

To dance professionally, he trained for years.

VERBAL AS SUBJECT

To dance professionally is his one desire.

34c Use a comma or commas to set off nonrestrictive elements.

Commas around part of a sentence often signal that the element is not essential to the meaning. This NONRESTRICTIVE ELEMENT may modify or rename the word it refers to, but it does not limit the word to a particular individual or group.

NONRESTRICTIVE ELEMENT

The company, *which is located in Oklahoma,* has an excellent reputation.

In contrast, a RESTRICTIVE ELEMENT *does* limit the word it refers to: the element cannot be omitted without leaving the meaning too general. Because it is essential, a restrictive element is *not* set off with commas, as the following example shows.

34c

KEY TERM

PREPOSITIONAL PHRASE A word group consisting of a preposition, such as *for* or *in,* followed by a noun or pronoun plus any modifiers: *in a jar, with a spoon.* Prepositional phrases usually serve as adjectives or adverbs.

A test for nonrestrictive and restrictive elements

1. Identify the element.

   Hai Nguyen *who emigrated from Vietnam* lives in Denver.
   Those *who emigrated with him* live elsewhere.

2. Remove the element. Does the fundamental meaning of the sentence change?

   Hai Nguyen lives in Denver. No.
   Those live elsewhere. YES.

3. If NO, the element is *nonrestrictive* and *should* be set off with punctuation.

   Hai Nguyen, who emigrated from Vietnam, lives in Denver.

   If YES, the element is *restrictive* and should *not* be set off with punctuation.

   Those who emigrated with him live elsewhere.

RESTRICTIVE ELEMENT

Any company *that treats employees well* deserves praise.

Nonrestrictive elements are *not* essential, but punctuation *is*. Restrictive elements *are* essential, but punctuation is *not*. When a nonrestrictive element falls in the middle of a sentence, be sure to set it off with a pair of commas, one *before* and one *after* the element.

NOTE Only restrictive clauses may begin with *that*. Some writers reserve *which* only for nonrestrictive clauses.

Nonrestrictive and restrictive elements may be modifiers, as in the examples so far, or appositives. A nonrestrictive appositive merely adds information about the word it refers to.

Toni Morrison's fifth novel, *Beloved*, won the Pulitzer Prize in 1988.

In contrast, a restrictive appositive limits or defines the word it refers to.

Morrison's novel *The Bluest Eye* is about an African-American girl who longs for blue eyes.

KEY TERM

APPOSITIVE   A noun or noun substitute that renames another noun immediately before it: *His wife, Emma Thompson, is also an actor.*

34d Use a comma or commas to set off other nonessential elements.

Like nonrestrictive modifiers or appositives, many other elements contribute to texture, tone, or overall clarity but are not essential to the meaning. Unlike nonrestrictive elements, these other nonessential elements generally do not refer to any specific word in the sentence.

ABSOLUTE PHRASES

Domestic recycling having succeeded, the city now wants to extend the program to businesses.

Many businesses, *their profits already squeezed,* resist recycling.

PARENTHETICAL EXPRESSIONS

Few people would know, *or even guess,* the most celebrated holiday on earth.

That holiday is, *in fact,* New Year's Day.

(Dashes and parentheses may also set off parenthetical expressions. See pp. 170–72.)

PHRASES OF CONTRAST

The essay needs less wit, *more pith.*

His generosity, *not his good looks,* won him friends.

It is not light that is needed, *but fire;* it is not the gentle shower, *but thunder.*   —FREDERICK DOUGLASS

TAG QUESTIONS

Jones should be allowed to vote, *should he not?*

They don't stop to consider others, *do they?*

34d

KEY TERMS

ABSOLUTE PHRASE A phrase modifying a whole main clause and consisting of a participle and its subject: *Their homework completed, the children watched TV.*

PARENTHETICAL EXPRESSION An explanatory, supplemental, or transitional word or phrase, such as *of course, however,* or a brief example or fact.

TAG QUESTION A question attached to the end of a statement, consisting of a pronoun, a helping verb, and sometimes *not: It isn't collapsing, is it?*

Yes AND *NO*

Yes, the editorial did have a point.
No, that can never be.

WORDS OF DIRECT ADDRESS

Cody, please bring me the newspaper.
With all due respect, *sir,* I will not.

MILD INTERJECTIONS

Well, you will never know who did it.
Oh, they forgot all about the baby.

34e Use commas between items in a series.

A SERIES consists of three or more items of equal importance.
The items may be words, phrases, or clauses.

> Anna Spingle *married at the age of seventeen, had three children by twenty-one, and divorced at twenty-two.*
> She worked as *a cook, a baby-sitter, and a crossing guard.*

Some writers omit the comma before the coordinating conjunction in a series (*Breakfast consisted of coffee, eggs and kippers*).
But the final comma is never wrong, and it always helps the reader
see the last two items as separate.

34f Use commas between two or more adjectives that equally modify the same word.

Adjectives that equally modify the same word—COORDINATE AD-
JECTIVES—may be separated either by *and* or by a comma.

> Spingle's *scratched and dented* car is an eyesore, but it gets her to
> work.
> She has dreams of a *sleek, shiny* car.

Adjectives are not coordinate—and should not be separated by
commas—when the one nearer the noun is more closely related to
the noun in meaning.

KEY TERM

INTERJECTION   A word that expresses feeling or commands attention: *Oh, must we?*

⌃
,
34f

Spingle's children work at *various odd* jobs.
They all expect to go to a *nearby community* college.

Tests for commas with adjectives

1. Identify the adjectives.

   She was a *faithful sincere* friend.
   They are *dedicated medical* students.

2. Can the adjectives be reversed without changing meaning?

   She was a *sincere faithful* friend. YES.
   They are *medical dedicated* students. No.

3. Can the word *and* be inserted between the adjectives without changing meaning?

   She was a *faithful and sincere* friend. YES.
   They are *dedicated and medical* students. No.

4. If YES to *both* questions, the adjectives *should* be separated by a comma.

   She was a *faithful, sincere* friend.

5. If NO to both questions, the adjectives should *not* be separated by a comma.

   They are *dedicated medical* students.

34g Use commas in dates, addresses, place names, and long numbers.

When they appear within sentences, dates, addresses, and place names punctuated with commas are also ended with commas.

DATES

July 4, 1776, was the day the Declaration was signed.

The bombing of Pearl Harbor on Sunday, December 7, 1941, prompted American entry into World War II.

Commas are not used between the parts of a date in inverted order (*15 December 1992*) or in dates consisting of a month or season and a year (*December 1941*).

ADDRESSES AND PLACE NAMES

Use the address 5262 Laurie Lane, Memphis, Tennessee, for all correspondence.

Columbus, Ohio, is the location of Ohio State University.

⌃
,
34g

Commas are not used between state names and zip codes in addresses: *Berkeley, California 94720, is the place of my birth.*

LONG NUMBERS

Use the comma to separate the figures in long numbers into groups of three, counting from the right. With numbers of four digits, the comma is optional.

The new assembly plant cost $7,525,000.
A kilometer is 3,281 feet (*or* 3281 feet).

34h Use commas with quotations according to standard practice.

The words *she said, he replied,* and so on identify the source of a quotation. These identifying words should be separated from the quotation by punctuation, usually a comma or commas.

Eleanor Roosevelt said, "You must do the thing you think you cannot do."

"Knowledge is power," wrote Francis Bacon.

"The shore has a dual nature," observes Rachel Carson, "changing with the swing of the tides." [The identifying words interrupt the quotation at a comma and thus end with a comma.]

EXCEPTIONS When explanatory words interrupt a quotation between main clauses, follow the explanatory words with a semicolon or a period. The choice depends on the punctuation of the original.

NOT "That part of my life was over," she wrote, "his words had sealed it shut."

BUT "That part of my life was over," she wrote. "His words had sealed it shut." [*She wrote* interrupts the quotation at a period.]

OR "That part of my life was over," she wrote; "his words had sealed it shut." [*She wrote* interrupts the quotation at a semicolon.]

Do not use a comma when identifying words follow a quotation ending in an exclamation point or a question mark.

"Claude!" Mrs. Harrison called.
"Why must I come home?" he asked.

Commas are often overused with quotations. Do not use a comma with a quotation introduced by *that* or with a short quotation that is merely one element in a longer sentence.

The warning that "cigarette smoking is dangerous to your health" has fallen on many deaf ears.

The children were trained to say "Excuse me" when they bumped into others.

Do not use a comma with a quoted title unless it is a nonrestrictive appositive (see p. 152).

The Beatles recorded "She Loves Me" in the early 1960s.

34i   Delete commas where they are not required.

Commas can make sentences choppy and even confusing if they are used more often than needed or in violation of rules 34a–34h. The most common spots for misused commas are discussed below.

1. Between subject and verb, verb and object, or preposition and object

NOT   The returning *soldiers, received* a warm welcome. [Separated subject and verb.]

BUT   The returning *soldiers received* a warm welcome.

NOT   They had *chosen, to fight* for their country *despite, the risks.* [Separated verb *chosen* and its object; separated preposition *despite* and its object.]

BUT   They had *chosen to fight* for their country *despite the risks.*

2. In compound constructions

Compound constructions consisting of two elements almost never require a comma. The only exception is the sentence consisting of two main clauses linked by a coordinating conjunction: *The computer failed,* but *employees kept working* (see pp. 149–50).

no ⌃ ⸴

34i

⌐ KEY TERMS ─────────────────────────────

NONRESTRICTIVE APPOSITIVE   A word or words that rename an immediately preceding noun but do not limit or define the noun: *The author's first story, "Biloxi," won a prize.*

COMPOUND CONSTRUCTION   Two or more words, phrases, or clauses connected by a coordinating conjunction, usually *and, but, or, nor*: *man and woman, old or young, leaking oil and spewing steam.*

NOT   Banks *could, and should* help older people manage their money. [Compound helping verbs.]

BUT   Banks could and should help older people manage their money.

NOT   Older people need special assistance *because they live on fixed incomes, and because they are not familiar with new accounts.* [Compound subordinate clauses.]

BUT   Older people need special assistance because they live on fixed incomes and because they are not familiar with new accounts.

NOT   *Banks, and community groups* can *help* the elderly, *and eliminate* the confusion they often feel. [Compound subject and compound predicate.]

BUT   Banks and community groups can help the elderly and eliminate the confusion they often feel.

3. Around restrictive elements

NOT   Hawthorne's work, *The Scarlet Letter,* was the first major American novel. [The title is essential to distinguish the novel from the rest of Hawthorne's work.]

BUT   Hawthorne's work *The Scarlet Letter* was the first major American novel.

NOT   The symbols, *that Hawthorne used,* influenced other novelists. [The clause identifies which symbols were influential.]

BUT   The symbols that Hawthorne used influenced other novelists.

4. Around a series

Commas separate the items *within* a series (p. 154) but do not separate the series from the rest of the sentence.

NOT   The skills of, *hunting, herding, and agriculture,* sustained the Native Americans.

BUT   The skills of hunting, herding, and agriculture sustained the Native Americans.

no ̂

34i

┌─ KEY TERM ──────────────────────────────────────
RESTRICTIVE ELEMENT   Limits (or restricts) the word it refers to and thus can't be omitted without leaving the meaning too general. See also pages 151–52.
└──

5. Before an indirect quotation

NOT   The report *concluded, that* dieting could be more dangerous than overeating.

BUT   The report concluded that dieting could be more dangerous than overeating.

35 The Semicolon

The semicolon (;) separates equal and balanced sentence elements—usually main clauses (35a, 35b) and occasionally items in series (35c).

35a   Use a semicolon between main clauses not joined by *and, but,* or another coordinating conjunction.

When no coordinating conjunction links two main clauses, the clauses should be separated by a semicolon.

A new ulcer drug arrived on the market with a mixed reputation; doctors find that the drug works but worry about its side effects.

The side effects are not minor; some leave the patient quite uncomfortable or even ill.

NOTE This rule prevents the errors known as comma splice and fused sentence. (See pp. 138–41.)

;
35a

┌─ **KEY TERMS** ─────────────────────────────

INDIRECT QUOTATION   Reports what someone said or wrote, but not in the exact words of the original.

MAIN CLAUSE   A word group that contains a subject and a verb and does not begin with a subordinating word: *Parks help cities breathe.*

COORDINATING CONJUNCTIONS   *And, but, or, nor,* and sometimes *for, so, yet.*

35b Use a semicolon between main clauses related by *however, thus,* or another conjunctive adverb.

When a conjunctive adverb relates two main clauses, the clauses should be separated by a semicolon. The adverb is usually followed by a comma.

> Blue jeans have become fashionable all over the world; *however,* the American originators still wear more jeans than anyone else.

The position of the semicolon between main clauses never changes, but the conjunctive adverb may move around within the second clause. When the adverb falls somewhere besides the beginning of the clause, set it off with a comma or commas. (The semicolon remains between clauses.)

> Blue jeans have become fashionable all over the world; the American originators, *however,* still wear more jeans than anyone else.

> Blue jeans have become fashionable all over the world; the American originators still wear more jeans than anyone else, *however.*

NOTE This rule prevents the errors known as comma splice and fused sentence. (See pp. 138–41.)

35c Use semicolons between main clauses or series items containing commas.

Normally, commas separate main clauses linked by coordinating conjunctions (*and, but, or, nor*) and items in a series. But when the clauses or series items contain commas, a semicolon between them makes the sentence easier to read.

> Lewis and Clark led the men of their party with consummate skill, inspiring and encouraging them, doctoring and caring for them; *and* they kept voluminous journals.   —PAGE SMITH

> The custody case involved Amy Dalton, the child; Ellen and Mark Dalton, the parents; and Ruth and Hal Blum, the grandparents.

;
35c

┌─ KEY TERM ───

CONJUNCTIVE ADVERBS   Modifiers that describe the relation of the ideas in two clauses, such as *consequently, hence, however, indeed, instead, nonetheless, otherwise, still, then, therefore, thus.* (See p. 140 for a fuller list.)

35d Delete or replace unneeded semicolons.

Too many semicolons can make writing choppy. And semicolons are often misused in certain constructions that call for other punctuation or no punctuation.

1. Between a main clause and subordinate clause or phrase

The semicolon does not separate unequal parts, such as main clauses and subordinate clauses or phrases.

> **Not**   According to African authorities; only about 35,000 Pygmies exist today.
>
> **But**   According to African authorities, only about 35,000 Pygmies exist today.
>
> **Not**   They are in danger of extinction; because of encroaching development.
>
> **But**   They are in danger of extinction because of encroaching development.

2. Before a series or explanation

Colons and dashes, not semicolons, introduce series, explanations, and so forth. (See pp. 162 and 170–71.)

> **Not**   Teachers have heard all sorts of reasons why students do poorly; psychological problems, family illness, too much work, too little time.
>
> **But**   Teachers have heard all sorts of reasons why students do poorly: psychological problems, family illness, too much work, too little time.

36 The Colon

The colon (:) is mainly a mark of introduction: it signals that the words following will explain or amplify (see 36a). The colon also has several conventional uses, such as in expressions of time (see 36b).

36a Use a colon to introduce a concluding explanation, series, appositive, or long or formal quotation.

As an introducer, a colon is always preceded by a complete main clause. It may or may not be followed by a main clause. This is one way the colon differs from the semicolon, which generally separates main clauses only. (See pp. 159–60.)

EXPLANATION

Soul food has a deceptively simple definition: the ethnic cooking of African-Americans.

Sometimes a concluding explanation is preceded by *the following* or *as follows* and a colon.

A more precise definition might be *the following*: soul food draws on ingredients, cooking methods, and dishes originating in Africa, brought to the New World by slaves, and modified or supplemented in the Caribbean and the American South.

NOTE A complete sentence *after* a colon may begin with a capital letter or a small letter (as in the example above). Just be consistent throughout an essay.

SERIES

At least three soul food dishes are familiar to most Americans: fried chicken, barbecued spareribs, and sweet potatoes.

APPOSITIVE

Soul food has one disadvantage: fat.

Namely, that is, and other expressions that introduce appositives *follow* the colon: *Soul food has one disadvantage*: *namely, fat.*

LONG OR FORMAL QUOTATION

One soul food chef has a solution: "Soul food doesn't have to be greasy to taste good. . . . Instead of using ham hocks to flavor beans, I use smoked turkey wings. The soulful, smoky taste remains, but without all the fat of pork."

:

36a

┌─ **KEY TERMS** ─────────────────────────────

MAIN CLAUSE A word group that contains a subject and a verb and does not begin with a subordinating word: *Soul food is varied.*

APPOSITIVE A noun or noun substitute that renames another noun immediately before it: *my brother, Jack.*

36b Use a colon after the salutation of a business letter, between a title and subtitle, between divisions of time, and in biblical citations.

SALUTATION OF BUSINESS LETTER

Dear Ms. Burak:

TITLE AND SUBTITLE

Charles Dickens: An Introduction to His Novels

TIME   BIBLICAL CITATION

12:26   6:00   1 Corinthians 3:6–7

36c Delete or replace unneeded colons.

Use the colon only at the end of a main clause. Do not use it inside a main clause, especially after *such as* or a verb.

NOT   The best-known soul food dish is: fried chicken. Many Americans have not tasted delicacies such as: chitlins and black-eyed peas.

BUT   The best-known soul food dish is fried chicken. Many Americans have not tasted delicacies such as chitlins and black-eyed peas.

37 The Apostrophe

The apostrophe (') appears as part of a word to indicate possession (37a), the omission of one or more letters (37c), or (in a few cases) plural number (37d).

37a Use the apostrophe and sometimes *-s* to form possessive nouns and indefinite pronouns.

A noun or indefinite pronoun shows possession with an apostrophe and, usually, an *s: the dog's hair, everyone's hope.*

┌ KEY TERM ───
INDEFINITE PRONOUN   A pronoun that does not refer to a specific person or thing, such as *anyone, each, everybody, no one,* or *something.*

ˇ

37a

Uses and misuses of the apostrophe

USES	MISUSES
Possessives of nouns and indefinite pronouns (37a)	Possessives of personal pronouns (37b)

SINGULAR	PLURAL
Ms. Park's	the Parks'
everyone's	two weeks'

NOT	BUT
it's toes	its toes
your's	yours

Contractions (37c)

it's a girl	shouldn't
you're	won't

Third-person singulars of verbs (37b)

NOT	BUT
swim's	swims

Plurals of letters, numbers, and words named as words (37d)

C's	*6*'s	*if*'s

Plurals of nouns (37b)

NOT	BUT
book's are	books are
the Freed's	the Freeds

NOTE Apostrophes are easy to misuse. For safety's sake, check your drafts to be sure that all words ending in *-s* neither omit needed apostrophes nor add unneeded ones. Also, remember that the apostrophe or apostrophe-plus-*s* is an *addition*. Before this addition, always spell the name of the owner or owners without dropping or adding letters.

ꞌ
v

37a

1. **Singular words: Add -'s.**

> Bill *Boughton's* skillful card tricks amaze children.
> *Anyone's* eyes would widen.
> Most tricks will pique an *adult's* curiosity, too.

The -'s ending for singular words pertains also to singular words ending in *-s*.

> Henry *James's* novels reward the patient reader.
> The *business's* customers filed suit.

EXCEPTION An apostrophe alone may be added to a singular word ending in *-s* when another *s* would make the word difficult to say: *Moses' mother, Joan Rivers' jokes*. But the added *-s* is never wrong (*Moses's, Rivers's*).

2. **Plural words ending in -s: Add -' only.**

Workers' incomes have fallen slightly over the past year.
Many students benefit from several *years'* work after high school.
The *Jameses'* talents are extraordinary.

Note the difference in the possessives of singular and plural words ending in -s. The singular form usually takes -'*s: James's.* The plural takes only the apostrophe: *Jameses'.*

3. **Plural words not ending in -s: Add -'s.**

Children's educations are at stake.
We need to attract the *media's* attention.

4. **Compound words: Add -'s only to the last word.**

The *brother-in-law's* business failed.
Taxes are always *somebody else's* fault.

5. **Two or more owners: Add -'s depending on possession.**

INDIVIDUAL POSSESSION

Youngman's and Mason's comedy techniques are similar. [Each comedian has his own technique.]

JOINT POSSESSION

The child recovered despite her *mother and father's* neglect. [The mother and father were jointly neglectful.]

 37b Delete or replace any apostrophe in a plural noun, a singular verb, or a possessive personal pronoun.

37b

1. **Plural nouns**

The plurals of nouns are generally formed by adding -s or -es: *boys, families, Joneses, Murphys.* Don't add an apostrophe to form the plural.

> **NOT** The *Jones'* were the family that controlled the *firm's* until 1993.
>
> **BUT** The *Joneses* were the family that controlled the *firms* until 1993.

2. Singular verbs

Verbs ending in *-s never* take an apostrophe.

Not   The subway *break's* down less often now.
But   The subway *breaks* down less often now.

3. Possessives of personal pronouns

His, hers, its, ours, yours, theirs, and *whose* are possessive forms of *he, she, it, we, you, they,* and *who.* They do not take apostrophes.

Not   The house is *her's. It's* roof leaks.
But   The house is *hers. Its* roof leaks.

Don't confuse possessive pronouns with contractions. See below.

37c   Use the apostrophe to form contractions.

A CONTRACTION replaces one or more letters, numbers, or words with an apostrophe.

it is	it's	cannot	can't
you are	you're	does not	doesn't
they are	they're	were not	weren't
who is	who's	class of 1997	class of '97

Note   Don't confuse contractions with personal pronouns.

CONTRACTIONS	PERSONAL PRONOUNS
It's a book.	*Its* cover is green.
They're coming.	*Their* car broke down.
You're right.	*Your* idea is good.
Who's coming?	*Whose* party is it?

37d   Use an apostrophe plus *-s* to form plurals of letters, numbers, and words named as words.

You may cite a character or word as a word rather than use it for its meaning. When such an element is plural, add an apostrophe plus *-s.*

This sentence has too many but's.
Remember to do your i's and cross your t's.
At the end of each poem, the author had written two 3's.

Notice that the cited element is underlined (italicized) but the apostrophe and added -s are not.

38 Quotation Marks

Quotation marks—either double (" ") or single (' ')—mainly enclose direct quotations from speech and from writing.

NOTE Always use quotation marks in pairs, one at the beginning of a quotation and one at the end.

38a Use double quotation marks to enclose direct quotations.

A DIRECT QUOTATION reports what someone said or wrote, in the exact words of the original.

"Life," said the psychoanalyst Karen Horney, "remains a very efficient therapist."

Do not use quotation marks with an INDIRECT QUOTATION, which reports what someone said or wrote but not in the exact words of the original.

" "

38b

The psychoanalyst Karen Horney said that life is a good therapist.

38b Use single quotation marks to enclose a quotation within a quotation.

"In formulating any philosophy," Woody Allen writes, "the first consideration must always be: What can we know? . . . Descartes hinted at the problem when he wrote, 'My mind can never know my body, although it has become quite friendly with my leg.'"

Notice that two different quotation marks appear at the end of the sentence—one single (to finish the interior quotation) and one double (to finish the main quotation).

38c Put quotation marks around the titles of works that are parts of other works.

Use quotation marks to enclose the titles of works that are published or released within larger works (see the box below). Use underlining (italics) for all other titles, such as books, plays, periodicals, movies, and works of art. (See p. 196.)

Titles to be enclosed in quotation marks
Other titles should be underlined (italicized). (See p. 196.)

SONG
"Lucy in the Sky with Diamonds"

SHORT STORY
"The Gift of the Magi"

SHORT POEM
"Stopping by Woods on a Snowy Evening"

ARTICLE IN A PERIODICAL
"Does 'Scaring' Work?"

ESSAY
"Joey: A 'Mechanical Boy'"

EPISODE OF A TELEVISION OR RADIO PROGRAM
"The Mexican Connection" (on Sixty Minutes)

SUBDIVISION OF A BOOK
"The Mast Head" (Chapter 35 of Moby-Dick)

" "

38e

NOTE Use single quotation marks for a quotation within a quoted title, as in the article and essay titles in the box. And enclose all punctuation in the title within the quotation marks, as in the article title.

38d Quotation marks may be used to enclose words being defined or used in a special sense.

By "charity" I mean the love of one's neighbor as oneself.

On movie sets movable "wild walls" make a one-walled room seem four-walled on film.

NOTE Underlining (italics) may also highlight defined words. (See p. 197.)

38e Delete quotation marks where they are not required.

TITLE OF YOUR PAPER

NOT "The Death Wish in One Poem by Robert Frost"

BUT The Death Wish in One Poem by Robert Frost

OR The Death Wish in "Stopping by Woods on a Snowy Evening"

COMMON NICKNAME

NOT As President, "Jimmy" Carter preferred to use his nickname.

BUT As President, Jimmy Carter preferred to use his nickname.

SLANG OR TRITE EXPRESSION

Quotation marks will not excuse slang or a trite expression that is inappropriate to your writing. If slang is appropriate, use it without quotation marks.

NOT We should support the President in his "hour of need" rather than "wimp out on him."

BUT We should give the President the support he needs rather than turn away like cowards.

38f Place other punctuation marks inside or outside quotation marks according to standard practice.

1. Commas and periods: Inside quotation marks

Swift uses irony in his essay "A Modest Proposal."

Many first-time readers are shocked to see infants described as "delicious."

"'A Modest Proposal,'" wrote one critic, "is so outrageous that it cannot be believed."

EXCEPTION When a parenthetical source citation immediately follows a quotation at the end of a sentence, the period follows the source citation: *One critic calls the essay "outrageous" (Olms 26).*

2. Colons and semicolons: Outside quotation marks

A few years ago the slogan in elementary education was "learning by playing"; now educators are concerned with teaching basic skills.

We all know the meaning of "basic skills": reading, writing, and arithmetic.

" "

38f

3. Dashes, question marks, and exclamation points: Inside quotation marks only if part of the quotation

When a dash, question mark, or exclamation point is part of the quotation, place it *inside* quotation marks. Don't use any other punctuation, such as a period or comma.

"But must you—" Marcia hesitated, afraid of the answer.
The stranger asked, "Where am I?"
"Go away!" I yelled.

When a dash, question mark, or exclamation point applies only to the larger sentence, not to the quotation, place it *outside* quotation marks—again, with no other punctuation.

One of the most evocative lines in English poetry—"After many a summer dies the swan"—was written by Alfred, Lord Tennyson.
Who said, "Now cracks a noble heart"?
The woman called me "stupid"!

When both the quotation and the larger sentence take a question mark or exclamation point, use only the one *inside* the quotation mark.

Did you say, "Who is she?"

39 Other Marks

39a

The other marks of punctuation are the dash (39a), parentheses (39b), the ellipsis mark (39c), brackets (39d), and the slash (39e).

 Use the dash or dashes to indicate shifts and to set off some sentence elements.

The dash (—) is mainly a mark of interruption: it signals a shift, insertion, or break.

NOTE In handwritten and typewritten papers, form a dash with two hyphens (--). Do not add extra space before, after, or between the hyphens.

1. Shifts in tone or thought

He tells us—does he really mean it?—that he will speak the truth from now on.

If she found out—he did not want to think what she would do.

2. Nonrestrictive elements

Dashes may be used instead of commas to set off and emphasize modifiers and other nonrestrictive elements, especially when these elements are internally punctuated. Be sure to use a pair of dashes when the element interrupts the sentence.

The qualities Monet painted—sunlight, rich shadows, deep colors—abounded near the rivers and gardens he used as subjects.

Though they are close together—separated by only a few blocks—the two neighborhoods could be in different countries.

3. Introductory series and concluding series and explanations

Shortness of breath, skin discoloration or the sudden appearance of moles, persistent indigestion, the presence of small lumps—all these may signify cancer. [Introductory series.]

The patient undergoes a battery of tests—CAT scan, bronchoscopy, perhaps even biopsy. [Concluding series.]

Many patients are disturbed by the CAT scan—by the need to keep still for long periods in an exceedingly small space. [Concluding explanation.]

A colon could be used instead of a dash in the last two examples. The dash is more informal.

4. Overuse

Too many dashes can make writing jumpy or breathy.

NOT In all his life—eighty-seven years—my great-grandfather never allowed his picture to be taken—not even once. He claimed the "black box"—the camera—would steal his soul.

BUT In all his eighty-seven years, my great-grandfather did not allow his picture to be taken even once. He claimed the "black box"—the camera—would steal his soul.

39a

KEY TERM

NONRESTRICTIVE ELEMENT Gives added information but does not limit (or restrict) the word it refers to. (See also pp. 151–52.)

39b Use parentheses to enclose nonessential elements.

Parentheses *always* come in pairs, one before and one after the punctuated material.

1. Parenthetical expressions

PARENTHETICAL EXPRESSIONS are explanatory, supplemental, or transitional words or phrases, such as *of course, however,* or a brief example or fact. Parentheses de-emphasize parenthetical expressions. (Commas emphasize them more and dashes still more.)

> The population of Philadelphia (now about 1.6 million) has declined since 1950.

NOTE Don't put a comma before a parenthetical expression enclosed in parentheses. Punctuation after the parenthetical expression should be placed outside the closing parenthesis.

> NOT   We were haunted by the dungeon, (really the basement.)
> BUT   We were haunted by the dungeon (really the basement**).**

When it falls between other complete sentences, a complete sentence enclosed in parentheses has a capital letter and end punctuation.

> In general, coaches will tell you that scouts are just guys who can't coach. (But then, so are brain surgeons**.)**   —ROY BLOUNT

2. Labels for lists

> My father could not, for his own special reasons, even *like* me. He spent the first twenty-five years of my life acting out that painful fact. Then he arrived at two points in his own life: **(1)** his last years, and **(2)** the realization that he had made a tragic mistake.
> —RAY WEATHERLY

39c Use the ellipsis mark to indicate omissions from quotations.

The ellipsis mark consists of three spaced periods (. . .). It generally indicates an omission from a quotation, as illustrated in the following excerpts from this quotation about the Philippines:

ORIGINAL QUOTATION

"It was the Cuba of the future. It was going the way of Iran. It was another Nicaragua, another Cambodia, another Vietnam. But all these places, awesome in their histories, are so different from each other that one couldn't help thinking: this kind of talk was a shorthand for a confusion. All that was being said was that something was happening in the Philippines. Or more plausibly, a lot of different things were happening in the Philippines. And a lot of people were feeling obliged to speak out about it."

—JAMES FENTON, "The Philippine Election"

OMISSION OF THE MIDDLE OF A SENTENCE

"But all these places . . . are so different from each other that one couldn't help thinking: this kind of talk was a shorthand for a confusion."

OMISSION OF THE END OF A SENTENCE

"It was another Nicaragua. . . ." [The sentence period, closed up to the last word, precedes the ellipsis mark.]

"It was another Nicaragua . . ." (Fenton 25). [When the quotation is followed by a parenthetical source citation, as here, the sentence period follows the citation.]

OMISSION OF PARTS OF TWO SENTENCES

"All that was being said was that . . . a lot of different things were happening in the Philippines."

OMISSION OF ONE OR MORE SENTENCES

"It was the Cuba of the future. It was going the way of Iran. It was another Nicaragua, another Cambodia, another Vietnam. . . . All that was being said was that something was happening in the Philippines."

Note these features of the examples:

* * *
39c

❖ The ellipsis mark indicates that material is omitted from the source when the omission would not otherwise be clear. Thus, use an ellipsis mark when the words you quote form a complete sentence that is different in the original (first through fourth examples above). Don't use an ellipsis mark at the beginning or end of a partial sentence: *Fenton calls the Philippines "another Nicaragua."*

❖ After a grammatically complete sentence, an ellipsis mark usually follows a sentence period and a space (second and last examples). The exception occurs when a parenthetical source citation follows the quotation (third example), in which case the sentence period falls after the citation.

NOTE If you omit one or more lines of poetry or paragraphs of prose from a quotation, use a separate line of ellipsis marks across the full width of the quotation to show the omission.

39d Use brackets to indicate changes in quotations.

Brackets have only one use: to indicate that you have altered a quotation to explain, clarify, or correct it.

"That Texaco station [just outside Chicago] is one of the busiest in the nation," said a company spokesperson.

The word *sic* (Latin for "in this manner") in brackets indicates that an error in the quotation appeared in the original and was not made by you.

According to the newspaper report, "The car slammed thru [*sic*] the railing and into oncoming traffic."

But don't use *sic* to make fun of a writer or to note errors in a passage that is clearly nonstandard.

39e Use the slash between options and between lines of poetry.

Use the slash between options:

Some teachers oppose pass/fail courses.

The slash also separates lines of poetry that you run into your text. (Surround the slash with space.)

Many readers have sensed a reluctant turn away from death in Frost's lines "The woods are lovely, dark and deep, / But I have promises to keep."

V

Conventions of Form and Appearance

❖

V

Conventions of Form and Appearance

❖

Form and Appearance

VI

Research
and
Documentation

❖

VI

Research and
Documentation

❖

40 Manuscript Format

Legible, consistent, and attractive papers and letters are a service to your readers. This chapter describes and illustrates formats for academic papers (40a), business letters and résumés (40b), business memos (40c), and fax transmissions and electronic mail (40d).

40a Use an appropriate format for your academic papers.

The guidelines below are adapted from the *MLA Handbook for Writers of Research Papers*, the style book for English and some other disciplines. Most of these guidelines are standard, but instructors in various courses may expect you to follow different conventions. Check with your instructor for his or her preferences.

1. Materials

Typewritten papers

For typewritten papers, use 8½" × 11" white bond paper of sixteen- or twenty-pound weight. Use the same type of paper throughout a project. Type on only one side of a sheet.

Use a black typewriter ribbon that is fresh enough to make a dark impression, and make sure the keys of the typewriter are clean. To avoid smudging the page when correcting mistakes, use correction fluid or tape. Don't use hyphens or *x*'s to cross out mistakes, and don't type corrections (strikeovers) on top of mistakes.

Papers produced on a word processor

If you use a dot-matrix printer, make sure the characters are legible. (Show your instructor a sample of the type to be sure it is acceptable.) Also be sure the printer ribbon or cartridge produces a dark impression. Use standard-sized (8½" × 11") white bond paper of sixteen- or twenty-pound weight. If you use continuous paper folded like a fan at perforations, remove the strips of holes along the sides, and separate the pages at the folds.

Handwritten papers

For handwritten papers, use regular white paper, 8½" × 11", with horizontal lines spaced between one-quarter and three-eighths

ms
40a

of an inch apart. Write on only one side of a sheet, using black or blue ink, not pencil. If possible, use an ink eraser or eradicator to correct mistakes. If you must cross out material, draw a single line through it. Don't scribble over mistakes or write corrections on top of mistakes.

2. Format

The samples below show the format of a paper. For the special formats of source citations and a list of works cited or references, see Chapters 49 (MLA style) and 50 (APA style).

FIRST PAGE OF PAPER

```
                                              ½"
                                           Perez 1

        Terry Perez

        Professor Christensen

        English 100                        All
                                           double-
        November 16, 1994                  spaced

                        America's Media Image  ←—Center
          5 spaces
                  ⌐—⌐Is the United States a monoculture, a
     1"
      ←—→ unified, homogeneous society?  Many Americans     1"
                                                           ←—→
```

A LATER PAGE OF THE PAPER

```
         ↑ 1"
         |                                    ½"
                                           Perez 2

      ←—→ present enough good news.  When it comes to    ←—→
     1"                                                  1"
          ethnic relations, this is certainly the case.




          Roseanne, the Cosbys, and more recent African-
     1"
      ←—→ American situation comedies and dramas.  How
          ↑ 1"
          |
```

ms
40a

Margins and spacing

Use one-inch margins on all sides of each page. The top margin will contain the page numbers. If you have a word processor or electronic typewriter that produces an even (or justified) right margin, use the feature only if it does not leave wide spaces between words and thus interfere with readability.

Indent the first line of every paragraph five spaces, and double-space throughout.

Paging

Begin numbering your paper in the upper right of the first text page, and number consecutively through the end. Use Arabic numerals (1, 2, 3), and place your last name before the page number in case the pages become separated after you submit your paper.

Title and identification

Provide your name and the date, plus any other information requested by your instructor, in the upper left of the first text page. Double-space between this identification and the title. Center the title, capitalize words in it according to the guidelines on page 195, and double-space between the title and the first line of text. (See pp. 19–20 for advice on creating titles.)

Punctuation

Type punctuation as follows:

❖ Leave one space after a comma, semicolon, colon, and apostrophe closing a word.
❖ Leave one space after a closing quotation mark, closing parenthesis, and closing bracket when these marks fall before a word within a sentence. When they fall after the sentence period, leave two spaces.
❖ Leave two spaces after a sentence period, question mark, or exclamation point.
❖ Do not add any space before or after a dash, a hyphen, or an apostrophe within a word. Form a dash with two hyphens (--).
❖ Leave one space before and after an ellipsis mark (. . .).

Quotations

POETRY

❖ When you quote a single line from a poem, song, or verse play, run the line into your text and enclose it in quotation marks.

ms

40a

```
Dylan Thomas remembered childhood as an idyllic time:

"About the lilting house and happy as the grass was

green."
```

❖ Poetry quotations of two or three lines may be placed in the text or displayed separately. In the text enclose the quotation in quotation marks and separate the lines with a slash surrounded by space.

```
An example of Robert Frost's incisiveness is in two

lines from "Death of the Hired Man": "Home is the place

where, when you have to go there / They have to take

you in."
```

❖ Quotations of more than three lines of poetry should always be separated from the text with space and an indention. *Do not add quotation marks.*

```
Emily Dickinson rarely needed more than a few lines to

express her complex thoughts:

              To wait an Hour - is long -

              If Love be just beyond -

              To wait Eternity - is short -

              If Love reward the end -
```

❖ Double-space above, below, and throughout a displayed quotation. Indent the quotation ten spaces from the left margin.

PROSE

❖ Run a prose quotation of four or fewer lines into your text, and enclose it in quotation marks.
❖ Separate quotations of five lines or more from the body of your paper. (Use such quotations sparingly. See p. 216.)

```
In his 1967 study of the lives of unemployed black men,

Elliot Liebow observes that "unskilled" construction

work requires more experience and skill than is gener-

ally assumed.

              A healthy, sturdy, active man of good intel-

              ligence requires from two to four weeks to

              break in on a construction job. . . . It

              frequently happens that his foreman or the
```

ms

40a

```
craftsman he services is not willing to wait
that long for him to get into condition or to
learn at a glance the difference in size be-
tween a rough 2 x 8 and a finished 2 x 10.
```

❖ Double-space before, after, and throughout a displayed quotation. Indent the quotation ten spaces from the left.
❖ *Do not add quotation marks.*

DIALOGUE

❖ When quoting conversations, begin a new paragraph for each speaker.

> "What shall I call you? Your name?" Andrews whispered rapidly, as with a high squeak the latch of the door rose.
> "Elizabeth," she said. "Elizabeth."
> —GRAHAM GREENE, *The Man Within*

❖ When you quote a single speaker for more than one paragraph, put quotation marks at the beginning of each paragraph but at the end of only the last paragraph.

40b Use standard formats for business letters and résumés.

1. Business letters

In a letter to a businessperson, you are addressing someone who wants to see quickly why you are writing and how to respond to you. State your purpose at the start. Be straightforward, clear, objective, and courteous.

For a job application, announce right off what job you are applying for and how you heard about it. (See the sample letter on the next page.) Summarize your qualifications for the job, including relevant facts about your education and employment history. Include your reason for applying, such as a specific career goal. At the end of the letter mention when you are available for an interview.

Use either unlined white paper measuring 8½" × 11" or what is called letterhead stationery with your address printed at the top of the sheet. Type the letter single-spaced (with double space between elements) on only one side of a sheet.

A common form for business letters is described and illustrated on the next two pages.

ms

40b

```
                              3712 Swiss Avenue  ⎤  Return
                              Dallas, TX 75204   ⎬  address
                              March 2, 1994      ⎦  heading

        Personnel Manager               ⎤
        Dallas News                     ⎬ Inside address
        Communications Center           ⎦
        Dallas, TX 75222

        Dear Personnel Manager: ⎬ Salutation

        In response to your posting in the English  ⎤
        Department of Southern Methodist University, │
        I am applying for the summer job of part-    │
        time editorial assistant for the Dallas      │
        News.                                        │
                                                     │
        I am now enrolled at Southern Methodist      │
        University as a sophomore, with a dual major │
        in English literature and journalism.   I    │
        have worked on the university newspaper for  ⎬ Body
        nearly two years, and I worked a summer on   │
        my hometown newspaper as a copy aide.   My   │
        goal is a career in journalism.   I believe  │
        my educational background and my work expe-  │
        rience qualify me for the opening you have.  │
                                                     │
        My résumé is enclosed.   I am available for  │
        an interview at any time and would be happy  │
        to show samples of my newspaper work.   My   │
        telephone number is 744-3816.                ⎦

                        Sincerely,      ⎬ Close

                        Ian M. Irvine   ⎬ Signature

                        Ian M. Irvine

        Enc.
```

❖ The RETURN-ADDRESS HEADING gives your address (but not your
  name) and the date. (If you are using stationery with a printed
  heading, you need only give the date.) Place your heading at
  least an inch from the top of the page. Align all lines of the
  heading on the left, and position the whole heading to the right
  of the center of the paper.

❖ The INSIDE ADDRESS shows the name, title, and complete address of the person you are writing to. Place the address at least two lines below the return-address heading.

❖ The SALUTATION greets the addressee. Position it at the left margin, two lines below the inside address and two lines above the body of the letter. Follow it with a colon. If you are not addressing someone whose name you know, use a job title (*Dear Personnel Manager*) or use a general salutation (*Dear Smythe Shoes*). Use *Ms.* as the title for a woman when she has no other title, when you don't know how she prefers to be addressed, or when you know that she prefers *Ms.*

❖ The BODY of the letter, containing its substance, begins at the left margin. Instead of indenting the first line of each paragraph, insert an extra line of space between paragraphs.

❖ The letter's CLOSE begins two lines below the last line of the body and aligns with the return-address heading to the right of the center of the page. The close should reflect the level of formality in the salutation: *Respectfully, Cordially, Yours truly,* and *Sincerely* are more formal closes; *Regards* and *Best wishes* are less formal. Capitalize only the first word, and follow the close with a comma.

❖ The SIGNATURE falls below the close and has two parts: your name typed four lines below the close, and your handwritten signature in the space between. Give your name as you sign checks and other documents.

❖ Below the signature at the left margin, you may want to include additional information such as *Enc.* (indicating an enclosure with the letter) or *cc: Margaret Zusky* (indicating that a copy is being sent to the person named).

❖ Use an envelope that will accommodate the letter once it is folded horizontally in thirds. The envelope should show your name and address in the upper left corner and the addressee's name, title, and address in the center. For easy machine reading, the United States Postal Service recommends all capital letters and no punctuation (spaces separate the elements on a line), as in this address:

```
PERSONNEL MANAGER
DALLAS NEWS
COMMUNICATIONS CENTER
DALLAS TX 75222
```

2. Résumés

The résumé that you enclose with a letter of application should contain, in table form, your name and address, career objective,

Ian M. Irvine
3712 Swiss Avenue
Dallas, Texas 75204
Telephone: 214-744-3816

Position desired
Part-time editorial assistant.

Education
Southern Methodist University, 1992 to present.
Current standing: sophomore.
Major: English literature and journalism.

Abilene (Texas) Senior High School, 1988-1992.
Graduated with academic, college preparatory
degree.

Employment history
Daily Campus, student newspaper of Southern
Methodist University, 1992 to present.
Responsibilities include writing feature sto-
ries and sports coverage.

Abilene Reporter-News, summer 1993.
Responsibilities as a copy aide included
routing copy, monitoring teleprinter, running
errands, and assisting reporters.

Longhorn Painters, summer 1992.
Responsibilities included exterior and interior
house painting.

References
Academic: Placement Office
                Southern Methodist University
                Dallas, TX 75275

Employment: Ms. Millie Stevens
                Abilene Reporter-News
                Abilene, TX 79604

Personal: Ms. Sheryl Gipstein
                26 Overland Drive
                Abilene, TX 79604

ms
40b

and education and employment history, along with information about how to obtain your references. (See the sample on the facing page.) Use headings to mark the various sections of the résumé, spacing around them and within sections so that important information stands out. Try to limit your résumé to one page so that it can be quickly scanned. However, if your experience and education are extensive, a two-page résumé is preferable to a single cramped, unreadable page.

In preparing your résumé, you may wish to consult one of the many books devoted to application letters, résumés, and other elements of a job search. Two helpful guides are Richard N. Bolles, *What Color Is Your Parachute? A Practical Manual for Job-Hunters and Career Changers,* and Tom Jackson, *The Perfect Résumé.*

40c Use a standard form for business memos.

Business memorandums (memos, for short) address people within the same organization. A memo reports briefly and directly on a very specific topic: an answer to a question, a progress report, an evaluation.

Both the form and the structure of a memo are designed to get to the point and dispose of it quickly. State your reason for writing in the first sentence. Devote the first paragraph to a concise presentation of your answer, conclusion, or evaluation. In the rest of the memo explain your reasoning or evidence. Use headings or lists as appropriate to highlight key information. (See the sample on the next page.)

Most companies have their own conventions for memo formats. The heading usually consists of the company name, the addressee's name, the writer's name, the date, and a subject description or title. (See the sample.) The body of the memo is usually single-spaced, with double spacing between paragraphs and no paragraph indentions. An indication of who receives copies of the memo can be given two spaces below the last line of the body.

40d Adapt other business formats for faxes and electronic mail.

Communicating via electronic devices, especially facsimile (fax) machines and computerized electronic mail (E-mail), speeds up correspondence but also creates new challenges. For both fax transmissions and E-mail, the standards are the same as for other

Bigelow Wax Company

TO: Aileen Rosen, Director of Sales
FROM: Patricia Phillips, Territory 12
DATE: March 15, 1994
SUBJECT: 1993 sales of Quick Wax in Territory 12

Since it was introduced in January 1993, Quick
Wax has been unsuccessful in Territory 12 and
has not affected the sales of our Easy Shine.
Discussions with customers and my own analysis
of Quick Wax suggest three reasons for its
failure to compete with our product.

1. Quick Wax has not received the promotion
   necessary for a new product. Advertising--
   primarily on radio--has been sporadic and
   has not developed a clear, consistent image
   for the product. In addition, the Quick
   Wax sales representative in Territory 12 is
   new and inexperienced; he is not known to
   customers, and his sales pitch (which I
   once overheard) is weak. As far as I can
   tell, his efforts are not supported by
   phone calls or mailings from his home
   office.

2. When Quick Wax does make it to the store
   shelves, buyers do not choose it over our
   product. Though priced competitively with
   our product, Quick Wax is poorly packaged.
   The container seems smaller than ours,
   though in fact it holds the same eight
   ounces. The lettering on the Quick Wax
   package (red on blue) is difficult to read,
   in contrast to the white-on-green lettering
   on the Easy Shine package.

3. Our special purchase offers and my
   increased efforts to serve existing customers have had the intended effect of
   keeping customers satisfied with our
   product and reducing their inclination to
   stock something new.

Copies: L. Goldberger, Director of Marketing
        L. MacGregor, Customer Service Manager

ms
40d

business correspondence: state your purpose at the outset and write straightforwardly, clearly, concisely, objectively, courteously, and correctly.

For fax transmissions, follow the format of a letter (p. 181) or memo (p. 185), as appropriate. Provide a cover sheet containing the addressee's name, company, and fax number; the date, time, and subject; your own name and fax and telephone numbers (the telephone number is important in case something goes wrong with the transmission); and the total number of pages (including the cover sheet) in the fax.

Because fax transmissions can go astray, it's often wise to advise your addressee to expect a fax. Such advice is essential if the fax is confidential, because the machine is often shared. Transmission by fax can imply that the correspondence is urgent. If yours isn't, consider using the mail. (Swamping your correspondents with needless faxes can make you the boy who cried wolf when you really have an urgent message to transmit.)

E-mail messages, sent over computer networks, are usually more informal and often more terse than standard business letters or memos. The headings in an E-mail message are usually dictated by the network, but you can still address the recipient(s) by name and sign off with your own name. In between, write clearly and correctly, use basic courtesies like *please* and *thank you,* and avoid "flashing," or attacking, the addressee. Also, be aware that E-mail is seldom confidential.

41 Spelling

You can train yourself to spell better, and this chapter will tell you how. But you can also improve instantly by acquiring three habits:

- ❖ Carefully proofread your writing.
- ❖ Cultivate a healthy suspicion of your spellings.
- ❖ Compulsively check a dictionary whenever you doubt a spelling.

NOTE The spelling checkers for computerized word processors can help you find and track spelling errors in your papers. But their

sp
41

usefulness is limited, mainly because they can't spot the very common error of confusing words with similar spellings, such as *their/there/they're* or *to/too/two*. A spelling checker can supplement but can't substitute for your own care and attention.

41a Anticipate typical spelling problems.

Certain situations, such as misleading pronunciation, commonly lead to misspelling.

1. Pronunciation

In English, pronunciation of words is an unreliable guide to how they are spelled. Pronunciation is especially misleading with HOMONYMS, words pronounced the same but spelled differently.

Some commonly confused homonyms and other pairs that sound similar are listed below.

accept (to receive)
except (other than)

affect (to have an influence on)
effect (result)

all ready (prepared)
already (by this time)

allusion (indirect reference)
illusion (erroneous belief or
    perception)

ascent (a movement up)
assent (agreement)

bare (unclothed)
bear (to carry, or an animal)

board (a plane of wood)
bored (uninterested)

brake (stop)
break (smash)

buy (purchase)
by (next to)

cite (to quote an authority)
sight (the ability to see)
site (a place)

desert (to abandon)
dessert (after-dinner course)

discreet (reserved, respectful)
discrete (individual, distinct)

fair (average, or lovely)
fare (a fee for transportation)

forth (forward)
fourth (after *third*)

hear (to perceive by ear)
here (in this place)

heard (past tense of *hear*)
herd (a group of animals)

hole (an opening)
whole (complete)

its (possessive of *it*)
it's (contraction of *it is*)

know (to be certain)
no (the opposite of *yes*)

meat (flesh)
meet (encounter)

passed (past tense of *pass*)
past (after, or a time gone by)

patience (forbearance)
patients (persons under medical
    care)

peace (the absence of war)
piece (a portion of something)

plain (clear)
plane (a carpenter's tool, or an
   airborne vehicle)

presence (the state of being at
   hand)
presents (gifts)

principal (most important, or
   the head of a school)
principle (a basic truth or law)

rain (precipitation)
reign (to rule)
rein (a strap for controlling an
   animal)

right (correct)
rite (a religious ceremony)
write (to make letters)

road (a surface for driving)
rode (past tense of *ride*)

scene (where an action occurs)
seen (past participle of *see*)

stationary (unmoving)
stationery (writing paper)

their (possessive of *they*)
there (opposite of *here*)
they're (contraction of *they are*)

to (toward)
too (also)
two (following *one*)

waist (the middle of the body)
waste (discarded material)

weak (not strong)
week (Sunday through Saturday)

weather (climate)
whether (*if*, or introducing a
   choice)

which (one of a group)
witch (a sorcerer)

who's (contraction of *who is*)
whose (possessive of *who*)

your (possessive of *you*)
you're (contraction of *you are*)

2. Different forms of the same word

Often, the noun form and the verb form of the same word are spelled differently: for example, *advice* (noun) and *advise* (verb). Sometimes the noun and the adjective forms of the same word differ: *height* and *high*. Similar changes occur in the parts of some irregular verbs (*know, knew, known*) and the plurals of irregular nouns (*man, men*).

41b Follow spelling rules.

1. *Ie* vs. *ei*

To distinguish between *ie* and *ei*, use the familiar jingle:

I before *e*, except after *c*, or when pronounced "ay" as in *neighbor* and *weigh*.

i BEFORE *e*	believe	thief	hygiene
ei AFTER *c*	ceiling	conceive	perceive
ei SOUNDED AS "AY"	sleigh	eight	beige

sp

41b

EXCEPTIONS For some of the exceptions, remember this sentence:

The weird foreigner neither seizes leisure nor forfeits height.

2. Final -*e*

When adding an ending to a word ending in -*e*, drop the -*e* if the ending begins with a vowel.

> advise + able = advisable
> surprise + ing = surprising

Keep the -*e* if the ending begins with a consonant.

> care + ful = careful
> like + ly = likely

EXCEPTIONS Retain the -*e* after a soft *c* or *g*, to keep the sound of the consonant soft rather than hard: *courageous, changeable.* And drop the -*e* before a consonant when the -*e* is preceded by another vowel: *argue + ment = argument, true + ly = truly.*

3. Final -*y*

When adding an ending to a word ending in -*y*, change the *y* to *i* if it follows a consonant.

> beauty, beauties   worry, worried   supply, supplies

But keep the *y* if it follows a vowel, if it ends a proper name, or if the ending is -*ing.*

> day, days   Minsky, Minskys   cry, crying

4. Final consonants

When adding an ending to a word ending in a consonant, double the consonant if it is preceded by a single vowel or if the stress, once the ending is added, falls on the syllable finished by the consonant.

> slap, slapping   submit, submitted   begin, beginning

Don't double the final consonant if it is preceded by two vowels or a vowel and another consonant or if the stress, once the ending is added, falls on some syllable other than the one finished by the consonant.

> pair, paired   park, parking   refer, reference

5. Prefixes

When adding a prefix, do not drop a letter from or add a letter to the original word.

u<u>nn</u>ecessary   <u>dis</u>appoint   <u>mis</u>spell

6. Plurals

Most nouns form plurals by adding -*s* to the singular form. For nouns ending in -*s*, -*sh*, -*ch*, or -*x*, add -*es* for the plural.

boy, boy<u>s</u>   kiss, kiss<u>es</u>   church, church<u>es</u>

Nouns ending in -*o* preceded by a vowel usually form the plural with -*s*. Those ending in -*o* preceded by a consonant usually form the plural with -*es*.

ratio, ratio<u>s</u>   hero, hero<u>es</u>

Some very common nouns form irregular plurals.

child, chil<u>dren</u>   man, m<u>e</u>n
mouse, m<u>ice</u>   woman, wom<u>e</u>n

Some English nouns that were originally Italian, Greek, Latin, or French form the plural according to their original language:

analysis, analys<u>es</u>   datum, dat<u>a</u>
basis, bas<u>es</u>   medium, medi<u>a</u>
beau, bea<u>ux</u>   phenomenon, phenomen<u>a</u>
crisis, cris<u>es</u>   piano, piano<u>s</u>
criterion, criteri<u>a</u>   thesis, thes<u>es</u>

A few such nouns may form irregular *or* regular plurals: for instance, *index, ind<u>ices</u>, ind<u>exes</u>; curriculum, curricul<u>a</u>, curricul<u>ums</u>.* The regular plural is more contemporary.

With compound nouns, add -*s* to the main word of the compound. Sometimes this main word is not the last word.

city-state<u>s</u>   father<u>s</u>-in-law   passer<u>s</u>by

 **The Hyphen**

Always use a hyphen to divide a word between syllables from one line to the next. Also use it to form some COMPOUND WORDS expressing a combination of ideas, such as *cross-reference*. The following rules cover many but not all compounds. When you doubt the spelling of a compound word, consult a dictionary.

42a Use the hyphen in some compound adjectives.

When two or more words serve together as a single modifier before a noun, a hyphen forms the modifying words clearly into a unit.

> She is a *well-known* actor.
> No *English-speaking* people were in the room.

When such a compound adjective follows the noun, the hyphen is unnecessary.

> The actor is *well known*.
> Those people are *English speaking*.

The hyphen is also unnecessary in a compound modifier containing an *-ly* adverb, even before the noun: *clearly defined terms*.

When part of a compound adjective appears only once in two or more parallel compound adjectives, hyphens indicate which words the reader should mentally join with the missing part.

> School-age children should have eight- or nine-o'clock bedtimes.

42b Use the hyphen in fractions and compound numbers.

Hyphens join the numerator and denominator of fractions: *three-fourths, one-half.* And the whole numbers *twenty-one* to *ninety-nine* are always hyphenated.

42c Use the hyphen to attach some prefixes and suffixes.

Prefixes are usually attached to word stems without hyphens: *predetermine, unnatural, disengage.* However, when the prefix precedes a capitalized word or when a capital letter is combined with a word, a hyphen usually separates the two: *un-American, non-European, A-frame.* And some prefixes, such as *self-, all-,* and *ex-* (meaning "formerly"), usually require hyphens no matter what follows: *self-control, all-inclusive, ex-student.* The only suffix that regularly requires a hyphen is *-elect,* as in *president-elect.*

43 Capital Letters

The following conventions and a desk dictionary can help you decide whether to capitalize a particular word. In general, capitalize only when a rule or the dictionary says you must.

43a Capitalize the first word of every sentence.

Every writer should own a good dictionary.

When quoting other writers, you should reproduce the capital letters beginning their sentences or indicate that you have altered the source. Whenever possible, integrate the quotation into your own sentence so that its capitalization coincides with yours.

"Psychotherapists often overlook the benefits of self-deception," the author argues.

The author argues that "the benefits of self-deception" are not always recognized by psychotherapists.

If you need to alter the capitalization in the source, indicate the change with brackets.

"[T]he benefits of self-deception" are not always recognized by psychotherapists, the author argues.

The author argues that "[p]sychotherapists often overlook the benefits of self-deception."

NOTE Capitalization of questions in a series is optional. Both of the following examples are correct.

Is the population a hundred? Two hundred? More?
Is the population a hundred? two hundred? more?

Also optional is capitalization of the first word in a complete sentence after a colon.

43b Capitalize proper nouns, proper adjectives, and words used as essential parts of proper nouns.

1. Proper nouns and proper adjectives

PROPER NOUNS name specific persons, places, and things: *Shake-*

cap
43b

speare, California, World War I. PROPER ADJECTIVES are formed from some proper nouns: *Shakespearean, Californian.* Capitalize all proper nouns and proper adjectives but not the articles (*a, an, the*) that precede them.

SPECIFIC PERSONS AND THINGS

Stephen King	Boulder Dam
Napoleon Bonaparte	the Empire State Building

SPECIFIC PLACES AND GEOGRAPHICAL REGIONS

New York City	the Mediterranean Sea
China	the Northeast, the South

But: northeast of the city, going south

DAYS OF THE WEEK, MONTHS, HOLIDAYS

Monday	Yom Kippur
May	Christmas

HISTORICAL EVENTS, DOCUMENTS, PERIODS, MOVEMENTS

the Vietnam War	the Renaissance
the Constitution	the Romantic Movement

GOVERNMENT OFFICES OR DEPARTMENTS AND INSTITUTIONS

House of Representatives	Polk Municipal Court
Department of Defense	Northeast High School

POLITICAL, SOCIAL, ATHLETIC, AND OTHER ORGANIZATIONS AND ASSOCIATIONS AND THEIR MEMBERS

Democratic Party, Democrats	League of Women Voters
Sierra Club	Boston Celtics
B'nai B'rith	Chicago Symphony Orchestra

RACES, NATIONALITIES, AND THEIR LANGUAGES

Native American	Germans
African-American, Negro	Swahili
Caucasian	Italian

But: blacks, whites

RELIGIONS, THEIR FOLLOWERS, AND TERMS FOR THE SACRED

Christianity, Christians	God
Catholicism, Catholics	Allah
Judaism, Orthodox Jew	the Bible (*but* biblical)
Islam, Moslems *or* Muslims	the Koran

cap

43b

2.   Common nouns used as essential parts of proper nouns

Capitalize the common nouns *street, avenue, park, river, ocean, lake, company, college, county,* and *memorial* when they are part of proper nouns naming specific places or institutions.

Main Street   Lake Superior
Central Park   Ford Motor Company
Mississippi River   Madison College
Pacific Ocean   George Washington Memorial

43c Capitalize most words in titles and subtitles of works.

In all titles and subtitles of works, capitalize the first and last words and all other words *except* articles (*a, an, the*), *to* in infinitives, and connecting words (prepositions and coordinating and subordinating conjunctions) of fewer than five letters. Capitalize even these short words when they are the first or last word in a title or when they fall after a colon or semicolon.

"Courtship Through the Ages"   *Management: A New Theory*
A Diamond Is Forever   "Once More to the Lake"
"Knowing Whom to Ask"   *An End to Live For*
Learning from Las Vegas   *File Under Architecture*

43d Capitalize titles preceding persons' names.

Before a person's name, capitalize his or her title. After the name, do not capitalize the title.

Professor Otto Osborne   Otto Osborne, a professor
Doctor Jane Covington   Jane Covington, a doctor
Senator Robert Dole   Robert Dole, the senator

NOTE Many writers capitalize a title denoting very high rank even when it follows a name or is used alone: *Lyndon Johnson, past President of the United States.*

44 Underlining (Italics)

und

44

Underlining and *italic type* indicate the same thing: the word or words are being distinguished or emphasized. In your papers use a ruler or the underscore on the keyboard to underline. If your typewriter or word processor can produce italic type, consult your instructor about whether to use it. Many instructors prefer underlining.

44a Underline the titles of works that appear independently.

Underline the titles of works, such as books and periodicals, that are published, released, or produced separately from other works. (See the box below.) Use quotation marks for all other titles, such as short stories, articles in periodicals, and episodes of television series. (See p. 168.)

Titles to be underlined (italicized)

Other titles should be placed in quotation marks (see p. 168).

BOOKS

Catch-22
War and Peace
And the Band Played On

PLAYS

Hamlet
The Phantom of the Opera

PAMPHLETS

The Truth About Alcoholism

LONG MUSICAL WORKS

Tchaikovsky's Swan Lake
The Beatles' Revolver
But: Symphony in C

TELEVISION AND RADIO PROGRAMS

60 Minutes
The Shadow
Seinfeld

LONG POEMS

Beowulf
Paradise Lost
The Song of Roland

PERIODICALS

Time
Philadelphia Inquirer

PUBLISHED SPEECHES

Lincoln's Gettysburg Address

MOVIES AND VIDEOTAPES

Schindler's List
Invasion of the Body Snatchers
How to Relax

WORKS OF VISUAL ART

Michelangelo's David
the Mona Lisa
Guernica

EXCEPTIONS Legal documents, the Bible, the Koran, and their parts are generally not underlined.

NOT   We studied the Book of Revelation in the Bible.

BUT   We studied the Book of Revelation in the Bible.

44b Underline the names of ships, aircraft, spacecraft, and trains.

Challenger   Orient Express   Queen Elizabeth 2
Apollo XI   Montrealer   Spirit of St. Louis

44c Underline foreign words that arc not part of the English language.

A foreign expression should be underlined when it has not been absorbed into our language. A dictionary will say whether a word is still considered foreign to English.

> The scientific name for the brown trout is <u>Salmo trutta</u>. [The Latin scientific names for plants and animals are always underlined.]

> The Latin <u>De gustibus non est disputandum</u> translates roughly as "There's no accounting for taste."

44d Underline words, letters, numbers, and phrases named as words.

> Some people say <u>th</u>, as in <u>thought</u>, with a faint <u>s</u> or <u>f</u> sound.

> Try pronouncing <u>unique New York</u> ten times fast.

> The word <u>syzygy</u> refers to a straight line formed by three celestial bodies, as in the alignment of the earth, sun, and moon. [Quotation marks may also be used for words being defined.]

44e Occasionally, underlining may be used for emphasis.

Underlining can stress an important word or phrase, especially in reporting how someone said something. But use such emphasis very rarely, or your writing may sound immature or hysterical.

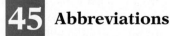

45 Abbreviations

ab
45

The following guidelines on abbreviations pertain to nontechnical writing. Technical writing, such as in the sciences and engineering, generally uses many more abbreviations.

45a Use standard abbreviations for titles immediately before and after proper names.

BEFORE THE NAME	AFTER THE NAME
Dr. James Hsu	James Hsu, M.D.
Mr., Mrs., Ms., Hon.,	D.D.S., D.V.M., Ph.D.,
St., Rev., Msgr., Gen.	Ed.D., O.S.B., S.J., Sr., Jr.

Do not use abbreviations such as *Rev., Hon., Prof., Rep., Sen., Dr.,* and *St.* (for *Saint*) unless they appear before a proper name.

45b Familiar abbreviations and acronyms are acceptable in most writing.

An ACRONYM is an abbreviation that spells a pronounceable word, such as WHO, NATO, and AIDS. These and other abbreviations using initials are acceptable in most writing as long as they are familiar to readers. Abbreviations of three or more words are usually written without periods.

INSTITUTIONS	LSU, UCLA, TCU
ORGANIZATIONS	CIA, FBI, YMCA, AFL-CIO
CORPORATIONS	IBM, CBS, ITT
PEOPLE	JFK, LBJ, FDR
COUNTRIES	U.S.A. (or USA)

NOTE If a name or term (such as *operating room*) appears often in a piece of writing, then its abbreviation (*O.R.*) can cut down on extra words. Spell out the full term at its first appearance, indicate its abbreviation in parentheses, and then use the abbreviation.

45c Use *B.C., A.D., A.M., P.M., no.,* and *$* only with specific dates and numbers.

44 B.C.	11:26 A.M. (*or* a.m.)	no. 36 (*or* No. 36)
A.D. 1492	8:05 P.M. (*or* p.m.)	$7.41

The abbreviation B.C. ("before Christ") always follows a date, whereas A.D. (*anno Domini,* Latin for "in the year of the Lord") precedes a date.

NOTE B.C.E. ("before the common era") and C.E. ("common era") are increasingly replacing B.C. and A.D., respectively. Both follow the date.

ab
45c

45d Generally, reserve Latin abbreviations for source citations and comments in parentheses.

i.e.   *id est:* that is
cf.   *confer:* compare
e.g.   *exempli gratia:* for example
et al.   *et alii:* and others
etc.   *et cetera:* and so forth
N.B.   *nota bene:* note well

He said he would be gone a fortnight (i.e., two weeks)
Bloom et al., editors, *Anthology of Light Verse*
Trees, too, are susceptible to disease (e.g., Dutch elm disease).

(Note that these abbreviations are generally not italicized or underlined.)

Some writers avoid these abbreviations in formal writing, even within parentheses.

45e Reserve *Inc., Bros., Co.,* or & (for *and*) for official names of business firms.

FAULTY   *The Santini bros.* operate a large moving firm in New York City & environs.

REVISED   *The Santini brothers* operate a large moving firm in New York City *and* environs.

REVISED   *Santini Bros.* is a large moving firm in New York City *and* environs.

45f Spell out units of measurement and names of places, calendar designations, people, and courses.

Units of measurement, geographical names, and other words are often abbreviated in technical writing. In other academic writing and general writing, however, such words should be spelled out.

UNITS OF MEASUREMENT
The dog is thirty *inches* (not *in.*) high.

GEOGRAPHICAL NAMES
The publisher is in *Massachusetts* (not *Mass.* or *MA*).

NAMES OF DAYS, MONTHS, AND HOLIDAYS
The truce was signed on *Tuesday* (not *Tues.*), *April* (not *Apr.*) 16.

ab

45f

NAMES OF PEOPLE

Robert (not *Robt.*) Frost writes accessible poems.

COURSES OF INSTRUCTION

I'm majoring in *political science* (not *poli. sci.*).

46 Numbers

In scientific and technical writing, all numbers are usually written as figures. In business writing, all numbers over ten are usually written as figures. In other academic and general writing—the subject of this chapter—numbers are more often spelled out.

46a Use figures for numbers that require more than two words to spell out.

The leap year has *366* days.
The population of Minot, North Dakota, is about *32,800*.

Spell out numbers of one or two words.

The ball game drew *forty-two thousand* people. [A hyphenated number may be considered one word.]

EXCEPTIONS Use a combination of figures and words for round numbers over a million: *26 million, 2.45 billion*. And use either all figures or all words when several numbers appear together in a passage, even if convention would require a mixture.

46b Use figures instead of words according to standard practice.

We conventionally use figures for certain information, even when the numbers could be spelled out in one or two words.

DAYS AND YEARS

June 18, 1985   A.D. 12   456 B.C.   1999

PAGES, CHAPTERS, VOLUMES, ACTS, SCENES, LINES

Chapter 9, page 123
Hamlet, Act 5, Scene 3

DECIMALS, PERCENTAGES, AND FRACTIONS

22.5   3½
48% (*or* 48 percent)

ADDRESSES

355 Clinton Avenue
Washington, D.C. 20036

SCORES AND STATISTICS

21 to 7   a ratio of 8 to 1

EXACT AMOUNTS OF MONEY

$3.5 million $4.50

THE TIME OF DAY

9:00   3:45

EXCEPTIONS Round dollar or cent amounts of only a few words may be expressed in words: *seventeen dollars; sixty cents.* When the word *o'clock* is used for the time of day, also express the number in words: *two o'clock* (not *2 o'clock*).

46c Spell out numbers that begin sentences.

For clarity, spell out any number that begins a sentence. If the number requires more than two words, reword the sentence so that the number falls later and can be expressed as a figure.

FAULTY   *103* visitors asked for refunds.

AWKWARD   *One hundred three* visitors asked for refunds.

REVISED   Of the visitors, *103* asked for refunds.

num

46c

47 Research Strategy

Research writing is a process involving diverse and overlapping activities. A thoughtful plan (47a), an appropriate topic (47b), and some preliminary thinking about the topic (47c) will give you a head start and help direct your progress.

47a Planning a research project

As soon as you receive an assignment for a research project, you can begin developing a strategy for completing it. The first step should be making a schedule that apportions the available time to the necessary work. A possible schedule appears below. (The section numbers in parentheses refer to relevant discussions in this book.)

Complete
by:

_____ 1. Finding a topic (47b–47c)
_____ 2. Finding information and refining the topic (48a–48b)

_____ 3. Evaluating and synthesizing sources (48c)
_____ 4. Taking notes using summary, paraphrase, and direct quotation (48d–48e)

_____ 5. Creating a focus and structure (3a–3b)
_____ 6. Drafting the paper (4a–4b, 48f)

_____ 7. Revising and editing the paper (5a–5d)
_____ 8. Citing sources in your text (49a, 50a)
_____ 9. Preparing the list of sources (49b, 50b)
_____ 10. Preparing and proofreading the final manuscript (5c, 40a)
_____ 11. Final paper due

You can estimate that each segment marked off by a horizontal line will occupy *roughly* one-quarter of the total time—for example, a week in a four-week assignment or two weeks in an eight-week assignment. The most unpredictable segments are the first two, so it's wise to get started early enough to accommodate the unexpected.

47b Finding a topic

Before reading this section, you may want to review the suggestions given in Chapter 1 for finding and limiting a topic and for defining a purpose (pp. 3–4). Selecting and refining a topic for a research paper present special opportunities and problems. If you have questions about your topic, consult your instructor.

A topic for a research paper has four primary requirements, each with corresponding pitfalls.

* Ample published sources of information are available on the topic.

  Avoid (*a*) very recent topics, such as the latest medical breakthrough, and (*b*) topics that are too removed geographically, such as a minor event in Australian history.

* The topic encourages research in the kinds and number of sources required by the assignment.

  Avoid (*a*) topics that depend entirely on personal opinion and experience, such as the virtues of your hobby, and (*b*) topics that require research in only one source, such as a straight factual biography.

* The topic will lead you to an objective assessment of sources and to defensible conclusions.

  Avoid topics that rest entirely on belief or prejudice, such as when human life begins or why women (or men) are superior. Your readers are unlikely to be swayed from their own beliefs.

* The topic suits the length of paper assigned and the time given for research and writing.

  Avoid broad topics that have too many sources to survey adequately, such as a major event in history.

47c Approaching the topic

Before you begin digging in the library for information about your topic, take some time to figure out what you already know and think.

* Consider your own ideas about the topic. What led you to choose it? What can you say about it without any research? What opinions do you have about it, and why?

❖ Ask some questions about the topic. What *don't* you know?
What kinds of information do you think you will need?

48 Using Sources

Research writing is mainly about finding sources and using
them to form, support, and extend your own ideas. This chapter discusses keeping track of sources (48a); the kinds of sources available
(48b); reading sources critically (48c); taking notes using summary,
paraphrase, and quotation (48d); avoiding plagiarism (48e); and introducing borrowed material in your own text (48f).

NOTE If sources you need are not in your library, your librarian
may be able to obtain them from another library. But plan ahead:
these interlibrary loans can take a week or even several weeks.

48a Keeping a working bibliography

Keep track of sources as you come across them with a WORKING
BIBLIOGRAPHY, a record of all the information you need to locate the
sources. Some instructors require that the working bibliography be
submitted on note cards (one source to a card), and this system has
the advantage of allowing the sources to be shuffled easily. But
many researchers have abandoned note cards because their library's computers can print out pages of bibliographic information
or even transfer data to the user's own disk. (See the next section
for more on computers in libraries.)

Whatever system you use, you should have a bibliographic reference for each source you think may be useful. Pages 229 and
236–37 show diagrams of the basic information you'll need for a
book and an article in a periodical. In addition, record the library's
catalog number for each source so that you can retrieve it easily.

48b Finding sources

Sources are of two basic kinds:

❖ PRIMARY SOURCES are firsthand accounts: historical documents
(letters, speeches, and so on), eyewitness reports, works of lit-

48b

erature, reports on experiments or surveys, or your own interviews, experiments, observations, or correspondence. Whenever possible, you should seek and rely on primary sources, drawing your own conclusions from them.

❖ SECONDARY SOURCES report and analyze information drawn from other sources, often primary ones: a historian's account of a battle, a critic's reading of a poem, a physicist's evaluation of several studies, an encyclopedia or other standard reference work. Secondary sources may contain helpful summaries and interpretations that direct, support, and extend your thinking. However, most research-writing assignments expect your own ideas to go beyond those you find in such sources.

Your library houses primary and secondary sources on computerized databases and in reference works, periodicals, and books. In addition, you can generate your own primary sources.

1. Computerized sources

Kinds of computerized sources

These days most libraries have at least some research sources on computer. Your library probably has a computerized catalog of its holdings, at least the more recent ones (see p. 211). The library may also provide some sources on compact disks called CD-ROMs (compact disk—read only memory). Many of the reference works, indexes, and other resources described on the following pages are available on CD-ROM.

Before you begin researching your topic, find out what resources your library has available electronically. (A librarian will help you.) A catalog of CD-ROMs is *CD-ROMs in Print*, but not all the listed works will be available in your library.

In addition to CD-ROMs, many libraries also provide access to

---

A tip for researchers

If you are unsure of how to locate or use your library's resources, ask a reference librarian. This person is familiar with all the library's resources and with general and specialized research techniques, and it is his or her job to help you and others with research. Even experienced researchers often consult reference librarians.

information networks and services through telephone connections between computers. The Internet is a huge network of networks linking diverse sources of information, such as publications, businesses, governments, schools, libraries, foundations, and millions of individuals. The largest information service, DIALOG, offers hundreds of separate databases (bibliographies, indexes, reports, and so on) in many disciplines. Both the Internet and DIALOG generally cost money to use and often require the assistance of a library staffer.

Policies and procedures

Libraries vary widely in their handling of searches on computer. For a search of the library's catalog, ample terminals, easy-to-follow instructions, and free use should encourage you to work independently (though of course you can ask questions). For other searches, you may opt or be required to obtain a librarian's assistance, and you may be charged a fee. Libraries sometimes discourage the use of comprehensive information sources such as DIALOG and the Internet for relatively small-scale research projects like ten- or twenty-page term papers.

Computer searches

Research by computer is usually faster than research in print sources. The opening screen of a CD-ROM will tell you what databases the disk holds. To search through them, you'll need to describe your topic using words that correspond to the database's own categories for indexing information. With some databases, you locate subject headings that come as close as possible to your own subject. Most library catalogs, for instance, use the categories listed in *Library of Congress Subject Headings*. Some other databases use this guide, too, but many have their own subject headings. These headings are usually available in the database's thesaurus, stored electronically with the database or located in printed form near the computer or at the reference desk. You can still search a database without the thesaurus by entering your subject headings and asking the computer to show you a list of its own related terms (usually those surrounding yours in alphabetical order).

In a more complicated search, you can give the computer key words to locate within the database, such as in the titles of books and summaries of articles. This kind of search goes beyond the database's menu of subject headings, but unless you carefully define your key words it can produce a flood of useless references or nothing at all. Key words should accurately describe your topic: they should be neither too narrow, excluding potentially relevant information, nor too broad, calling up many irrelevant sources. Ask a librarian if you need help developing key words.

2. Reference works

REFERENCE WORKS (often available on computer) include encyclopedias, dictionaries, digests, bibliographies, indexes, atlases, almanacs, and handbooks. Your research *must* go beyond these sources, but they can help you decide whether your topic really interests you and whether it meets the requirements for a research paper (p. 206). Preliminary research in reference works will also direct you to more detailed sources on your topic. A comprehensive catalog and explanation is Eugene P. Sheehy, *Guide to Reference Books,* 10th edition plus supplement (1986, 1992).

3. Periodicals

PERIODICALS—journals, magazines, and newspapers—are invaluable sources of information in research. The difference between journals and magazines lies primarily in their content, readership, and frequency of issue.

* Magazines—such as *Psychology Today, Newsweek,* and *Esquire*—are nonspecialist publications intended for diverse readers. Most magazines appear weekly or monthly, and their pages are numbered anew with each issue.
* Journals often appear quarterly and contain specialized information intended for readers in a particular field. Examples include *American Anthropologist, Journal of Black Studies,* and *Journal of Chemical Education.* Many journals page each issue separately, but others number their pages consecutively through all the issues in a year (an annual volume).

Various indexes to periodicals—many available on computer—provide information on the articles in journals, magazines, and newspapers. The following are a few of the most widely used indexes:

* *InfoTrac:* more than a thousand business, government, technical, and general-interest publications.
* *Humanities Index:* journals in language and literature, history, philosophy, and other humanities.

- *MLA International Bibliography of Books and Articles on the Modern Languages and Literatures:* books and periodicals on literature, linguistics, and languages.
- *New York Times Index:* articles in the most complete U.S. newspaper.
- *Social Sciences Index:* journals in economics, psychology, political science, and other social sciences.
- *General Science Index:* journals in biology, chemistry, physics, and other sciences.
- *Readers' Guide to Periodical Literature:* over a hundred popular magazines.

Every library lists its complete periodical holdings either in its main catalog (see below) or in a separate catalog. The recent issues of a periodical are usually held in the library's periodical room. Back issues are usually stored elsewhere, either in bound volumes or on film that requires a special machine to read. A librarian will show you how to operate the machine.

4. Books

The library's main catalog lists books alphabetically by author's name, title of book, and subject. The catalog may be in a card file, in a printed volume, on film, or, increasingly, on a computerized database that you reach by a keyboard and a monitor. Ask a librarian if you are uncertain about the location, form, or use of the catalog.

To search the catalog, you will need specific key words relating to your subject. See pages 209–10 for advice on key-word searches.

5. Your own sources

Academic writing will often require you to conduct primary research for information of your own. For instance, you may need to analyze a poem, conduct an experiment, survey a group of people, or interview an expert. Such primary research may be the sole basis of your paper or may supplement and extend the information you find in other sources.

48c Reading sources critically

Research writing is much more than finding sources and reporting their contents. The challenge and interest come from *inter-*

acting with sources, discovering their meanings, judging their quality, and creating relationships among them.

Such engagement requires CRITICAL READING, reading that looks beyond the surface of the words. To read critically, you analyze a text, identifying its main ideas, structure, evidence, or other relevant elements; you evaluate its usefulness or quality; and you relate it to other texts and to your own ideas.

1. Evaluation

Not all the sources in your working bibliography will be useful to you. Some may prove irrelevant to your subject; others may prove unreliable. Before you settle in to take notes, examine your sources' introductions, tables of contents, and headings. Look for information about authors' backgrounds that will help you understand their expertise and bias. Try to answer the following questions about each source:

❖ Is the work relevant?

Does the source devote some attention to your topic?

Where in the source are you likely to find relevant information or ideas?

Is the source appropriately specialized for your needs? Check the source's treatment of a topic you know something about, to ensure that it is neither too superficial nor too technical.

How important is the source likely to be for your writing?

❖ Is the work reliable?

How up to date is the source? Check the publication date.

Is the author an expert in the field? Look for an author biography, or look up the author in a biographical reference.

What is the author's bias? Check biographical information or the author's own preface or introduction. Consider what others have written about the author or the source.

Whatever his or her bias, does the author reason soundly, provide adequate evidence, and consider opposing views?

Don't expect to find harmony among sources, for reasonable people often disagree in their opinions. Thus you must deal hon-

---

┌─ KEY TERM ───
ANALYSIS Separating something (such as a text) into its elements and interpreting the meaning, relationships, and significance of the elements.
└──

48d

estly with the gaps and conflicts in sources. Old sources, superficial ones, slanted ones—these should be offset in your research and your writing by sources that are more recent, more thorough, or more objective.

2. Synthesis

When you begin to locate the differences and similarities among sources, you move into the most significant part of research writing: forging relationships for your own purpose. This SYNTHESIS is an essential step in reading sources critically and continues through the drafting and revision of a research paper. You infer connections—say, between one writer's ideas and another's or between two works by the same author. Doing so, you create something different from what you started with: you create new knowledge.

Your synthesis of sources will grow more detailed and sophisticated as you proceed through the research-writing process. Unless you are analyzing primary sources such as the works of a writer, at first read your sources quickly and selectively to obtain an overview of your topic and a sense of how the sources approach it. Don't get bogged down in taking detailed notes, but *do* write down important connections between sources and general ideas that seem fundamental to your topic. Be especially careful to record ideas of your own, such as your reaction to a writer's theories, because these may not occur to you later.

As you read, digest, and organize source information, your own ideas should gain more and more prominence. A common trap of research writing is allowing your sources to control you, rather than vice versa. To avoid this trap, ask how each source illuminates the idea you are building. When you are taking notes, assign each note a heading from an outline (even a rough one) that you have devised to develop your idea. When you are drafting, make sure each paragraph focuses on a conclusion you have drawn from your reading (the support for the idea will come from your sources). In this way, your paper will synthesize existing work into something wholly your own.

48d **Taking notes using summary, paraphrase, and direct quotation**

You can accomplish a great deal of synthesis while taking notes from your sources. Note taking is not a mechanical process of copying from books. Rather, as you read and take notes you assess and organize the information in your sources.

1. Note form

Most researchers take notes on note cards, on computer, or by photocopying sources. Each system has advantages and disadvantages.

- ❖ Note cards are easy to rearrange, but handwriting can be tedious.
- ❖ Notes on computer are also easy to rearrange and easy to incorporate into your drafts, but they require a handy computer.
- ❖ Photocopied notes save time, but they usually cost money, they can be difficult to rearrange, and, most important, they postpone critical thinking about sources.

Whatever system of note taking you use, record the source author's name and the source page number (without this information, you won't be able to use the note). Also give the note a topic heading that corresponds to a part of your subject, so you can see at a glance where the note fits.

2. Summary

When you SUMMARIZE, you condense an extended idea or argument into a sentence or more in your own words. Summary is most useful when you want to record the gist of an author's idea without the background or supporting evidence. The sample note card at the top of the facing page shows a summary of the following passage. The source is used in the sample paper on pages 245–51.

ORIGINAL

Most commercial [diet] programs are also beginning to pay more attention to counseling and exercise. Scientists say that developing new habits of eating and activity is the real key to long-term maintenance—and the only hope for breaking ties with a diet machine.

"They are trying to improve programs, but it's very variable," says Dr. Thomas A. Wadden, a weight-loss specialist at Syracuse University. "Some have lectures. But most people who are overweight need more than a lecture. Most people who are overweight know what they have to do—they know they should walk more and put their fork down in between bites—but have trouble doing it."

—ELISABETH ROSENTHAL, "Commercial Diets Lack Proof of Their Long-Term Success," *New York Times*, p. C11

SUMMARY

> *Need for behavior modification*
>
> Rosenthal, p. C11
>
> Commercial diets are now stressing the essentials
> of long-term weight loss that overweight people
> know but find difficult: exercise more, and change
> eating habits (quotes Dr. Thomas A. Wadden,
> Syracuse U).

3. Paraphrase

When you PARAPHRASE, you follow much more closely the author's original presentation, but you still restate it in your own words. Paraphrase is most useful when you want to reconstruct an author's line of reasoning but don't feel the original words merit direct quotation. Here is a paraphrase of the quotation from Thomas Wadden in the *New York Times* passage opposite:

PARAPHRASE

> *Need for behavior modification*
>
> Rosenthal, p. C11
>
> Dr. Thomas A. Wadden (weight-loss expert,
> Syracuse U) holds that although most overweight
> people are aware that they need to get more
> exercise and eat differently, they find behavior
> change difficult.

Notice that the paraphrase follows the original but uses different words and different sentence structures. To achieve such a paraphrase, use these guidelines:

48d

❖ Read the relevant material several times to be sure you understand it.
❖ Restate the source's ideas in your own words and sentence structures. You need not put down in new words the whole passage or all the details. Select what is relevant to your topic, and restate only that. If complete sentences seem too detailed or cumbersome, use phrases, as in this example: *Exercising and changing eating habits—essential for weight loss but hard to do.*
❖ Be careful not to distort meaning. Don't change the source's emphasis or omit connecting words, qualifiers, and other material whose absence will confuse you later or cause you to misrepresent the source.

4. Direct quotation

In a paper analyzing primary sources such as literary works, you will use direct quotation extensively to illustrate and support your analysis. But you should quote from secondary sources only in the following circumstances:

❖ The author's original satisfies one of these requirements:

The language is unusually vivid, bold, or inventive.
The quotation cannot be paraphrased without distortion or loss of meaning.
The words themselves are at issue in your interpretation.
The quotation represents and emphasizes the view of an important expert.
The quotation is a graph, diagram, or table.

❖ The quotation is as short as possible.

It includes only material relevant to your point.
It is edited to eliminate examples and other unneeded material. (See below.)

When taking a quotation from a source, copy the material *carefully.* Take down the author's exact wording, spelling, capitalization, and punctuation. Proofread every direct quotation *at least twice,* and be sure you have supplied big quotation marks so that later you won't confuse the direct quotation with a paraphrase or summary. If you want to make changes for clarity, use brackets (see p. 174). If you want to omit irrelevant words or sentences, use ellipsis marks, usually three spaced periods (see pp. 172–74).

48e Avoiding plagiarism

PLAGIARISM (from a Latin word for "kidnapper") is the presentation of someone else's ideas or words as your own. Whether deliberate or accidental, plagiarism is a serious and often punishable offense.

❖ *Deliberate* plagiarism:

Copying a phrase, a sentence, or a longer passage from a source and passing it off as your own by omitting quotation marks and a source citation.

Summarizing or paraphrasing someone else's ideas without acknowledging your debt in a source citation.

Handing in as your own work a paper you have bought, had a friend write, or copied from another student.

❖ *Accidental* plagiarism:

Forgetting to place quotation marks around another writer's words.

Omitting a source citation for another's idea because you are unaware of the need to acknowledge the idea.

Carelessly copying a source when you mean to paraphrase.

1. What you need not acknowledge

Your independent material

Your own observations, thoughts, compilations of facts, or experimental results, expressed in your words and format, do not require acknowledgment. Though you generally should describe the basis for your conclusions so that readers can evaluate your thinking, you need not cite sources for them.

Common knowledge

Common knowledge consists of the standard information on a subject as well as folk literature and commonsense observations.

❖ Standard information includes the major facts of history, such as the dates of Charlemagne's rule as emperor of Rome (800–814). It does not include interpretations of facts, such as a historian's opinion that Charlemagne was sometimes needlessly cruel in extending his power.

48e

Checklist for avoiding plagiarism

❖ What type of source are you using: your own independent material, common knowledge, or someone else's independent material? You must acknowledge someone else's material.

❖ If you are quoting someone else's material, is the quotation exact? Have you inserted quotation marks around quotations run into the text? Have you shown omissions with ellipsis marks and additions with brackets?

❖ If you are paraphrasing or summarizing someone else's material, have you used your own words and sentence structures? Does your paraphrase or summary employ quotation marks when you resort to the author's exact language? Have you represented the author's meaning without distortion?

❖ Is each use of someone else's material acknowledged in your text? Are all your source citations complete and accurate? (See 49a or 50a.)

❖ Does your list of works cited include all the sources you have drawn from in writing your paper? (See 49b or 50b.)

❖ Folk literature, such as the fairy tale "Snow White," is popularly known and cannot be traced to a particular writer. Literature traceable to a writer is not folk literature, even if it is very familiar.

❖ A commonsense observation is something most people know, such as that inflation is most troublesome for people with low and fixed incomes. An economist's argument about the effects of inflation on Chinese immigrants is not a commonsense observation.

If you do not know a subject well enough to determine whether a piece of information is common knowledge, make a record of the source as you would for any other quotation, paraphrase, or summary. As you read more about the subject, the information may come up repeatedly without acknowledgment, in which case it is probably common knowledge. But if you are still in doubt when you finish your research, always acknowledge the source.

2. What you must acknowledge

You must always acknowledge other people's independent material—that is, any facts or ideas that are not common knowledge or your own. The source may be anything, including a book, an article, a movie, an interview, a microfilmed document, or a computer program. You must acknowledge not only ideas or facts themselves but also the language and format in which the ideas or facts appear, if you use them. That is, the wording, sentence structures, arrangement of ideas, and special graphics (such as a diagram) created by another writer belong to that writer just as his or her ideas do.

The following example baldly plagiarizes both the structure and the words of the original quotation from Jessica Mitford's *Kind and Usual Punishment,* page 9.

ORIGINAL | The character and mentality of the keepers may be of more importance in understanding prisons than the character and mentality of the kept.

PLAGIARISM | But the character of prison officials (the keepers) is more important in understanding prisons than the character of prisoners (the kept).

The next example is more subtle plagiarism, because it changes Mitford's sentence structure. But it still uses her words.

PLAGIARISM | In understanding prisons, we should know more about the character and mentality of the keepers than of the kept.

The plagiarism in these examples can be remedied by placing Mitford's exact words in quotation marks, changing her sentence structure when not quoting, and citing the source properly (here, in MLA style).

REVISION (QUOTATION) | According to one critic of the penal system, "The character and mentality of the keepers may be of more importance in understanding prisons than the character and mentality of the kept" (Mitford 9).

REVISION (PARAPHRASE) | One critic of the penal system maintains that we may be able to learn more about prisons from the psychology of the prison officials than from that of the prisoners (Mitford 9).

48f Introducing borrowed material

Summarizing, paraphrasing, or quoting your sources is a key step in research writing (see pp. 214–16 for guidelines), but you also want to integrate any borrowed material smoothly into your own ideas and sentences. The evidence of others' information and opinions should back up your conclusions: you want to *synthesize* evidence (see p. 213), not allow it to overwhelm your own point of view and voice.

To integrate borrowed material into your text, you need, first, to mesh the structures of your own and your source's sentences.

48f

AWKWARD   One editor disagrees with this view and "a good reporter does not fail to separate opinions from facts"
(Lyman 52).

REVISED   One editor disagrees with this view, <u>maintaining that</u> "a
good reporter does not fail to separate opinions from
facts" (Lyman 52).

Even when not conflicting with your own sentence structure,
borrowed material will be ineffective if you merely dump it in readers' laps without explaining how you intend it to be understood.

DUMPED   Many news editors and reporters maintain that it is impossible to keep personal opinions from influencing the
selection and presentation of facts. "True, news reporters, like everyone else, form impressions of what
they see and hear. However, a good reporter does not
fail to separate opinions from facts" (Lyman 52).

REVISED   Many news editors and reporters maintain that it is impossible to keep personal opinions from influencing the
selection and presentation of facts. <u>Yet not all authorities agree with this view. One editor grants that</u> "news
reporters, like everyone else, form impressions of what
they see and hear." But, <u>he insists,</u> "a good reporter
does not fail to separate opinions from facts" (Lyman
52).

The words *grants* and *insists* in the revised passage tell the reader
what to expect in the quotations following. Below are some other
verbs that indicate the source author's attitude or approach to what
he or she is saying. (Note that these verbs are in the present tense,
the appropriate tense for discussions of others' writings.)

AUTHOR IS NEUTRAL	AUTHOR INFERS OR SUGGESTS	AUTHOR ARGUES	AUTHOR IS UNEASY OR DISPARAGING
comments	analyzes	claims	belittles
describes	asks	contends	bemoans
explains	assesses	defends	complains
illustrates	concludes	disagrees	condemns
notes	considers	holds	deplores
observes	finds	insists	deprecates
points out	predicts	maintains	derides
records	proposes		laments
relates	reveals	**AUTHOR AGREES**	warns
reports	shows	admits	
says	speculates	agrees	
sees	suggests	concedes	
thinks	supposes	concurs	
writes		grants	

48f

Besides meshing sentence structures and interpreting meaning, you can do even more to introduce borrowed material. If your readers will recognize it, you can provide the author's name in the text:

AUTHOR **NAMED**	. . . Harold Lyman grants that "news reporters, like everyone else, form impressions of what they see and hear." But, Lyman insists, "a good reporter does not fail to separate opinions from facts" (52).

If the source title contributes information about the author or the context of the quotation, you can provide it in the text:

TITLE **GIVEN**	. . . Harold Lyman, in his book *The Conscience of the Journalist*, grants that "news reporters, like everyone else, form impressions of what they see and hear." But, Lyman insists, "a good reporter does not fail to separate opinions from facts" (52).

Finally, if the quoted author's background and experience clarify or strengthen the quotation, you can provide these credentials in the text:

CREDENTIALS **GIVEN**	. . . Harold Lyman, a newspaper editor for more than forty years, grants that "news reporters, like everyone else, form impressions of what they see and hear." But, Lyman insists, "a good reporter does not fail to separate opinions from facts" (52).

You need not name the author, source, or credentials in your text when you are simply establishing facts or weaving together facts and opinions from varied sources. In the following passage, the information is more important than the source, so the name of the source is confined to a parenthetical acknowledgment:

> To end the abuses of the British, many colonists were urging three actions: forming a united front, seceding from Britain, and taking control of their own international trade and diplomacy (Wills 325–36).

NOTE Several other conventions of quotations are discussed elsewhere in this handbook:

- ❖ See page 156 for the punctuation of identifying words with quotations, such as *he insists.*
- ❖ See pages 179–81 for when to run quotations into your text and when to display them separately from your text.
- ❖ See page 174 for the use of brackets around words you add to quotations for clarity.
- ❖ See pages 172–74 for the use of the ellipsis mark (. . .) to indicate omissions from quotations.

49 Documenting Sources: MLA Style

Every time you borrow the words, facts, or ideas of others, you must DOCUMENT the source—that is, supply a reference (or document) telling readers that you borrowed the material and where you borrowed it from.

Editors and teachers in most academic disciplines require special documentation formats (or styles) in their scholarly journals and in students' papers. This chapter concentrates on a style of in-text citation widely used in the arts and humanities: that of the Modern Language Association, published in the *MLA Handbook for Writers of Research Papers*, 3rd ed. (1988). The next chapter presents a style widely used in the social sciences, that of the American Psychological Association (APA). Beyond this book several guides outline other documentation styles:

> American Anthropological Association. "Style Guide and Information for Authors." *American Anthropologist* (1977): 774–79.
>
> American Chemical Society. *ACS Style Guide: A Manual for Authors and Editors*. 1986.
>
> American Institute of Physics. *Style Manual for Guidance in the Preparation of Papers*. 4th ed. 1990.
>
> American Mathematical Society. *A Manual for Authors of Mathematical Papers*. 8th ed. 1980.
>
> American Medical Association. *Style Book: Editorial Manual*. 6th ed. 1976.
>
> American Sociological Association. "Editorial Guidelines." Inside front cover of each issue of *American Sociological Review*.
>
> *The Chicago Manual of Style*. 14th ed. 1993.
>
> Council of Biology Editors. *Scientific Style and Format: A Manual for Authors, Editors, and Publishers*. 6th ed. 1994.
>
> Turabian, Kate L. *A Manual for Writers of Term Papers, Theses, and Dissertations*. 5th ed. Rev. and exp. Bonnie Birtwistle Honigsblum. 1987.

Ask your instructor which style he or she prefers.

49a Writing MLA parenthetical citations

The documentation system of the *MLA Handbook* employs brief parenthetical citations within the text that direct readers to the list of works cited at the end of the text. The following pages describe this documentation system: what must be included in a citation (below), where to place citations (p. 227), and when to use footnotes or endnotes in addition to parenthetical citations (p. 228).

1. Citation formats

The in-text citations of sources have two requirements:

❖ They must include just enough information for the reader to locate the appropriate source in your list of works cited.
❖ They must include just enough information for the reader to locate the place in the source where the borrowed material appears.

Usually, you can meet both these requirements by providing the author's last name and the page(s) in the source on which the material appears. The reader can find the source in your list of works cited and find the borrowed material in the source itself.

1. AUTHOR NOT NAMED IN YOUR TEXT

```
One researcher concludes that "women impose a distinc-
tive construction on moral problems, seeing moral
dilemmas in terms of conflicting responsibilities"
(Gilligan 105).
```

When you have not already named the author in your sentence, provide the author's last name and the page number(s), with no punctuation between them, in parentheses.

Index to MLA parenthetical citations

2. AUTHOR NAMED IN YOUR TEXT

One researcher, Carol Gilligan, concludes that "women
impose a distinctive construction on moral problems,
seeing moral dilemmas in terms of conflicting responsibilities" (105).

If the author's name is already given in your text, you need not repeat it in the parenthetical citation. The citation gives just the page
number(s).

3. A WORK WITH TWO OR THREE AUTHORS

As Frieden and Sagalyn observe, "The poor and the
minorities were the leading victims of highway and
renewal programs" (29).

According to one study, "The poor and the minorities
were the leading victims of highway and renewal programs" (Frieden and Sagalyn 29).

If the source has two or three authors, give all their names in the
text or in the citation.

4. A WORK WITH MORE THAN THREE AUTHORS

It took the combined forces of the Americans, Euro-
peans, and Japanese to break the rebel siege of Beijing
in 1900 (Lopez et al. 362).

It took the combined forces of the Americans, Euro-
peans, and Japanese to break the rebel siege of Beijing
in 1900 (Lopez, Blum, Cameron, and Barnes 362).

If the source has more than three authors, you may list all their last
names or use only the first author's name followed by "et al." (the
abbreviation for the Latin "and others"). The choice depends on
what you do in your list of works cited (see p. 231).

5. AN ENTIRE WORK (NO PAGE NUMBERS)

Boyd deals with the need to acknowledge and come to
terms with our fear of nuclear technology.

When you cite an entire work rather than a part of it, the reference will not include any page number. If the author's name appears in the text, no parenthetical reference is needed. But remember that the source must appear in the list of works cited, even if a parenthetical citation does not appear in the text.

6. A MULTIVOLUME WORK

```
After issuing the Emancipation Proclamation, Lincoln

said, "What I did, I did after very full deliberations,

and under a very heavy and solemn sense of responsibil-

ity" (5: 438).
```

If you consulted only one volume of a multivolume work, your list of works cited will indicate as much (see pp. 233–34), and you can treat the volume as any book. But if you consulted two or more volumes, your citation must indicate which one you are referring to. In the example the number 5 indicates the volume from which the quotation was taken; the number 438 indicates the page number in that volume.

7. A WORK BY AN AUTHOR OF TWO OR MORE WORKS

```
At about age seven, most children begin to use appro-

priate gestures to reinforce their stories (Gardner,

Arts 144-45).
```

If your list of works cited includes two or more works by the same author, give the appropriate title or a shortened version of it in the parenthetical citation. For this reference the full title is *The Arts and Human Development.*

8. AN UNSIGNED WORK

```
One article notes that a death-row inmate may demand

his own execution to achieve a fleeting notoriety

("Right").
```

Anonymous works are alphabetized by title in the list of works cited. In the text they are referred to by full or shortened title. This citation refers to an unsigned article titled "The Right to Die." (A page number is unnecessary because the article is no longer than a page.)

9. A GOVERNMENT DOCUMENT OR A WORK WITH A CORPORATE AUTHOR

```
A 1983 report by the Hawaii Department of Education

predicts a gradual increase in enrollments (6).
```

If the author of the work is listed as a government body or a corporation, cite the work by that organization's name. If the name is long, work it into the text to avoid an intrusive parenthetical citation.

10. AN INDIRECT SOURCE

```
George Davino maintains that "even small children have

vivid ideas about nuclear energy" (qtd. in Boyd 22).
```

When you quote or paraphrase one source's quotation of someone else, your citation must indicate as much. In the citation above, "qtd. in" ("quoted in") says that Davino was quoted by Boyd. The list of works cited then includes only Boyd (the work consulted), not Davino.

11. A LITERARY WORK

```
Toward the end of James's novel, Maggie suddenly feels

"the intimate, the immediate, the familiar, as she

hadn't had them for so long" (535; pt. 6, ch. 41).
```

Novels, plays, and poems are often available in many editions, so your instructor may ask you to provide information that will help readers find the passage you cite no matter what edition they consult. For novels, as in the example above, the page number comes first, followed by a semicolon and then information on the appropriate part or chapter of the work.

For poems, you can omit the page number and supply the line number(s) for the quotation. To prevent confusion with page numbers, preceded the numbers with "line" or "lines" in the first citation; then just use the numbers.

```
In Shakespeare's Sonnet 73 the speaker identifies with

the trees of late autumn, "Bare ruined choirs, where

late the sweet birds sang" (line 4). "In me," Shake-

speare writes, "thou seest the glowing of such fire /

That on the ashes of his youth doth lie" (9-10).
```

For verse plays, omit a page number and cite the appropriate part or act (and scene, if any) plus the line number(s). Use Arabic numerals for acts and scenes ("3.4") unless your instructor specifies Roman numerals ("III.iv").

> Later in King Lear Shakespeare has the disguised Edgar
>
> say, "The prince of darkness is a gentleman" (3.4.147).

For prose plays, provide the page number followed by the act and scene, if any (see the reference to *Death of a Salesman* on the next page).

12. MORE THAN ONE WORK

> Two recent articles point out that a computer badly
>
> used can be less efficient than no computer at all
>
> (Richards 162; Gough and Hall 201).

If you use a parenthetical citation to refer to more than a single work, separate the references by a semicolon. Since long citations in the text can distract the reader, you may choose to cite several or more works in an endnote or footnote rather than in the text. See the next page.

2. Placement of parenthetical citations

Generally, place a parenthetical citation at the end of the sentence in which you summarize, paraphrase, or quote a work. The citation should follow a closing quotation mark but precede the sentence punctuation. (See the examples in the previous section.) When a citation pertains to only part of a sentence, place the citation after the borrowed material and at the least intrusive point— usually at the end of a clause.

> Though Spelling argues that American automobile manu-
>
> facturers "did the best that could be expected" in
>
> meeting consumer needs (26), not everyone agrees with
>
> him.

When a citation appears after a quotation that ends in an ellipsis mark (. . .), place the citation between the closing quotation mark and the sentence period.

```
One observer maintains that "American manufacturers

must bear the blame for their poor sales . . ." (Rosen-

baum 12).
```

When a citation appears at the end of a quotation set off from the text, place it two spaces *after* the punctuation ending the quotation. No additional punctuation is necessary.

```
In Arthur Miller's Death of a Salesman, the most

poignant defense of Willie Loman comes from his wife,

Linda:

          He's not the finest character that ever

          lived.  But he's a human being, and a terri-

          ble thing is happening to him. . . . Atten-

          tion, attention must finally be paid to such

          a person.  (56; act 1)
```

(This citation of a play includes the act number as well as the page number. See model 11 on pp. 226–27.)

3. Footnotes or endnotes in special circumstances

Footnotes or endnotes may replace parenthetical citations when you cite several sources at once, when you comment on a source, or when you provide information that does not fit easily in the text. Signal a footnote or endnote in your text with a numeral raised above the appropriate line. Then write a note with the same numeral.

TEXT   ```At least five subsequent studies have confirmed```

```these results.[1]```

NOTE   ```[1] Abbott and Winger 266-68; Casner 27;```

```Hoyenga 78-79; Marino 36; Tripp, Tripp, and Walk```

```179-83.```

In a note the raised numeral is indented five spaces and followed by a space. If the note appears as a footnote, place it at the bottom of the page on which the citation appears, set it off from the text with quadruple spacing, and single-space the note itself. If the note appears as an endnote, place it in numerical order with the other endnotes on a page between the text and the list of works cited; double-space all the endnotes.
```

49b Preparing the MLA list of works cited

At the end of your paper, a list titled "Works Cited" includes all the sources you quoted, paraphrased, or summarized in your paper. (If your instructor asks you to include sources you examined but did not cite, title the list "Works Consulted.")

For the list of works cited, arrange your sources in alphabetical order by the last name of the author. If an author is not given in the source, alphabetize the source by the first main word of the title (excluding *A, An,* or *The*). Type the entire list double-spaced (both within and between entries). Indent the second and subsequent lines of each entry five spaces from the left. (See the sample on pp. 251–52.)

NOTE You may have to combine some of the following formats for particular sources. For example, to list a work by four authors appearing in a monthly periodical, you will have to draw on model 3 ("A book with more than three authors") and model 23 ("A signed article in a monthly or bimonthly magazine").

1. Books

The basic format for a book includes the following elements:

```
     ⓐ               ⓑ
Gilligan, Carol.  In a Different Voice: Psychological
                                              ⓒ
     Theory and Women's Development.  Cambridge:
                                          ①
     Harvard UP, 1982.
        ②          ③
```

a. The author's full name: the last name first, followed by a comma, and then the first name and any middle name or initial. End the name with a period and two spaces.

b. The full title of the book, including any subtitle. Underline the complete title, capitalize all important words (see p. 195), separate the main title and the subtitle with a colon and one space, and end the title with a period and two spaces.

c. The publication information:

   (1) The city of publication, followed by a colon and one space.

   (2) The name of the publisher, followed by a comma. Shorten most publishers' names—in many cases to a single word. For instance, use "Little" for Little, Brown. For university presses, use the abbreviation "UP," as in the example above.

   (3) The date of publication, ending with a period.

Index to MLA works-cited models

1. A BOOK WITH ONE AUTHOR

```
Gilligan, Carol.  In a Different Voice: Psychological
     Theory and Women's Development.  Cambridge:
     Harvard UP, 1982.
```

2. A BOOK WITH TWO OR THREE AUTHORS

```
Frieden, Bernard J., and Lynne B. Sagalyn.  Downtown,
     Inc.: How America Rebuilds Cities.  Cambridge:
     MIT, 1989.
```

Give the authors' names in the order provided on the title page. Reverse the first and last names of the first author *only,* and separate the authors' names with a comma.

3. A BOOK WITH MORE THAN THREE AUTHORS

```
Lopez, Robert S., et al.  Civilizations: Western and
     World.  Boston: Little, 1975.
```

You may, but need not, give all authors' names if the work has more than three authors. If you do not give all names, provide the name of the first author only, and follow the name with a comma and the abbreviation "et al." (for the Latin *et alii,* meaning "and others").

4. TWO OR MORE WORKS BY THE SAME AUTHOR(S)

```
Gardner, Howard.  The Arts and Human Development.  New
     York: Wiley, 1973.
---.  The Quest for Mind: Piaget, Lévi-Strauss, and the
     Structuralist Movement.  New York: Knopf, 1973.
```

Give the author's name only in the first entry. For the second and any subsequent works by the same author, substitute three hyphens for the author's name. Within the set of entries for the author, list the sources alphabetically by the first main word of the title. Note that the three hyphens stand for *exactly* the same name or names. If the second source above were by Gardner and somebody else, both names would have to be given in full.

5. A BOOK WITH AN EDITOR

```
Ruitenbeek, Hendrick, ed.  Freud as We Knew Him.
     Detroit: Wayne State UP, 1973.
```

The abbreviation "ed.," separated from the name by a comma, identifies Ruitenbeek as the editor of the work.

6. A BOOK WITH AN AUTHOR AND AN EDITOR

Melville, Herman.   The Confidence Man: His Masquerade.

    Ed. Hershel Parker.   New York: Norton, 1971.

When citing the work of the author, give his or her name first, and give the editor's name after the title, preceded by "Ed." ("Edited by"). When citing the work of the editor, use model 5 for a book with an editor, and give the author's name after the title preceded by "By": "Parker, Hershel, ed. The Confidence Man: His Masquerade. By Herman Melville."

7. A TRANSLATION

Alighieri, Dante.   The Inferno.   Trans. John Ciardi.

    New York: NAL, 1971.

When citing the work of the author, give his or her name first, and give the translator's name after the title, preceded by "Trans." ("Translated by"). When citing the work of the translator, give his or her name first, followed by a comma and "trans.," and after the title give the author's name preceded by "By": "Ciardi, John, trans. The Inferno. By Dante Alighieri."

8. A BOOK WITH A CORPORATE AUTHOR

Lorenz, Inc.   Research in Social Studies Teaching.

    Baltimore: Arrow, 1992.

List the name of the corporation, institution, or other body as author.

9. AN ANONYMOUS BOOK

Merriam-Webster's Collegiate Dictionary.   10th ed.

    Springfield: Merriam-Webster, 1993.

List the book under its title. Do not use either "anonymous" or "anon."

10. A LATER EDITION

Bollinger, Dwight L. Aspects of Language. 2nd ed.

New York: Harcourt, 1975.

For any edition after the first, place the edition number between the title and the publication information. Use the appropriate designation for editions that are named or dated rather than numbered—for instance, "Rev. ed." for "Revised edition."

11. A REPUBLISHED BOOK

James, Henry. The Golden Bowl. 1904. London: Pen-

guin, 1966.

Place the original date of publication after the title, and then provide the full publication information for the source you are using.

12. A BOOK WITH A TITLE IN ITS TITLE

Eco, Umberto. Postscript to The Name of the Rose.

Trans. William Weaver. New York: Harcourt, 1983.

When a book's title contains another book title (as here: The Name of the Rose), do not underline the shorter title. When a book's title contains the title of a work normally placed in quotation marks, keep the quotation marks and underline both titles: Critical Response to Henry James's "Beast in the Jungle." (Note that the underlining extends under the closing quotation mark.)

13. A WORK IN MORE THAN ONE VOLUME

Lincoln, Abraham. The Collected Works of Abraham

Lincoln. Ed. Roy P. Basler. 8 vols. New

Brunswick: Rutgers UP, 1953.

Lincoln, Abraham. The Collected Works of Abraham

Lincoln. Ed. Roy P. Basler. Vol. 5. New

Brunswick: Rutgers UP, 1953. 8 vols.

If you use two or more volumes of a multivolume work, give the work's total number of volumes before the publication information

("8 vols." in the first example). Your text citation will indicate which volume you are citing (see p. 225). If you use only one volume, give that volume number before the publication information ("Vol. 5" in the second example). You may add the total number of volumes to the end of the entry ("8 vols." in the second example).

14. A WORK IN A SERIES

Bergman, Ingmar. <u>The Seventh Seal</u>. Modern Film

Scripts Series. New York: Simon, 1968.

Place the name of the series (no quotation marks or underlining) after the title.

15. PUBLISHED PROCEEDINGS OF A CONFERENCE

<u>Watching Our Language: A Conference Sponsored by the</u>

<u>Program in Architecture and Design Criticism</u>. 6-8

May 1994. New York: Parsons School of Design,

1994.

Whether in or after the title of the conference, supply information about who sponsored the conference, when it was held, and who published the proceedings. If you are citing a particular presentation at the conference, treat it as a selection from an anthology or collection (model 17).

16. AN ANTHOLOGY

Martin, Richard, ed. <u>The New Urban Landscape</u>. New

York: Rizzoli, 1990.

When citing an entire anthology, give the name of the editor (followed by "ed.") and then the title of the anthology.

17. A SELECTION FROM AN ANTHOLOGY

Brooks, Rosetta. "Streetwise." <u>The New Urban Land-</u>

<u>scape</u>. Ed. Richard Martin. New York: Rizzoli,

1990. 38-39.

Give the author and the title of the selection you are citing, placing the title in quotation marks and ending it with a period. Then give the title of the anthology. If the anthology has an editor, add the name after "Ed.," as above. At the end of the entry give the inclusive page numbers for the entire selection, but do not include the abbreviation "pp."

If the work you cite comes from a collection of works by one author and with no editor, use the following form:

Auden, W. H.   "Family Ghosts."   The Collected Poetry of

W. H. Auden.   New York: Random, 1945.   132-33.

If the work you cite was previously printed elsewhere, provide the complete information for the earlier publication of the piece, followed by "Rpt. in" ("Reprinted in") and the information for the source in which you found the piece.

Gibian, George.   "Traditional Symbolism in Crime and

Punishment."   PMLA 70 (1955): 979-96.   Rpt. in

Crime and Punishment.   By Feodor Dostoevsky.   Ed.

George Gibian.   Norton Critical Editions.   New

York: Norton, 1964.   575-92.

18. Two or more selections from the same anthology

Brooks, Rosetta.   "Streetwise."   Martin 38-39.

Martin, Richard, ed.   The New Urban Landscape.   New

York: Rizzoli, 1990.

Plotkin, Mark J.   "Tropical Forests and the Urban

Landscape."   Martin 50-51.

When citing more than one selection from the same source, you may avoid unnecessary repetition by giving the source in full (as in the Martin entry) and then simply cross-referencing it in entries for the works you used. Thus, instead of full information for the Brooks and Plotkin articles, give Martin's name and the appropriate pages in his book. Note that each entry appears in its proper alphabetical place among other works cited.

19. An introduction, preface, foreword, or afterword

Donaldson, Norman.   Introduction.   The Claverings.   By

Anthony Trollope.   New York: Dover, 1977.   vii-xv.

An introduction, foreword, or afterword is often written by someone other than the book's author. When citing such a work, give its name without quotation marks or underlining. Follow the title of the book with its author's name preceded by "By." Give the inclusive page numbers of the part you cite. (In the example above, the small Roman numerals indicate that the cited work is in the front matter of the book, before page 1.)

When the author of a preface or introduction is the same as the author of the book, give only the last name after the title:

```
Gould, Stephen Jay.  Prologue.  The Flamingo's Smile:

     Reflections in Natural History.  By Gould.  New

     York: Norton, 1985.  13-20.
```

20. AN ENCYCLOPEDIA OR ALMANAC

```
"Mammoth."  The Columbia Encyclopedia.  1993.

Mark, Herman F.  "Polymers."  Encyclopaedia Britannica:

     Macropaedia.  1974.
```

Give the name of an author only when the article is signed; otherwise, give the title first. If the articles are alphabetized in the reference work, you needn't list any page numbers. For familiar sources like those in the examples, full publication information is not needed. Just provide the year of publication.

2. Periodicals: Journals, magazines, and newspapers

The basic format for an article from a periodical includes the following information:

```
        ┌──────ⓐ──────┐   ┌────────────ⓑ────────────
        Lever, Janet.   "Sex Differences in the Games Children
             ┌──────┐  ┌───────ⓒ───────┐
             Play."  Social Problems 23 (1976): 478-87.
                        ①          ②  ③       ④
```

a. The author's full name: last name first, followed by a comma, and then the first name and any middle name or initial. End the name with a period and two spaces.

b. The full title of the article, including any subtitle. Place the title in quotation marks, capitalize all important words in the title (see p. 195), and end the title with a period (inside the final quotation mark) and two spaces.

c. The publication information:

(1) The underlined title of the periodical (minus any *A, An,* or *The* at the beginning).

(2) The volume or issue number (in Arabic numerals).

(3) The date of publication, followed by a colon and a space.
(4) The inclusive page numbers of the article (without the abbreviation "pp."). For the second number in inclusive page numbers over 100, provide only as many digits as needed for clarity (usually two): 100–01, 1190–206, 398–401.

21. A SIGNED ARTICLE IN A JOURNAL WITH CONTINUOUS PAGINATION THROUGHOUT THE ANNUAL VOLUME

```
Lever, Janet.   "Sex Differences in the Games Children

     Play."   Social Problems 23 (1976): 478-87.
```

Some journals page all issues of an annual volume consecutively, so that issue 3 may begin on page 261. For this kind of journal, give the volume number after the title ("23" in the example above) and place the year of publication in parentheses.

22. A SIGNED ARTICLE IN A JOURNAL THAT PAGES ISSUES SEPARATELY OR THAT NUMBERS ONLY ISSUES, NOT VOLUMES

```
Dacey, June.   "Management Participation in Corporate

     Buy-Outs."   Management Perspectives 7.4 (1994):

     20-31.
```

Some journals page each issue separately (starting each issue at page 1). For these journals, give the volume number, a period, and the issue number (as in "7.4" in the Dacey entry). When citing an article in a journal that numbers only issues, not annual volumes, treat the issue number as if it were a volume number (model 21).

23. A SIGNED ARTICLE IN A MONTHLY OR BIMONTHLY MAGAZINE

```
Stein, Harry.   "Living with Lies."   Esquire Dec. 1981:

     23.
```

Follow the magazine title with the month (abbreviated) and the year of publication. Don't place the date in parentheses, and don't provide a volume or issue number.

24. A SIGNED ARTICLE IN A WEEKLY OR BIWEEKLY MAGAZINE

```
Stevens, Mark.   "Low and Behold."   New Republic 24 Dec.

     1990: 27-33.
```

Follow the magazine title with the day, the month (abbreviated), and the year of publication. Don't place the date in parentheses, and don't provide a volume or issue number.

25. A SIGNED ARTICLE IN A DAILY NEWSPAPER

Ramirez, Anthony. "Computer Groups Plan Standards."

New York Times 14 Dec. 1993: D5.

Give the name of the newspaper as it appears on the first page (but without *A, An,* or *The*). Then follow model 24, with one difference if the newspaper is divided into sections that are paged separately. In that case, provide the section designation before the page number when the newspaper does the same (as in "D5" above), or provide the section designation before the colon when the newspaper does not combine the two in its numbering (as in "sec. 1: 1+" below).

26. AN UNSIGNED ARTICLE

"The Right to Die." Time 11 Oct. 1976: 101.

"Protests Greet Pope in Holland." Boston Sunday Globe

12 May 1985, sec. 1: 1+.

Begin the entry for an unsigned article with the title of the article. The number "1+" indicates that the article does not run on consecutive pages but starts on page 1 and continues later in the issue.

27. AN EDITORIAL OR LETTER TO THE EDITOR

"Bodily Intrusions." Editorial. New York Times 29

Aug. 1990: A20.

Don't use quotation marks or underlining for the word "Editorial." For a signed editorial, give the author's name first.

Dowding, Michael. Letter. Economist 5-11 Jan. 1985:

4.

Don't use quotation marks or underlining for the word "Letter."

28. A REVIEW

Dunne, John Gregory. "The Secret of Danny Santiago."

Rev. of Famous All over Town, by Danny Santiago.

New York Review of Books 16 Aug. 1984: 17-27.

"Rev." is an abbreviation for "Review." The name of the author of the work being reviewed follows the work's title, a comma, and "by."

29. An abstract of a dissertation

```
Steciw, Steven K.   "Alterations to the Pessac Project
       of Le Corbusier."   DAI 46 (1986): 565C.   U of
       Cambridge, England.
```

For an abstract appearing in *Dissertation Abstracts (DA)* or *Dissertation Abstracts International* (*DAI*), give the author's name and the title as for any article. Then give publication information for the source and the name of the institution granting the author's degree.

3. Other sources

30. A government document

```
Hawaii.  Dept. of Education.  Kauai District Schools,
       Profile 1983-84.  Honolulu: Hawaii Dept. of Edu-
       cation, 1983.
United States.  Cong.  House.  Committee on Ways and
       Means.  Medicare Payment for Outpatient Occupa-
       tional Therapy Services.  102nd Cong., 1st sess.
       Washington: GPO, 1991.
```

Unless an author is listed for a government document, give the appropriate agency as author. Begin with the name of the government, then the name of the agency (which may be abbreviated), then the title and publication information. For a congressional document (second example), give the house and committee involved before the title, and give the number and session of Congress after the title. In the second example, "GPO" stands for the U.S. Government Printing Office.

31. A pamphlet

```
Medical Answers About AIDS.  New York: GMHC, 1994.
```

Most pamphlets can be treated as books. In the example above, the pamphlet has no listed author, so the title comes first. If the pamphlet has an author, list his or her name first.

32. AN UNPUBLISHED DISSERTATION OR THESIS

```
Wilson, Stuart M.   "John Stuart Mill as a Literary

     Critic."  Diss.  U of Michigan, 1970.
```

The title is quoted rather than underlined. "Diss." stands for "Dissertation." "U of Michigan" is the institution that granted the author's degree.

33. A MUSICAL COMPOSITION OR WORK OF ART

```
Mozart, Wolfgang Amadeus.  Piano Concerto no. 20 in D

     Minor, K. 466.
```

Don't underline musical compositions identified only by form, number, and key. Do underline titled operas, ballets, and compositions (Carmen, Sleeping Beauty).

```
Sargent, John Singer.  Venetian Doorway.  Metropolitan

     Museum of Art, New York.
```

Underline the title of a work of art. Include the name and location of the institution housing the work.

34. A FILM OR VIDEOTAPE

```
Spielberg, Steven, dir.  Schindler's List.  With Liam

     Neeson and Ben Kingsley.  Universal, 1993.
```

Start with the name of the individual whose work you are citing. (If you are citing the work as a whole, start with the title, as in the next model.) Give additional information (writer, lead actors, and so on) as seems appropriate. For a film, end with the film's distributor and date.

```
Serenade.  Videotape.  Chor. George Balanchine.  With

     San Francisco Ballet.  Dir. Hilary Bean.  San

     Francisco Ballet, 1987.  24 min.
```

For a videotape, filmstrip, or slide program, include the name of the medium after the title, without underlining or quotation marks. Add the running time to the end.

35. A TELEVISION OR RADIO PROGRAM

<u>A Life Together</u>.   With Donald Hall and Jane Kenyon.

    Bill Moyers' Journal.   PBS.   WNET, New York.   17

    Dec. 1993.

Start with the title of the program or the name of the individual whose work you are citing, and provide other participants' names as seems appropriate. Also give the series title (if any), the broadcasting network (if any), and the local station, city, and date.

36. A PERFORMANCE

<u>The English Only Restaurant</u>.   By Silvio Martinez Palau.

    Dir. Susana Tubert.   Puerto Rico Traveling The-

    ater, New York.   27 July 1990.

Ozawa, Seiji, cond.   Boston Symphony Orch. Concert.

    Symphony Hall, Boston.   25 Apr. 1991.

Place the title first unless you are citing the work of an individual (second example). Provide additional information about participants after the title, as well as the theater, city, and date. Note that the orchestra concert in the second example is neither quoted nor underlined.

37. A RECORDING

Mitchell, Joni.   <u>For the Roses</u>.   Asylum, SD-5057, 1972.

Brahms, Johannes.   Concerto no. 2 in B-flat, op. 83.

    Perf. Artur Rubinstein.   Cond. Eugene Ormandy.

    Philadelphia Orch.   RCA, RK-1243, 1972.

Begin with the name of the individual whose work you are citing. Then provide the title of the recording (first example) or the title of the work recorded (second example), the names of any artists not already listed, the manufacturer of the recording, the catalog number, and the date.

38. A LETTER

Buttolph, Mrs. Laura E.   Letter to Rev. and Mrs. C. C.

    Jones.   20 June 1857.   In <u>The Children of Pride: A</u>

> *True Story of Georgia and the Civil War*. Ed.
> Robert Manson Myers. New Haven: Yale UP, 1972.
> 334-35.

A published letter is listed under the writer's name. Specify that the source is a letter and to whom it was addressed, and give the date on which it was written.

> Packer, Ann E. Letter to the author. 15 June 1994.

For a letter you receive, give the name of the writer, note the fact that the letter was sent to you, and provide the date of the letter.

39. A LECTURE OR ADDRESS

> Carlone, Dennis J. "Urban Design in the 1990s." Sixth
> Symposium on Urban Issues. City of Cambridge.
> Cambridge, 16 Oct. 1988.

Give the speaker's name, the title if known (in quotation marks), the title of the meeting, the name of the sponsoring organization, the location of the lecture, and the date.

40. AN INTERVIEW

> Graaf, Vera. Personal interview. 19 Dec. 1993.
> Martin, William. Interview. "Give Me That Big Time
> Religion." *Frontline*. PBS. WGBH, Boston. 13
> Feb. 1984.

Begin with the name of the person interviewed. Then specify "Personal interview" (if you conducted the interview in person), "Telephone interview" (if you conducted the interview over the phone), or "Interview" (if you did not conduct the interview)—without quotation marks or underlining. Finally, provide a date (first example) or provide other bibliographic information and then a date (second example).

41. A MAP OR OTHER ILLUSTRATION

> *Women in the Armed Forces*. Map. *Women in the World:*
> *An International Atlas*. By Joni Seager and Ann
> Olson. New York: Touchstone, 1992. 44-45.

List the illustration by its title (underlined). Provide a descriptive label ("Map," "Chart," "Table"), without underlining or quotation marks, and the publication information. If the creator of the illustration is credited in the source, put his or her name first in the entry, as with any author.

42. AN INFORMATION OR COMPUTER SERVICE

Jolson, Maria K. Music Education for Preschoolers.

ERIC, 1981. ED 264 488.

Palfry, Andrew. "Choice of Mates in Identical Twins."

Modern Psychology Jan. 1992: 16-27. DIALOG file

261, item 5206341.

A source you get from an information or computer service should be treated like a book or a periodical article, as appropriate, with the author's name and then the title. If the source has not been published before, simply name the service (ERIC in the Jolson entry above), and give the year of release and the service's identifying number. If the source has been published before, give full publication information and then the name of the service and its identifying numbers, as in the Palfry entry.

43. COMPUTER SOFTWARE

Project Scheduler 7000. Computer software. Scitor,

1993. MS-DOS, 256 KB, disk.

Include the title of the software, the name of the writer (if known), the name of the distributor, and the date. As in this example, you may also provide information about the computer or operating system for which the software is designed, the amount of computer memory it requires, and its format.

49c Examining a sample research paper in MLA style

The sample paper beginning on p. 245 follows the guidelines of the *MLA Handbook* for manuscript format, as outlined on pages 177–81, and for parenthetical citations and the list of works cited, as outlined in this chapter. Marginal annotations highlight features of the paper.

A note on outlines

Some instructors ask students to submit a formal outline of the final paper. Advice on constructing such an outline appears on pages 14–15, along with an example written in phrases (a topic outline). Below is an outline of the sample paper following, written in complete sentences. Note that the thesis sentence precedes either a topic or a sentence outline.

THESIS SENTENCE

Most liquid-diet programs fail to emphasize that successful weight loss demands a fundamental change in behavior, not a tasty low-calorie shake.

   I. Although once dangerous, liquid diet programs are now safer.
      A. All programs have improved the calories and protein in liquid diets.
      B. Supervised programs monitor dieters' health.
  II. Unsupervised programs, such as Slim·Fast and Dynatrim, concern health-care professionals.
      A. They do not involve supervision.
      B. They encourage too-rapid weight loss.
      C. They do not encourage behavior modification.
 III. Most diet professionals consider behavior modification essential for long-term weight loss.
      A. Liquid-diet programs, which do not involve behavior modification, have poor results.
      B. Behavior modification involves a number of factors.
         1. Nutritionists suggest such practices as regular meals, small portions, and rewards.
         2. Weight Watchers and some other group programs emphasize eating real foods, understanding nutrition, and changing unhealthful habits.

If you attach an outline to your paper, use standard outline form (p. 14) and double-space all the lines. Place the outline before page 1 of the paper, and cover it with a title page containing the title, your name, and the course information; center this information on the page, and use double space or more between elements. If you use a title page, you do not need to repeat your name and the course information on page 1 of the paper, but do repeat the title.

Joseph 1

Andrea Joseph

English 101

Ms. Diodati

April 19, 1994

MLA

49c

Drinking the Pounds Away

"Give us a week, we'll take off the
weight" is a familiar jingle advertising
the Slim·Fast liquid diet. In our weight-
conscious society, liquid-diet programs such
as Slim·Fast and Optifast promise quick weight
loss with little effort on the dieter's part.
But most of these programs fail to emphasize
that successful weight loss demands a fundamental change in behavior, not a tasty low-
calorie shake.

When liquid diets were first introduced
in the 1970s, they were so deficient nutri-
tionally that they were actually dangerous.
But according to Victor Frattali, a nutrition-
ist at the U.S. Food and Drug Administration,
manufacturers have now raised calorie levels
and use "high-quality protein" (qtd. in Sachs
48). In addition, liquid diets are now
divided into two categories: those sold over
the counter in drugstores and markets and
those supervised by health-care professionals
(Simko et al. 231).

Medically supervised programs, such as
Optifast and Medifast, became popular when the
talk-show host Oprah Winfrey broadcast that
she lost sixty-seven pounds on the Optifast
diet (Kirschner et al. 902). The twenty-six-

Writer's name
and page
number.

Writer's name,
course,
instructor's
name, date.

Title centered.

Double-space
throughout.

Thesis sen-
tence.

Background
information.

Citation form:
indirect source
(Frattali quot-
ed by Sachs).
Citation falls
between quo-
tation mark
and sentence
period.

Citation form:
source with
more than
three authors.

Discussion of
supervised pro-
grams.

week Optifast regimen consists of three
stages: a fasting period when patients consume
only liquid-protein shakes providing 420 to
800 calories a day; a "refeeding" stage when
food is reintroduced into the diet; and a
maintenance stage when patients practice eating sensibly (Beek 56).

Summary of
source.

Citation form:
author not
named in the
text.

Medical supervision and psychological
counseling are crucial parts of the Optifast
program. Before admittance, patients must
pass a physical examination to ensure that
they do not have any conditions that might
make the diet dangerous for them. During the
diet, patients undergo frequent weight checks
and blood and urine tests (Stocker-Ferguson
57). The Mayo Clinic Diet Manual notes that
unmonitored patients can suffer dehydration
and loss of vital minerals (Pemberton et al.
190).

Discussion of
risks of liquid
diets.

Paragraph in-
tegrates
information
from two
sources to
describe risks.

Oprah Winfrey's weight loss "provoked a
new frenzy of public interest" in liquid diets
(Kirschner et al. 902), but most people were
medically ineligible for programs like Optifast. Over-the-counter liquid diets such as
Slim·Fast and Dynatrim quickly appeared to
meet consumer demand, and now celebrities
speaking for these products almost guarantee
weight loss. The drinks are indeed easy to
obtain and inexpensive (less than a dollar a
serving), and their packaging makes losing
weight seem effortless. According to the
Slim·Fast instructions, the dieter can shed

Transition to
unsupervised
programs.

The writer
uses Slim·Fast
packaging as
a primary
source. Her
analysis and
conclusions
are her own
unless
otherwise
acknowledged.

Joseph 3

one or two pounds per week with a simple regimen: "Enjoy a Slim·Fast shake for breakfast, a
mid-morning snack, another shake for lunch, a
mid-afternoon snack. . . , then a satisfying,
well-balanced dinner." Unlike with medically
supervised programs, dieters are not required
to attend meetings or consult health-care
professionals. Medical supervision is not
required because the addition of snacks and
regular meals raises the calorie intake to at
least 1200 compared to Optifast's maximum 800
(Lowe 48).

Citation form:
no parentheti-
cal citation
needed here
because the
author's name
(Slim·Fast) is
in the text and
the product
packaging has
no pages.

Citation form:
paraphrased
source not
named in the
text.

    Although consumers overwhelmingly support
the over-the-counter liquid diets, some
health-care professionals are concerned about
how the products are marketed. Kirschner et
al., writing in New Jersey Medicine, believe
that the marketing has "sensationalized weight
loss and deemphasized the role of carefully
supervised programs" (902). A can of
Slim·Fast shake mix does post a warning in
small type:

Transition to
professionals'
concerns.

Citation form:
author named
in the text.

        Slim·Fast shakes should not be used
        as a sole source of nutrition; eat
        at least one well-balanced meal
        daily. . . . Anyone who is preg-
        nant, nursing, has a health problem,
        is under the age of 18, or wants to
        lose more than 15 percent of their
        starting body weight should consult
        a physician before starting this or
        any weight loss program.

Quotation over
four lines is in-
dented ten
spaces and
double-spaced.

But the advertisements for Slim·Fast make the
required meal sound like an optional treat,
and they do not advise users to have a physical exam. Without supervision, dieters might
easily undereat, losing weight faster than is
safe for anyone, not just the categories of
people listed in the warning (Beek 53).

> Writer's own analysis of the Slim·Fast packaging (through the next paragraph).

    The insert in a can of Slim·Fast mentions
regular exercise and other forms of behavior
modification, but the can label does not, nor,
again, do the advertisements. And the insert
actually encourages the use of the product as
a crutch: "Behavior modification is a way of
learning to change habits and Slim·Fast can
help you. . . . Drink a satisfying Slim·Fast
shake every day for breakfast or lunch."
This advice shifts the responsibility for
weight loss from the dieter to the product.

> Ellipsis mark indicating omission from the quotation.

    Most doctors and nutritionists agree that
the will and effort of the dieter--especially
in changing lifelong eating habits--are essential for long-term weight loss. Dr. Thomas A.
Wadden, a leading expert in weight loss,
observes that although most overweight people
are aware they must get more exercise and eat
differently, they find behavior change difficult (qtd. in Rosenthal C11). Still, as
Newsweek's Melinda Beek observes, people who
have followed a liquid diet without behavior
modification "haven't done anything to improve
their eating habits--unless they plan to drink
the powder for the rest of their lives" (55).

> Introduction to a para-phrase, giving source's name and creden-tials. (See the note card for this para-phrase on p. 215.)

Joseph 5

Indeed, long-term results with Slim·Fast and other liquid diets are poor. One study of dieters on the closely monitored Optifast program found that only 32 percent of the patients reached their goal weights, and only 10 percent of these maintained their new weight after eighteen months (Segal 13). (Oprah Winfrey's well-publicized battles with her weight provide anecdotal evidence of the diet's weakness.) Dieters using over-the-counter products have even less success at losing pounds and keeping them off (Kirschner et al. 903; Segal 14).

What is the alternative? Two nutritionists offer some simple modifications in behavior that can help dieters learn to manage eating:

> Eat only at specified times and places; learn to eat more slowly; omit other activities, such as reading or watching television, while eating; use smaller plates and place portions directly on the plate rather than serve family style; and use a reward system. (Robinson and Lawler 481)

Weight Watchers and some other group programs combine sensible eating of real foods (as opposed to shakes and other substitutes) with counseling in nutrition and behavior modification. During group sessions conducted by nutritionists or therapists, dieters try to

MLA
49c

Paragraph integrates evidence from several sources.

Summary of supporting data.

Citation form: two sources.

Question emphasizing transition to behavior modification.

Citation form: after displayed quotation, citation follows sentence period and two spaces.

Joseph 6

identify and correct unhealthful eating

habits. One Weight Watchers participant, Ann

Lorden, explains that the counseling "helps

you realize what triggers your desire to eat,

other than hunger, so that you can keep your-

self from having food you really don't want

or need."

Primary source: personal interview.

Liquid diets lure consumers with promises

of quick and easy weight loss, but the formu-

las are not magic potions that absorb excess

weight. A liquid diet just lets a person

avoid food. Only behavior modification helps

a dieter learn to eat.

Conclusion: sharp contrast between liquid diets and behavior modification.

Joseph 7

Works Cited

Beek, Melinda. "The Losing Formula." News-

week 17 Apr. 1990: 53-58.

Kirschner, M. A., et al. "Responsible Weight

Loss in New Jersey." New Jersey Medicine

87 (1990): 901-04.

Lorden, Ann. Personal interview. 22 Mar.

1992.

Lowe, Carl. "Diet in a Glass." Health Oct.

1989: 48-50.

Pemberton, Cecelia M., et al. Mayo Clinic

Diet Manual: A Handbook of Dietary

Practices. 6th ed. Philadelphia:

Decker, 1988.

Robinson, Corrine H., and Marilyn R. Lawler.

Normal and Therapeutic Nutrition. New

York: Macmillan, 1982.

Rosenthal, Elisabeth. "Commercial Diets Lack

Proof of Their Long-Term Success." New

York Times 24 Nov. 1992: A1+.

Sachs, Andrea. "Drinking Yourself Skinny."

Time 22 Dec. 1988: 48-49.

Segal, Marian. "Modified Fast: A Sometime

Solution to a Weighty Problem." FDA

Consumer Apr. 1990: 11-15.

Simko, Margaret D., et al. Practical Nutri-

tion: A Quick Reference for Health Care

Practitioners. Rockville: Aspen, 1989.

Slim·Fast Foods. Label and insert with a can

of Slim·Fast powdered mix. New York:

Slim·Fast, 1994.

New page for
works cited.

MLA

49c

Heading cen-
tered.

Sources are al-
phabetized by
authors' last
names.

Second and
subsequent
lines of each
source are in-
dented five
spaces.

Double-space
throughout.

Joseph 8

```
Stocker-Ferguson, Sharon. "Inside America's

    Hottest Diet Programs." Prevention Jan.

    1990: 53-57.
```

50 Documenting Sources: APA Style

The documentation style of the American Psychological Association is used in psychology and some other social sciences and is very similar to the styles in sociology, economics, and other disciplines. The following adapts the APA style from the *Publication Manual of the American Psychological Association,* 4th ed. (1994).

NOTE The APA style resembles the MLA style (Chapter 49), but there are important differences. For instance, APA parenthetical citations include the date of publication, whereas MLA citations do not. Don't confuse the two styles.

50a Writing APA parenthetical citations

In the APA style, parenthetical citations in the text refer to a list of sources at the end of the text. The basic parenthetical citation contains the author's last name, the date of publication, and often the page number from which material is borrowed.

1. AUTHOR NOT NAMED IN YOUR TEXT

```
One critic of Milgram's experiments insisted that the

subjects "should have been fully informed of the

possible effects on them" (Baumrind, 1968, p. 34).
```

When you do not name the author in your text, place in parentheses the author's name, the date of the source, and the page number(s) preceded by "p." or "pp." Separate the elements with commas. Position the reference so that it is clear what material is being documented *and* so that the reference fits as smoothly as possible into your sentence structure.

2. AUTHOR NAMED IN YOUR TEXT

```
Baumrind (1968, p. 34) insisted that the subjects in
Milgram's study should have been fully informed of the
possible effects on them.
```

When you use the author's name in the text, do not repeat it in the reference. Position the reference next to the author's name. If you cite the same source again in the paragraph, you need not repeat the reference as long as the page number (if any) is the same and it is clear that you are using the same source.

3. A WORK WITH TWO AUTHORS

```
Pepinsky and DeStefano (1987) demonstrate that a
teacher's language often reveals hidden biases.
```

```
One study (Pepinsky & DeStefano, 1987) demonstrates
hidden biases in teachers' language.
```

When given in the text, two authors' names are connected by "and." In a parenthetical citation, they are connected by an ampersand, "&."

4. A WORK WITH THREE TO FIVE AUTHORS

```
Pepinsky, Dunn, Rentl, and Corson (1983) further
demonstrate the biases evident in gestures.
```

In the first citation of a work with three to five authors, name all the authors, as in the example above. In the second and subsequent references to the work, give only the first author's name, followed by "et al." (Latin for "and others"):

In the work of Pepinsky et al. (1983), the loaded
gestures include head shakes and eye contact.

5. A WORK WITH SIX OR MORE AUTHORS

One study (Rutter et al., 1976) attempts to explain
these geographical differences in adolescent experience.

For six or more authors, even in the first citation of the work, give
only the first author's name, followed by "et al."

6. A WORK WITH A CORPORATE AUTHOR

An earlier prediction was even more somber (Lorenz,
Inc., 1990).

For a work with a corporate or group author, treat the name of the
corporation or group as if it were an individual's name.

7. AN ANONYMOUS WORK

One article ("Right to Die," 1976) noted that a death-
row inmate may crave notoriety.

For an anonymous or unsigned work, use the first two or three
words of the title in place of an author's name, excluding an initial
The, A, or *An.* Underline book and journal titles. Place quotation
marks around article titles. (In the list of references, however, do
not use quotation marks for article titles. See pp. 259–60.) Capitalize the significant words in all titles cited in the text. (But in the reference list, treat only journal titles this way. See pp. 259–60.)

8. ONE OF TWO OR MORE WORKS BY THE SAME AUTHOR(S)

At about age seven, most children begin to use appropriate gestures to reinforce their stories (Gardner,
1973a, pp. 144-145).

If your reference list includes two or more works published by the
same author(s) *in the same year,* the works should be lettered in the
reference list (see p. 258). Then your parenthetical citation should
include the appropriate letter, as in "1973a" above.

9. TWO OR MORE WORKS BY DIFFERENT AUTHORS

```
Two studies (Herskowitz, 1984; Marconi & Hamblen, 1990)
found that periodic safety instruction can dramatically
reduce employees' accidents.
```

List the sources in alphabetical order by the first author's name. Insert a semicolon between sources.

10. AN INDIRECT SOURCE

```
Supporting data appear in a study by Wong (cited in
Marconi & Hamblen, 1990).
```

The phrase "cited in" indicates that the reference to Wong's study was found in Marconi and Hamblen. You are obliged to acknowledge that you did not consult the original source (Wong) yourself. In the list of references, give only Marconi and Hamblen.

50b Preparing the APA reference list

In APA style, the in-text parenthetical citations refer to the list of sources at the end of the text. This list, titled "References," includes full publication information on every source cited in the paper. (See p. 268 for a sample.) Prepare APA references as follows:

- ❖ Arrange the sources alphabetically by the author's last name or, if there is no author, by the first main word of the title.
- ❖ Double-space all entries. Type the first line of each entry at the left margin, and indent all subsequent lines three spaces. (This so-called hanging indent is clearest for student papers. For manuscripts that will be published, the APA specifies an indention for the first line and not the others.)
- ❖ List all authors last-name first, separating names and parts of names with commas. Use initials for first and middle names. Use an ampersand (&) rather than "and" before the last author's name.
- ❖ In titles of books and articles, capitalize only the first word of the title, the first word of the subtitle, and proper names; all other words begin with small letters. In titles of journals, capitalize all significant words. Underline the titles of books and journals, along with any comma or period following. Do not underline or use quotation marks around the titles of articles.

APA

50b

Index to APA references

❖ Generally, give full names of publishers, but exclude "Co.," "Inc.," and the like.

❖ Use the abbreviation "p." or "pp." before page numbers in books and in newspapers, but *not* in other periodicals. For inclusive page numbers, include all figures: "667–668."

❖ Separate the parts of the reference (author, date, title, and publication information) with a period and one space.

NOTE You may have to combine models to provide the necessary information on a source—for instance, combining "A book with one author" (1) and "A book with an editor" (3) for a book with only one editor.

1. A BOOK WITH ONE AUTHOR

```
Rodriguez, R. (1982). A hunger of memory: The education

    of Richard Rodriguez. Boston: David R. Godine.
```

The initial "R" appears instead of the author's first name, even though the author's full first name appears on the source. In the title, only the first words of title and subtitle and the proper name are capitalized.

2. A BOOK WITH TWO OR MORE AUTHORS

```
Nesselroade, J. R., & Baltes, P. B. (1979). Longitudi-

    nal research in the study of behavioral development.

    New York: Academic Press.
```

An ampersand (&) separates the authors' names.

3. A BOOK WITH AN EDITOR

```
Dohrenwend, B. S., & Dohrenwend, B. P. (Eds.). (1974).

    Stressful life events: Their nature and effects. New

    York: John Wiley.
```

List the editors' names as if they were authors, but follow the last name with "(Eds.)."—or "(Ed.)." with only one editor. Note the periods inside and outside the final parenthesis.

4. A BOOK WITH A TRANSLATOR

```
Trajan, P. D. (1927). Psychology of animals. (H.

    Simone, Trans.). Washington, DC: Halperin.
```

The name of the translator appears in parentheses after the title, followed by a comma, "Trans.," a closing parenthesis, and a final period.

5. A BOOK WITH A CORPORATE AUTHOR

```
Lorenz, Inc. (1992). Research in social studies teach-

    ing. Baltimore: Arrow Books.
```

For a work with a corporate or group author, begin the entry with the corporate or group name. In the reference list, alphabetize the work as if the first main word (excluding *The, A,* and *An*) were an author's last name.

6. AN ANONYMOUS BOOK

```
Merriam-Webster's collegiate dictionary (10th ed.).

    (1993). Springfield, MA: Merriam-Webster.
```

When no author is named, list the work under its title, and alphabetize it by the first main word (excluding *The, A, An*).

7. TWO OR MORE WORKS BY THE SAME AUTHOR(S)

Gardner, H. (1973a). The arts and human development.

New York: John Wiley.

Gardner, H. (1973b). The quest for mind: Piaget, Lévi-

Strauss, and the structuralist movement. New York:

Alfred A. Knopf.

When citing two or more works by exactly the same author(s), arrange the sources in order of their publication dates, earliest first. When citing two or more works by exactly the same author(s), published in the same year—as in the examples above—arrange them alphabetically by the first main word of the title and distinguish the sources by adding a letter to the date. Both the date *and* the letter are used in citing the source in the text (see p. 254).

8. A LATER EDITION

Bollinger, D. L. (1975). Aspects of language (2nd ed.).

New York: Harcourt Brace Jovanovich.

The edition number in parentheses follows the title and is followed by a period.

9. A WORK IN MORE THAN ONE VOLUME

Lincoln, A. (1953). The collected works of Abraham

Lincoln (R. P. Basler, Ed.). (Vol. 5). New

Brunswick, NJ: Rutgers University Press.

Lincoln, A. (1953). The collected works of Abraham

Lincoln (R. P. Basler, Ed.). (Vols. 1-8). New

Brunswick, NJ: Rutgers University Press.

The first entry cites a single volume (5) in the eight-volume set. The second cites all eight volumes. In the absence of an editor's name, the description of volumes would follow the title directly: "The collected works of Abraham Lincoln (Vol. 5)."

10. AN ARTICLE OR CHAPTER IN AN EDITED BOOK

Paykel, E. S. (1974). Life stress and psychiatric

disorder: Applications of the clinical approach. In

B. S. Dohrenwend & B. P. Dohrenwend (Eds.), <u>Stress-</u>

<u>ful life events: Their nature and effects</u> (pp. 239-

264). New York: John Wiley.

Give the publication date of the collection (1974 above) as the publication date of the article or chapter. After the word "In," provide the editors' names (in normal order), "(Eds.)," a comma, the title of the book, and the page numbers of the selection in parentheses.

11. AN ARTICLE IN A JOURNAL WITH CONTINUOUS PAGINATION THROUGHOUT THE ANNUAL VOLUME

Emery, R. E. (1982). Marital turmoil: Interpersonal

conflict and the children of discord and divorce.

<u>Psychological Bulletin, 92,</u> 310-330.

Some journals page all issues of an annual volume consecutively, so that issue 3 may begin on page 261. For these journals, include only the volume number, underlined and separated from the title by a comma and a space. No "pp." precedes the page numbers.

12. AN ARTICLE IN A JOURNAL THAT PAGES ISSUES SEPARATELY

Dacey, J. (1994). Management participation in corporate

buy-outs. <u>Management Perspectives, 7</u>(4), 20-31.

For journals that page issues separately (each beginning with page 1), give the issue number in parentheses immediately after the volume number. The issue number and its parentheses are *not* underlined.

13. AN ARTICLE IN A MAGAZINE

Van Gelder, L. (1986, December). Countdown to mother-

hood: When should you have a baby? <u>Ms.,</u> 37-39, 74.

Give the full date of the issue: year, followed by a comma, month, and day (if any). (If a magazine has volume and issue numbers, give them as in models 11 and 12.) Give all page numbers even when the article appears on discontinuous pages, without "pp."

14. AN ARTICLE IN A NEWSPAPER

Ramirez, A. (1993, December 14). Computer groups plan

standards. <u>The New York Times,</u> p. D5.

Give month *and* date along with year of publication. Use The in the
newspaper name if the paper itself does.

15. AN UNSIGNED ARTICLE

```
The right to die. (1976, October 11). Time, 121, 101.
```

List and alphabetize the article under its title, as you would an
anonymous book (model 6, p. 257).

16. A REVIEW

```
Dinnage, R. (1987, November 29). Against the master and
    his men. [Review of A mind of her own: The life of
    Karen Horney]. The New York Times Book Review, 10-
    11.
```

If the review is not titled, use the bracketed information as the title,
keeping the brackets.

17. A REPORT

```
Gerald, K. (1958). Micro-moral problems in obstetric
    care (Report No. NP-71). St. Louis, MO: Catholic
    Hospital Association.
```

Treat the report like a book, but provide any report number in
parentheses after the title, with no punctuation between them.

18. AN INFORMATION SERVICE

```
Jolson, Maria K. (1981). Music education for preschool-
    ers. New York: Teachers College, Columbia Univer-
    sity. (ERIC Document Reproduction Service No. ED 264
    488)
```

Place the name of the service and the document number in parentheses after the original publisher and a period. No period follows
the number.

19. A GOVERNMENT DOCUMENT

```
United States Commission on Civil Rights. (1983).
```

Greater Baltimore commitment. Washington, DC:

Author.

APA

50b

If no individual is listed as author, list the document under the name of the sponsoring agency. When the agency is both the author and the publisher, use "Author" in place of the publisher's name.

20. AN INTERVIEW

Brisick, W. C. (1988, July 1). [Interview with Ishmael

Reed]. Publishers Weekly, 41-42.

List a published interview under the interviewer's name. Provide the publication information appropriate for the kind of source the interview appears in (here, a magazine). Immediately after the title (if any), specify in brackets that the piece is an interview and, if necessary, provide other identifying information.

Note that interviews you conduct yourself are not included in the list of references. Instead, use an in-text parenthetical citation: if the subject is already named, "(personal communication, July 7, 1991)"; if not, "(L. Kogod, personal communication, July 7, 1991)."

21. A VIDEOTAPE, FILM, PERFORMANCE, OR ARTWORK

Heeley, D. (Director), & Kramer, J. (Producer). (1988).

Bacall on Bogart [Videotape]. New York: WNET Films.

Begin with the names of major contributors and (in parentheses) their function. Specify the medium in brackets after the title, with no intervening punctuation.

22. A SOURCE ON COMPUTER

Palfry, A. (1992, January). Choice of mates in identi-

cal twins [12 paragraphs]. Modern Psychology [On-

line serial], 26. Available FTP: host.publisher.com

Directory: pub/journals/modern.psychology/1992

Willard, B. L. (1992). Changes in occupational safety

standards, 1970-1990 [CD-ROM]. Abstract from: Pro-

Quest File: Dissertation Abstract Item: 7770763

In citing a source located on computer, give the information readers will need to track down the source themselves. Generally, some of that information is the same as for books and periodical articles: author(s), date, title(s), volume. In addition, computerized sources require the following: (1) for an article, the length in paragraphs (in brackets after the article title); (2) the electronic medium, such as on-line, on-line serial, or CD-ROM (in brackets after the book or periodical title; and (3) an "availability statement" that tells exactly where to find the source. This statement may include the name of an information service, a directory, and a file name or item number. Do not add any extra punctuation to an availability statement, not even a period at the end, because it could interfere with a reader's search.

Note that correspondence on electronic mail or bulletin boards may be cited in the text as "personal communication" but is not listed in the references. See the discussion of model 20 for an in-text form to use.

23. COMPUTER SOFTWARE

```
Project scheduler 7000. (1993). [Computer software].

    Orlando, FL: Scitor.
```

If no individual is given as author, list the software under its title (not underlined). Identify the entry as "Computer software" in brackets, add a period, and provide the name of the producer. If there is a catalog or other reference number, give it at the end of the entry, as in model 18.

50c Examining a sample research paper in APA style

The following excerpts from a sociology paper illustrate elements of a research paper using APA documentation style.

❖ The title page, abstract, opening of the paper, and reference list should all begin on new pages.
❖ The paper is double-spaced throughout.
❖ Pages are numbered consecutively, starting with the title page. Each page (including the title page) is identified by a shortened version of the title as well as a page number.
❖ Different levels of headings are distinct: the title and main headings are centered and are not underlined; subheadings begin at the left margin and are underlined.

[New page.]

Dating Violence   1

Heading:
shortened
title and page
number

APA

50c

An Assessment of

Dating Violence on Campus

Karen M. Tarczyk

Sociology 213

Mr. Durkan

May 6, 1992

Title page:
copy centered
vertically and
horizontally,
double-spaced

[New page.]

Dating Violence   2

Abstract

Little research has examined the patterns of
abuse and violence occurring within couples
during courtship. A questionnaire adminis-
tered to a sample of college students investi-
gated the extent and nature of such abuse and
violence. Results, interpretations, and implications for further research are discussed.

Abstract:
summary of
subject,
research
method,
conclusions.
Heading
centered.
Double-space.

[New page.]

Dating Violence   3

An Assessment of

Dating Violence on Campus

In recent years, a great deal of attention has been devoted to family violence.
Numerous studies have been done on spouse and
child abuse. However, violent behavior occurs
in dating relationships as well. The problem
of dating violence has been relatively ignored
by sociological research. It should be exam-

Double-space
throughout.

Title repeated
on first text
page.

Introduction:
presentation
of the problem
researched by
the writer.

Dating Violence   4

ined further since the premarital relationship is one context in which individuals learn and adopt behaviors that surface in marriage.

The sociologist James Makepeace (1979) contends that courtship violence is a "potential mediating link" between violence in one's family of orientation and violence in one's later family of procreation (p. 103). His provocative study examining dating behaviors at Bemidji State University in Minnesota caused a controversy. Makepeace reported that one-fifth of the respondents had had at least one encounter with dating violence. He concluded by extending these percentages to students nationwide, suggesting the existence of a major hidden social problem.

Citation form: author named in the text followed by date; combined quotation and paraphrase followed by page number.

Supporting Makepeace's research, another study found that 22.3% of respondents at Oregon State University had been either the victim or the perpetrator of premarital violence (Cates, Rutter, Karl, Linton, & Smith, 1982). In addition, in over one-half of the cases, the abuse was reciprocal. Cates et al. concluded that premarital violence was a problem of "abusive relationships" as well as "abusive individuals" (p. 90).

Citation form: authors not named in text; all authors named for first citation.

Citation form: after first citation of multiple authors, "et al." is used.

[The introduction continues.]

All these studies indicate a problem that is being neglected. The present study's objective was to gather information on the extent and nature of premarital violence and to discuss some possible interpretations.

Objective of the study being reported.

Dating Violence   5

Method

APA

50c

Sample

I conducted a survey of 200 students (134 females, 66 males) at a large state university in the northeast United States. The sample consisted of students enrolled in an introductory sociology course.

[The explanation of method continues.]

The Questionnaire

A questionnaire exploring the personal dynamics of relationships was distributed during regularly scheduled class. Questions were answered anonymously in a 30-minute period. The survey consisted of three sections.

[The explanation of method continues.]

Section 3 required participants to provide information about their current dating relationships. Levels of stress and frustration, communication between partners, and patterns of decision making were examined. These variables were expected to influence the amount of violence in a relationship. The next part of the survey was adopted from Murray Strauss's Conflict Tactics Scales (1982). These scales contain 19 items designed to measure conflict and the means of conflict resolution, including reasoning, verbal aggression, and actual violence. The final page of the questionnaire contained general questions on the couple's use of alcohol, sexual activity, and overall satisfaction with the relationship.

Main heading.

Subheading.

"Method" section: how writer conducted her own research (primary source).

APA
50c

Results

The incidence of verbal aggression and
threatened and actual dating violence was
examined. A high number of students, 50% (62
of 123 subjects), reported that they had been
the victim of verbal abuse, either being in-
sulted or sworn at. In addition, almost 14%
(17 of 123) of respondents admitted being
threatened with some type of violence,
and more than 14% (18 of 123) reported
being pushed, grabbed, or shoved. (See Table
1.)

[The explanation of results continues.]

[Table on a page by itself.]

Table 1

Incidence of Courtship Violence

Type of violence	Number of students reporting	Percentage of sample
Insulted or swore	62	50.4
Threatened to hit or throw something	17	13.8
Threw something	8	6.5
Pushed, grabbed, or shoved	18	14.6
Slapped	8	6.6
Kicked, bit, or hit with fist	7	5.7
Hit or tried to hit with something	2	1.6
Threatened with a knife or gun	1	0.8
Used a knife or gun	1	0.8

"Results"
section:
summary and
presentation
of data.

Illustration
presents
data in clear
format.

Dating Violence   7

Discussion

APA

50c

Violence within premarital relationships
has been relatively ignored. The results of
the present study indicate that abuse and
force do occur in dating relationships. Although the percentages are small, so was the
sample. Extending them to the entire campus
population of 5000 would mean significant
numbers. For example, if the nearly 6% incidence of being kicked, bitten, or hit with a
fist is typical, then 300 students might have
experienced this type of violence.

"Discussion" section: inter-pretation of data and presentation of conclu-sions.

[The discussion continues.]

If the courtship period is characterized
by abuse and violence, what accounts for it?
The other sections of the survey examined some
variables that appear to influence the relationship. Level of stress and frustration,
both within the relationship and in the re-
spondent's life, was one such variable. The
communication level between partners, both the
frequency of discussion and the frequency of
agreement, was another.

[The discussion continues.]

The method of analyzing the data in this
study, utilizing frequency distributions, provided a clear overview. However, more tests of
significance and correlation and a closer look
at the social and individual variables affect-
ing the relationship are warranted. The courtship period may set the stage for patterns of
married life. It merits more attention.

[New page.]

Dating Violence   8

References

Cates, R. L., Rutter, C. H., Karl, J., Linton,

M., & Smith, K. (1982). Premarital abuse: A

social psychological perspective. Journal

of Family Issues, 3(1), 79-90.

Glaser, R., and Rutter, C. H. (Eds.). (1984).

Familial violence [Special issue]. Family

Relations, 33.

Laner, M. (1983). Recent increases in dating

violence. Social Problems, 22, 152-166.

Makepeace, J. M. (1979). Courtship violence

among college students. Family Relations,

28, 97-103.

Socko performance on campus. (1981, June 7).

Time, 126, 66-67.

Strauss, M. L. (1982). Conflict tactics

scales. New York: Sociological Tests.

New page for
reference list.

Heading
centered.

Sources are
alphabetized
by authors'
last names.

Double-space
throughout.

Second and
subsequent
lines of each
source are
indented three
spaces.

VII

Special Types of Writing

VII

Special Types of Writing

❖

51 Writing an Argument

ARGUMENT is writing that attempts to change readers' minds or move readers to action. A good argument is neither a cold exercise in logic nor an attempt to beat others into submission. It is a work of negotiation and problem solving in which both writer and reader search for the knowledge that will create common ground between them.

51a Using the elements of argument

In one simple scheme, an argument has three elements: assertions, evidence, and assumptions.

1. Assertions

ASSERTIONS are statements that require support. In an argument you state the central assertion outright as the thesis sentence: it is what the argument is about. For instance:

> The college needs a new chemistry laboratory to replace the existing outdated lab.

Assertions are usually statements of fact, opinion (a judgment based on facts), or belief. The thesis sentence of an argument should always assert an opinion (such as the example above) because it is based on facts and is arguable on the basis of facts. Facts, in contrast, are not generally arguable because they are potentially verifiable—for example, *The cost of medical care is rising.* And beliefs, while seemingly arguable, are not based on facts and so cannot be contested on the basis of facts—for example, *The primary goal of government should be to provide equality of opportunity for all.* (Statements of fact and belief do not make thesis sentences, but they may serve as secondary assertions supporting the thesis.)

KEY TERM

THESIS SENTENCE   A sentence or sentences expressing the THESIS, the main idea of a piece of writing. All the ideas and evidence develop and support the thesis. See Chapter 3.

2. Evidence

EVIDENCE demonstrates the validity of your assertions. The evidence to support the assertion above about the need for a new chemistry lab might include the present lab's age, an inventory of facilities and equipment, and the testimony of chemistry professors.

There are several kinds of evidence:

- FACTS, statements whose truth can be verified: *Poland is slightly smaller than New Mexico.*
- STATISTICS, facts expressed as numbers: *Of those polled, 62 percent prefer a flat tax.*
- EXAMPLES, specific instances of the point being made: *Many groups, such as the elderly and the disabled, would benefit from this policy.*
- EXPERT OPINIONS, the judgments formed by authorities on the basis of their own examination of the facts: *Affirmative action is necessary to right past injustices, a point argued by Howard Glickstein, a past director of the U.S. Commission on Civil Rights.*
- APPEALS to readers' beliefs or needs, statements that ask readers to accept an assertion in part because it states something they already accept as true without evidence: *The shabby, antiquated chemistry lab shames the school, making it seem a second-rate institution.*

Evidence must be reliable to be convincing. Ask these questions about your evidence:

- Is it accurate—trustworthy, exact, and undistorted?
- Is it relevant—authoritative, pertinent, and current?
- Is it representative—true to its context, neither under- nor overrepresenting any element of the sample it's drawn from?
- Is it adequate—plentiful and specific?

3. Assumptions

An ASSUMPTION is an opinion or belief that ties evidence to an assertion: the assumption explains why a particular piece of evidence is relevant to a particular assertion. For instance:

Assertion: The college needs a new chemistry laboratory.
Evidence (in part): The testimony of chemistry professors.
Assumption: Chemistry professors are the most capable of evaluating the present lab's quality.

Assumptions are not flaws in arguments but necessities. In writing an argument, however, you need to be aware of your own assumptions and how they influence your argument. If your readers do not share your assumptions or perceive that you are not forthright about your biases, they will be less receptive to your argument. (See the following discussion of reasonableness.)

51b Being reasonable

51b

Reasonableness is essential if your argument is to establish common ground between you and your readers. Readers expect logical thinking, appropriate appeals, fairness toward the opposition, and, combining all of these, writing that is free of fallacies.

1. Logical thinking

The thesis of your argument is a conclusion you reach by reasoning about evidence. Two processes of reasoning, induction and deduction, are familiar to you even if you aren't familiar with their names.

Induction

When you're about to buy a used car, you consult friends, relatives, and consumer guides before deciding what kind of car to buy. Using INDUCTION, or INDUCTIVE REASONING, you make specific observations about cars (your evidence) and you induce, or infer, a GENERALIZATION about which car is most reliable. You might also use inductive reasoning in a term paper on print advertising:

> Analyze advertisements in newspapers and magazines (evidence).
> Read comments by advertisers, publishers, and critics (more evidence).
> Form a conclusion about print advertising (generalization).

Reasoning inductively, you connect your evidence to your generalization (or assertion) by assuming that what is true in one set of circumstances (the ads you look at) is true in a similar set of circumstances (other ads). With induction you create new knowledge out of old.

The more evidence you accumulate, the more probable it is that your generalization is true. Note, however, that absolute certainty is not possible. At some point you must *assume* that your evidence justifies your generalization, for yourself and your readers. Most errors in inductive reasoning involve oversimplifying either the evidence or the generalization. See pages 276–77 on fallacies.

Deduction

You use DEDUCTION, or DEDUCTIVE REASONING, when you proceed from your generalization that Model X is the most reliable used car to your own specific circumstances (you want to buy a used car) to the conclusion that you should buy a Model X car. In deduction your assumption is the generalization you believe to be true. It links the evidence (new information) to the assertion (the conclusion you draw). With deduction you apply old information to new.

Say that you want the school administration to postpone new room fees for one dormitory. You can base your argument on a deductive SYLLOGISM:

> *Premise:* The administration should not raise fees on dorm rooms in bad condition. [A generalization or belief that you assume to be true.]
> *Premise:* The rooms in Polk Hall are in bad condition. [New information: a specific case of the first premise.]
> *Conclusion:* The administration should not raise fees on the rooms in Polk Hall.

As long as the premises of a syllogism are true, the conclusion derives logically and certainly from them. Errors in constructing syllogisms lie behind many of the fallacies discussed on pages 276–77.

2. Appropriate appeals

In most arguments you will combine RATIONAL APPEALS to readers' capacities for logical reasoning with EMOTIONAL APPEALS to readers' beliefs and feelings. The following example illustrates both: the second sentence makes a rational appeal (to the logic of financial gain), and the third sentence makes an emotional appeal (to the sense of fairness and open-mindedness).

> Advertising should show more physically challenged people. The millions of disabled Americans have considerable buying power, yet so far advertisers have made no attempt to tap that power. Further, by keeping the physically challenged out of the mainstream depicted in ads, advertisers encourage widespread prejudice against disability, prejudice that frightens and demeans those who hold it.

51b

For an emotional appeal to be successful, it must be appropriate for the audience and the argument.

❖ It must not misjudge readers' actual feelings.
❖ It must not raise emotional issues that are irrelevant to the assertions and the evidence. (See the next page for a discussion of specific inappropriate appeals, such as bandwagon and ad hominem.)

A third kind of approach to readers, the ETHICAL APPEAL, is the sense you give of being a competent, fair person who is worth heeding. A rational appeal and an appropriate emotional appeal contribute to your ethical appeal, and so does your acknowledging your opposition (see below). In addition, a sincere and even tone will assure readers that you are a balanced person who wants to reason with them.

51b

A sincere and even tone need not exclude language with emotional appeal—words such as *frightens* and *demeans* at the end of the example about advertising. But avoid certain forms of expression that will mark you as unfair:

❖ Insulting words such as *idiotic* or *fascist*.
❖ Biased language such as *fags* or *broads* (see pp. 57–58.)
❖ Sarcasm—for instance, using the sentence *What a brilliant idea* to indicate contempt for the idea and its originator.
❖ Exclamation points! They'll make you sound shrill!

3. Acknowledgment of the opposition

A good test of your fairness in argument is how you handle possible objections. Assuming your thesis is indeed arguable, then others can marshal their own evidence to support a different view or views. You need to find out what these other views are and what the support is for them. Then, in your argument, you need to take these views on, refute those you can, grant the validity of others, and demonstrate why, despite their validity, the opposing views are less compelling than your own.

Before you draft your essay, list for yourself all the opposing views you can think of. You'll find them in your research, by talking to friends, and by critically thinking about your own ideas. Figure out which opposing views you can refute (do more research if necessary), and prepare to concede those views you can't refute. It's not a mark of weakness or failure to admit that the opposition has a point or two. Indeed, by showing yourself to be honest and fair, you strengthen your ethical appeal and thus your entire argument.

4. Fallacies

FALLACIES—errors in argument—either evade the issue of the argument or treat the argument as if it were much simpler than it is.

Evasions

An effective argument squarely faces the central issue or question it addresses. An ineffective argument may dodge the issue in one of the following ways:

❖ BEGGING THE QUESTION: treating an opinion that is open to question as if it were already proved or disproved.

The college library's expenses should be reduced by cutting subscriptions to useless periodicals. [Begged questions: Are some of the library's periodicals useless? Useless to whom?]

❖ NON SEQUITUR (Latin: "It does not follow"): linking two or more ideas that in fact have no logical connection.

If high school English were easier, fewer students would have trouble with the college English requirement. [Presumably, if high school English were easier, students would have *more* trouble.]

❖ APPEAL TO READERS' FEAR OR PITY: substituting emotions for reasoning.

She should not have to pay taxes because she is an aged widow with no friends or relatives. [Appeals to people's pity. Should age and loneliness, rather than income, determine a person's tax obligation?]

❖ BANDWAGON: inviting readers to accept an assertion because everyone else does.

As everyone knows, marijuana use leads to heroin addiction. [What is the evidence?]

❖ AD HOMINEM (Latin: "to the man"): attacking the qualities of the people holding an opposing view rather than the substance of the view itself.

One of the scientists has been treated for emotional problems, so his pessimism about nuclear waste merits no attention. [Do the scientist's previous emotional problems invalidate his current views?]

Oversimplifications

In a vain attempt to create something neatly convincing, an in-

51b

effective argument may conceal or ignore complexities in one of the following ways.

❖ HASTY GENERALIZATION: making an assertion on the basis of inadequate evidence.

People who care about the environment recycle their trash. [Many people who care about the environment may not have the option of recycling.]

❖ REDUCTIVE FALLACY: oversimplifying (reducing) the relation between causes and effects.

Poverty causes crime. [If so, then why do people who are not poor commit crimes? And why aren't all poor people criminals?]

❖ POST HOC FALLACY (from Latin, *post hoc, ergo propter hoc,* "after this, therefore because of this"): assuming that because *A* preceded *B,* then *A* must have caused *B.*

The town council erred in permitting the adult bookstore to open, for shortly afterward two women were assaulted. [It cannot be assumed without evidence that the women's assailants visited or were influenced by the bookstore.]

❖ EITHER/OR FALLACY: assuming that a complicated question has only two answers, one good and one bad, both good, or both bad.

Either we permit mandatory drug testing in the workplace or productivity will continue to decline. [Productivity is not necessarily dependent on drug testing.]

51c

51c   Organizing an argument

One trusty scheme for organizing an argument appears below. You can modify it to suit your subject, purpose, and audience.

❖ *Introduction:* Statement of the significance of the argument; background on the issue; statement of thesis. (See pp. 40–41 on introductions, p. 11 on the thesis sentence.) The introduction may be one or more paragraphs, depending on the complexity of the issue, readers' knowledge of it, and the length of the whole paper.

❖ *Body:* Assertions relating to the thesis, each developed in one or more paragraphs with the evidence for the assertion. If the argument consists of a string of supporting assertions, they are usually best arranged in order of increasing importance or persuasiveness. Sometimes the body of the argument will break into distinct sections, such as description of a problem, proposal for solving the problem, and advantages of the proposal. However arranged, the body is the meat of the argument and will run as long as needed.

❖ *Answering the opposition:* Refutation of opposing views, with evidence; concession to views more valid than your own; demonstration of your argument's greater strength. This material may come elsewhere in the argument, after the introduction or throughout the body. The choice depends mainly on whether you think readers need the opposition to be dealt with right away or can wait.

❖ *Conclusion:* Restatement of the thesis; summary of the argument; last appeal to readers. (See pp. 41–42 on conclusions.) The conclusion may be one or more paragraphs, depending on the complexity and the length of your argument.

51d   Examining a sample argument

The following student essay illustrates the principles discussed in this chapter. As you read the essay, note especially the structure, the relation of assertions and supporting evidence, and signs of the writer's reasonableness.

Share the Ride

Every year we encounter more bad news about the environment, and a good portion of it is due to the private automobile. Respected scientists warn that carbon dioxide emissions, such as those from cars, may produce disastrous global warming. Soot, sulfur, and other automobile emissions are contributing to reduced air quality almost everywhere. The oil that powers cars comes from rapidly depleting reserves, leading to an unhappy choice between imports of foreign oil and exploration, such as offshore drilling, that threatens the environment.

Introduction: identification of problem

In its own way Beverly Community College contributes to the problem. School administrators report that campus parking lots are filled with about 1800 cars every weekday, so that means 3600 trips a day are made to and from campus. If just a third of the solo drivers shared rides with one another, the total trips to and from campus would be reduced by at least 600. It is time for the BCC community to make a difficult move toward an organized car-pooling system that would achieve this modest goal.

Thesis sentence: proposal for a solution

The first step in getting car-pools going is to form a task force of administrators, faculty, and students to devise a workable system. School records would be used to connect people who live near each other and would be willing to car-pool. With administration backing, the task force would initiate a school-wide campaign of meetings, rallies, posters, and other public-relations efforts to overcome resistance to car-pooling, answer questions, and win converts. The administration would assign staff to help with records and to keep the system current each term, since schedules and the student population change. As soon as administrators thought it was feasible, they could give a big boost to the system by creating monetary incentives to car-pool. Students who participate in car-pooling could receive a tuition rebate—say, $100 a term for full-time students. Faculty and staff could receive equivalent bonuses. In addition, parking fees could be instituted to discourage driving to school.

Explanation of the proposal

51d

The most obvious advantage of this proposal is that it would reduce car trips and thus air pollution and needless use of oil. Burning a single gallon of gasoline produces 20 pounds of carbon dioxide. If the average length of a trip to or from BCC is 10 miles (a conservative number) and the average car gets 30 miles to the gallon (a generous number), then it takes only 3 trips to burn a gallon of gasoline. Saving just 600 trips a day would keep 4000 pounds of carbon dioxide out of the air. It would also keep 200 gallons of gasoline in the pumps.

Support for the proposal: first advantage

That unused gasoline would also save money for participants. If a full-time student drove half as often as now, the gasoline savings would be about $30 a term, plus the savings in wear and tear on the car. If the school instituted a $100 tuition rebate, the cash savings would rise to $130 a term. If the school instituted a parking fee of, say, $1 a day, the cash savings would rise to more than $160 a term. (All figures assume that car-pools consist of two people who share driving and expenses equally.)

Support for the proposal: second advantage

There are more abstract advantages, too. Individual freedom is a cherished right in our society, but it has no meaning outside the community.

Support for the proposal: third advantage

Like recycling and other environmental efforts, car-pooling would ask the individual to make a sacrifice on behalf of the community. Car-poolers would be actively participating in something larger than themselves, instead of just furthering their own self-interest.

Members of the BCC administration may point out that the proposed program asks for sacrifice from the school as well. They may object that rebates or bonuses and the costs of running the program are not feasible given the school's tight budget. True, $100 rebates or bonuses for an estimated 600 participants would cost $60,000 a term, and administrative time would also cost something. But considerable money could be raised by instituting a dollar parking fee, which could produce as much as $1500 a day, nearly $100,000 a term, in revenue. Furthermore, sponsoring a car-pooling system is no more than many corporations do that encourage their employees to take public transportation by contributing to their monthly passes. Businesses, schools, and other institutions that require their people to assemble in one place should help reduce the environmental cost of commuting.

Probable objection and response

Of course, it is the cost of commuters' convenience that will probably make or break the program. Students and faculty may have to arrive at school earlier than they want or leave later because of their car-pools. While considerable, this inconvenience could over time be turned to an advantage if car-poolers learned to use their extra on-campus time wisely to prepare for classes (work they would have do at home anyway). In addition, this inconvenience might seem worthwhile in exchange for helping the environment and the concrete rewards of a rebate or bonus and savings on parking.

Probable objection and response

It is no small flaw in the proposal that not all commuters would be able to participate in the program, even if they wanted to. The fact is that many part-time faculty and students have schedules that are too complicated or erratic to permit car-pooling. Many teachers and students must make intermediate stops between their homes and BCC, such as for work. These commuters would not have access to the rebates or bonuses and still would be subject to the parking fee.

Probable objection

This unfairness is regrettable but, for now, unavoidable; we have to start somewhere. A change away from single-passenger cars to car-pools is like

Response to probable objection and conclusion

all other significant changes we must make on behalf of the environment. The shift in consciousness
and responsibility will be halting and prolonged,
and the costs and benefits will not always be distributed equally. One thing we can be sure of, however, is that the shift will not occur at all if we don't
take the difficult first steps.

—LEE MORRISON (student)

52 Reading and Writing About Literature

52a

By Sylvan Barnet

Writers of literature—stories, novels, poems, and plays—are
concerned with presenting human experience concretely, with
showing rather than *telling*, with giving a sense of the "feel" of life.
Reading and writing about literature thus require extremely close
attention to the feel of the words. For instance, the word *woods* in
Robert Frost's "Stopping by Woods on a Snowy Evening" has a
rural, folksy quality that *forest* doesn't have, and many such small
distinctions contribute to the poem's effect. When you read and
write about literature, you interpret distinctions like these, forming
an idea of a work that you support with evidence from it.

52a Reading literature

Reading literature critically involves interacting with a text, not
in order to make negative judgments but in order to understand the
work and evaluate its significance or quality. Such interaction is
not passive, like scanning a newspaper or watching television. Instead, it is a process of engagement, of diving into the words themselves. You will become more engaged if you write while you read.
If you own the book you're reading, don't hesitate to underline or
highlight passages that especially interest you for one reason or another. Don't hesitate to annotate the margins, indicating your plea-
sures, displeasures, and uncertainties with remarks such as *Nice
detail* or *Do we need this long description?* or *Not believable.* If you
don't own the book, make these notes on separate sheets.

An effective way to interact with a text is to keep a READING JOURNAL. A journal is not a diary in which you record your doings but a place in which you develop and store your reflections on what you read, such as an answer to a question you may have posed in the margin of the text or a response to something said in class. You may, for instance, want to reflect on why your opinion is so different from that of another student. You may even make an entry in the form of a letter to the author or from one character to another.

52b

52b Analyzing literature

In analyzing literature, you face right off the question of *meaning.* Readers disagree all the time over the meanings of works of literature, partly because (as noted above) literature *shows* rather than *tells:* it gives concrete images of imagined human experiences, but it usually does not say how we ought to understand the images. Further, readers bring different experiences to their reading and thus understand images differently. In writing about literature, then, we can offer only our *interpretation* of the meaning rather than *the* meaning. Still, most people agree that there are limits to interpretation: it must be supported by evidence that a reasonable person finds at least plausible if not totally convincing.

Possible meanings reside in many elements of a literary work. The following are the elements most often discussed. Asking yourself the questions for each element can help you think constructively and imaginatively about what you read.

❖ PLOT: the relationships and patterns of events. (Even a poem has a plot—for instance, a change in mood from grief to resignation.)

What actions happen?
What conflicts occur?
How do the events connect to each other and to the whole?

❖ CHARACTERS: the people the author creates (including the narrator of a story or the speaker of a poem).

Who are the principal people in the work?

┌─ KEY TERM ──

ANALYSIS   Separating something (such as a literary text) into its elements and interpreting the meaning, relationships, and significance of the elements.

How do they interact?

What do their actions, words, and thoughts reveal about their personalities and the personalities of others?

Do the characters stay the same, or do they change? Why?

❖ POINT OF VIEW: the perspective or attitude of the speaker in a poem or the voice who tells a story. The point of view may be FIRST PERSON (a participant, using *I*) or THIRD PERSON (an outsider, using *he, she, it, they*). A first-person narrator may be a major or a minor character in the narrative, and may be RELIABLE or UNRELIABLE (unable to report events wholly or accurately). A third-person narrator may be OMNISCIENT (knows what goes on in all characters' minds), LIMITED (knows what goes on in the mind of only one character), or OBJECTIVE (knows only what is external to the characters).

52b

Who is the narrator (or the speaker of a poem)?

How does the narrator's point of view affect the narrative?

❖ TONE: the narrator's or speaker's attitude, perceived through the words (for instance, joyful, bitter, or confident).

What tone (or tones) do you hear? If there is a change, how do you account for it?

Is there an ironic contrast between the narrator's tone (for instance, confidence) and what you take to be the author's attitude (for instance, pity for human overconfidence)?

❖ IMAGERY: word pictures or visual details involving the senses (sight, sound, touch, smell, taste).

What images does the writer use? What senses do they draw on?

What patterns are evident in the images (for instance, religious or commercial images)?

What is the significance of the imagery?

❖ SYMBOLISM: concrete things standing for larger and more abstract ideas (for instance, the American flag may symbolize freedom, or a dead flower may symbolize mortality).

What symbols does the author use? What do they seem to signify?

How does the symbolism relate to the theme of the work?

❖ SETTING: the place where the action happens.

What does the locale contribute to the work?

Are scene shifts significant?

❖ FORM: the shape or structure of the work.

What *is* the form? (For example, a story might divide sharply in the middle, moving from happiness to sorrow.)
What parts of the work does the form emphasize, and why?

❖ THEME: the main idea, the gist of what the work adds up to.

How might the theme be stated?
How do the parts of the work develop the theme?

❖ APPEAL: the degree to which the story pleases you.

What do you especially like or dislike about the work? Why?
Do you think your responses are unique, or would they be common to most readers? Why?

52c Examining two literary works and sample papers

The following pages reprint two works of literature (a short story and a poem), each followed by a student paper on the work. In each student paper the author supports his or her ideas with quotations, paraphrases, and summaries from the work being discussed, a primary source. In the second paper (p. 290), the author also draws sparingly on secondary sources (other critics' views), which further support his own views.

Note the following features of the students' papers:

❖ The students follow the manuscript format of the Modern Language Association, or MLA, which calls for name and course

┌─ KEY TERMS ──

QUOTATION   An exact repetition of an author's words, placed in quotation marks. (See also pp. 167–68, 179–81.)

PARAPHRASE   A restatement of an author's words, closely following the author's line of thought but using different words and sentence structures. (See also pp. 215–16.)

SUMMARY   A condensation of an extended passage into a sentence or more. (See also pp. 214–15.)

PRIMARY SOURCE   A firsthand account: for instance, a historical document, a work of literature, or your own observations.

SECONDARY SOURCE   A report on or analysis of other sources, often primary ones: for instance, a historian's account of a battle or a critic's view of a poem.

information on the first page, double-spacing throughout, and the "Works Cited" beginning on a new page. (See pp. 177–81 for complete guidelines on MLA manuscript format.)

❖ The authors use the MLA documentation style (pp. 222–43).

❖ The authors use ellipsis marks (. . .) to indicate omissions from quotations (pp. 172–74). (If the authors had added to quotations, they would have used brackets around the additions; see p. 174.)

❖ The authors use the present tense of verbs (*Chopin shows; Mrs. Mallard dies*) to describe both the literature author's work and the action in the work.

1. A short story and an essay about it

52c

Short story

Kate Chopin
The Story of an Hour

Knowing that Mrs. Mallard was afflicted with a heart trouble, great care was taken to break to her as gently as possible the news of her husband's death.

It was her sister Josephine who told her, in broken sentences, veiled hints that revealed in half concealing. Her husband's friend Richards was there, too, near her. It was he who had been in the newspaper office when intelligence of the railroad disaster was received, with Brently Mallard's name leading the list of "killed." He had only taken the time to assure himself of its truth by a second telegram, and had hastened to forestall any less careful, less tender friend in bearing the sad message.

She did not hear the story as many women have heard the same, with a paralyzed inability to accept its significance. She wept at once with sudden, wild abandonment, in her sister's arms. When the storm of grief had spent itself she went away to her room alone. She would have no one follow her.

There stood, facing the open window, a comfortable, roomy armchair. Into this she sank, pressed down by a physical exhaustion that haunted her body and seemed to reach into her soul.

She could see in the open square before her house the tops of trees that were all aquiver with the new spring life. The delicious breath of rain was in the air. In the street below a peddler was crying his wares. The notes of a distant song which some one was singing reached her faintly, and countless sparrows were twittering in the eaves.

There were patches of blue sky showing here and there through the clouds that had met and piled above the other in the west facing her window.

She sat with her head thrown back upon the cushion of the chair quite motionless, except when a sob came up into her throat and shook her, as a child who has cried itself to sleep continues to sob in its dreams.

She was young, with a fair, calm face, whose lines bespoke repression and even a certain strength. But now there was a dull stare in her eyes, whose gaze was fixed away off yonder on one of those patches of blue sky. It was not a glance of reflection, but rather indicated a suspension of intelligent thought.

There was something coming to her and she was waiting for it, fearfully. What was it? She did not know; it was too subtle and elusive to name. But she felt it creeping out of the sky, reaching toward her through the sounds, the scents, the color that filled the air.

52c

Now her bosom rose and fell tumultuously. She was beginning to recognize this thing that was approaching to possess her, and she was striving to beat it back with her will—as powerless as her two white slender hands would have been.

When she abandoned herself a little whispered word escaped her slightly parted lips. She said it over and over under her breath: "Free, free, free!" The vacant stare and the look of terror that had followed it went from her eyes. They stayed keen and bright. Her pulses beat fast, and the coursing blood warmed and relaxed every inch of her body.

She did not stop to ask if it were not a monstrous joy that held her. A clear and exalted perception enabled her to dismiss the suggestion as trivial.

She knew that she would weep again when she saw the kind, tender hands folded in death; the face that had never looked save with love upon her, fixed and gray and dead. But she saw beyond that bitter moment a long procession of years to come that would belong to her absolutely. And she opened and spread her arms out to them in welcome.

There would be no one to live for her during those coming years; she would live for herself. There would be no powerful will bending her in the blind persistence with which men and women believe they have a right to impose a private will upon a fellow creature. A kind intention or a cruel intention made the act seem no less a crime as she looked upon it in that brief moment of illumination.

And yet she had loved him—sometimes. Often she had not. What did it matter! What could love, the unsolved mystery, count for in face of this possession of self-assertion which she suddenly recognized as the strongest impulse of her being.

"Free! Body and soul free!" she kept whispering.

Josephine was kneeling before the closed door with her lips to the keyhole, imploring for admission. "Louise, open the door! I beg; open the door—you will make yourself ill. What are you doing, Louise? For heaven's sake open the door."

"Go away. I am not making myself ill." No; she was drinking in the very elixir of life through that open window.

Her fancy was running riot along those days ahead of her. Spring days, and summer days, and all sorts of days that would be her own. She breathed a quick prayer that life might be long. It was only yesterday she had thought with a shudder that life might be long.

She arose at length and opened the door to her sister's importunities. There was a feverish triumph in her eyes, and she carried herself unwittingly like a goddess of Victory. She clasped her sister's waist and together they descended the stairs. Richards stood waiting for them at the bottom.

Some one was opening the front door with a latchkey. It was Brently Mallard who entered, a little travel-stained, composedly carrying his grip-sack and umbrella. He had been far from the scene of accident, and did not even know there had been one. He stood amazed at Josephine's piercing cry; at Richards' quick motion to screen him from the view of his wife.

But Richards was too late.

When the doctors came they said she had died of heart disease—of joy that kills.

52c

Student essay (no secondary sources)

Janet Vong

English 102

Mr. Romano

February 20, 1993

Ironies of Life in Kate Chopin's

"The Story of an Hour"

Kate Chopin's "The Story of an Hour"--which takes only a few minutes to read--turns out to have an ironic ending. On rereading it, however, one sees that the irony is not concentrated only in the outcome of the plot--Mrs. Mallard dies just when she is beginning to live--but is also present in many details.

After we know how the story turns out, if we reread it we find irony at the very start. Because Mrs. Mallard's friends and her sister assume, mistakenly, that she was deeply in love with her husband, Brently Mallard, they

take great care to tell her gently of his death. They
mean well, and in fact they do well, bringing her an hour
of life, an hour of joyous freedom, but it is ironic that
they think their news is sad. True, Mrs. Mallard at first
expresses grief when she hears the news, but soon (unknown
to her friends) she finds joy in it. So Richards's "sad
message" (12), though sad in Richards's eyes, is in fact a
happy message.

    Among the small but significant ironic details is the
statement near the end of the story that when Mallard
entered the house, Richards tried to conceal him from Mrs.
Mallard, but "Richards was too late" (13). This is ironic
because almost at the start of the story, in the second
paragraph, Richards "hastened" (12) to bring his sad
message; if he had at the start been "too late" (13),
Brently Mallard would have arrived at home first, and Mrs.
Mallard's life would not have ended an hour later but
would simply have gone on as it had been. Yet another
irony at the end of the story is the diagnosis of the
doctors. They say she died of "heart disease--of joy that
kills" (14). In one sense they are right: Mrs. Mallard
has for the last hour experienced a great joy. But of
course the doctors totally misunderstand the joy that
kills her. It is not joy at seeing her husband alive, but
her realization that the great joy she experienced during
the last hour is over.

    All of these ironic details add richness to the
story, but the central irony resides not in the well-
intentioned but ironic actions of Richards, or in the
unconsciously ironic words of the doctors, but in Mrs.
Mallard's own life. She "sometimes" (13) loved her husband, but in a way she has been dead, a body subjected to
her husband's will. Now, his apparent death brings her

52c

new life. Appropriately, this new life comes to her at the
season of the year when "the tops of trees . . . were all
aquiver with the new spring life" (12). But, ironically,
her new life will last only an hour. She is "Free, free,
free"--but only until her husband walks through the door-
way. She looks forward to "summer days" (13), but she
will not see even the end of this spring day. If her
years of marriage were ironic, bringing her a sort of
living death instead of joy, her new life is ironic too,
not only because it grows out of her moment of grief for
her supposedly dead husband, but also because her vision
of "a long progression of years" (13) is cut short within
an hour on a spring day.

[New page.]

Work Cited

Chopin, Kate.   "The Story of an Hour."   <u>Literature for
     Composition</u>.   Ed. Sylvan Barnet et al.   3rd ed.   New
     York: Harper, 1992.   12-13.

2. A poem and an essay about it

Poem

Gwendolyn Brooks
The Bean Eaters

They eat beans mostly, this old yellow pair.
Dinner is a casual affair.
Plain chipware on a plain and creaking wood,
Tin flatware.

Two who are Mostly Good.   5
Two who have lived their day,
But keep on putting on their clothes
And putting things away.

And remembering . . .
Remembering, with tinklings and twinges,   10
As they lean over the beans in their rented back room that is
     full of beads and receipts and dolls and cloths, tobacco
     crumbs, vases and fringes.

Student essay (with secondary sources)

Kenneth Scheff

Professor MacGregor

English 101A

February 7, 1994

Marking Time Versus Enduring in

Gwendolyn Brooks's "The Bean Eaters"

52c

"The Bean Eaters," by Gwendolyn Brooks, is a poem of
only eleven lines. It is written in plain language about
very plain people. Yet its meaning is ambiguous. One
critic, George E. Kent, says the old couple who eat beans
"have had their day and exist now as time-markers" (141).
However, another reader, D. H. Melhem, perceives not so
much time marking as "endurance" in the old couple (123).
Is this poem a despairing picture of old age or a more
positive portrait?

"The Bean Eaters" describes an "old yellow pair" who
"eat beans mostly" (line 1) off "Plain chipware" (3) with
"Tin flatware" (4) in "their rented back room" (11).
Clearly, they are poor. Their existence is accompanied
not by friends or relatives--children or grandchildren are
not mentioned--but by memories and a few possessions (9-
11). They are "Mostly Good" (5), words Brooks capitalizes
at the end of a line, perhaps to stress the old people's
adherence to traditional values as well as their lack of
saintliness. They are unexceptional, whatever message
they have for readers.

The isolated routine of the couple's life is something Brooks draws attention to with a separate stanza:

> Two who are Mostly Good.
>
> Two who have lived their day,
>
> But keep on putting on their clothes
>
> And putting things away. (5-8)

Brooks emphasizes how isolated the couple is by repeating "Two who." Then she emphasizes how routine their life is by repeating "putting."

A pessimistic reading of this poem seems justified. The critic Harry B. Shaw reads the lines just quoted as perhaps despairing: "they are putting things away as if winding down an operation and readying for withdrawal from activity" (80). However, Shaw observes, the word "But" also indicates the couple's "determination to go on living, a refusal to give up and let things go" (80). This dual meaning is at the heart of Brooks's poem: the old people live a meager existence, yes, but their will, their self-control, and their connection with another person-- their essential humanity--are unharmed.

52c

The truly positive nature of the poem is revealed in the last stanza. In Brooks's words, the old couple remember with some "twinges" perhaps, but also with "tinklings" (10). As Melhem says, these people are "strong in mutual affection and shared memories" (123). And the final line, which is much longer than all the rest and which catalogs the evidence of the couple's long life together, is almost musically affirmative: "As they lean over the beans in their rented back room that is full of beads and receipts and dolls and cloths, tobacco crumbs, vases and fringes" (11).

What these people have is not much, but it is something.

[New page.]

Works Cited

Brooks, Gwendolyn. "The Bean Eaters." Literature: An
    Introduction to Fiction, Poetry, and Drama. Ed.
    X. J. Kennedy. 5th ed. New York: Harper, 1991.
    565.

Kent, George E. A Life of Gwendolyn Brooks. Lexington:
    UP of Kentucky, 1990.

Melhem, D. H. Gwendolyn Brooks: Poetry and the Heroic
    Voice. Lexington: UP of Kentucky, 1987.

Shaw, Harry B. Gwendolyn Brooks. Boston: Twayne, 1980.

52c

Glossary
of Usage

❖

Index

Glossary
of Usage

❖

This glossary provides notes on words or phrases that often cause problems for writers. The recommendations for standard written English are based on current dictionaries and usage guides. Items labeled NONSTANDARD should be avoided in speech and especially in writing. Those labeled COLLOQUIAL and SLANG occur in speech and in some informal writing but are best avoided in the more formal writing usually expected in college and business. (Words and phrases labeled *colloquial* include those labeled by many dictionaries with the equivalent term *informal.*)

Usage

a, an Use *a* before words beginning with consonant sounds, including those spelled with an initial pronounced *h* and those spelled with vowels that are sounded as consonants: *a̲ historian, a̲ one-o'clock class, a̲ university.* Use *an* before words that begin with vowel sounds, including those spelled with an initial silent *h: an̲ orgy, an̲ L, an̲ honor.*

The article before an abbreviation depends on how the abbreviation is to be read: *She was once an AEC undersecretary* (*AEC* is to be read as three separate letters); *Many Americans opposed a̲ SALT treaty* (*SALT* is to be read as one word, *salt*).

See also pp. 127–30 on the uses of *a/an* versus *the.*

accept, except *Accept* is a verb meaning "receive." *Except* is usually a preposition or conjunction meaning "but for" or "other than"; when it is

295

used as a verb, it means "leave out." *I can <u>accept</u> all your suggestions <u>except</u> the last one. I'm sorry you <u>excepted</u> my last suggestion from your list.*

advice, advise   *Advice* is a noun, and *advise* is a verb: *Take my <u>advice</u>; do as I <u>advise</u> you.*

affect, effect   Usually *affect* is a verb, meaning "to influence," and *effect* is a noun, meaning "result": *The drug did not <u>affect</u> his driving; in fact, it seemed to have no <u>effect</u> at all.* But *effect* occasionally is used as a verb meaning "to bring about": *Her efforts <u>effected</u> a change.* And *affect* is used in psychology as a noun meaning "feeling or emotion": *One can infer much about <u>affect</u> from behavior.*

agree to, agree with   *Agree to* means "consent to," and *agree with* means "be in accord with": *How can they <u>agree to</u> a treaty when they don't <u>agree with</u> each other about the terms?*

all ready, already   *All ready* means "completely prepared," and *already* means "by now" or "before now": *We were <u>all ready</u> to go to the movie, but it had <u>already</u> started.*

all right   *All right* is always two words. *Alright* is a common misspelling.

all together, altogether   *All together* means "in unison" or "gathered in one place." *Altogether* means "entirely." *It's not <u>altogether</u> true that our family never spends vacations <u>all together</u>.*

allusion, illusion   An *allusion* is an indirect reference, and an *illusion* is a deceptive appearance: *Paul's constant <u>allusions</u> to Shakespeare created the <u>illusion</u> that he was an intellectual.*

almost, most   *Almost* means "nearly"; *most* means "the greater number (or part) of." In formal writing, *most* should not be used as a substitute for *almost: We see each other <u>almost</u> (not <u>most</u>) every day.*

a lot   *A lot* is always two words, used informally to mean "many." *Alot* is a common misspelling.

among, between   In general, use *among* for relationships involving more than two people or for comparing one thing to a group to which it belongs. *The four of them agreed <u>among</u> themselves that the choice was <u>between</u> New York and Los Angeles.*

amount, number   Use *amount* with a singular noun that names something not countable (a noncount noun): *The <u>amount</u> of <u>food</u> varies.* Use *number* with a plural noun that names more than one of something countable (a plural count noun): *The <u>number</u> of <u>calories</u> must stay the same.*

and/or   *And/or* indicates three options: one or the other or both (*The decision is made by the mayor <u>and/or</u> the council*). If you mean all three options, *and/or* is appropriate. Otherwise, use *and* if you mean both, *or* if you mean either.

ante-, anti-   The prefix *ante-* means "before" (*antedate, antebellum*); *anti-* means "against" (*antiwar, antinuclear*). Before a capital letter or *i*, *anti-* takes a hyphen: *anti-Freudian, anti-isolationist.*

anxious, eager   *Anxious* means "nervous" or "worried" and is usually followed by *about*. *Eager* means "looking forward" and is usually followed by *to*. *I've been anxious about getting blisters. I'm eager* (not *anxious*) *to get new running shoes.*

anybody, any body; anyone, any one   *Anybody* and *anyone* are indefinite pronouns; *any body* is a noun modified by *any; any one* is a pronoun or adjective modified by *any*. *How can anybody communicate with any body of government? Can anyone help Amy? She has more work than any one person can handle.*

any more, anymore   *Any more* means "no more"; *anymore* means "now." Both are used in negative constructions. *He doesn't want any more. She doesn't live here anymore.*

anyplace   Colloquial for *anywhere.*

anyways, anywheres   Nonstandard for *anyway* and *anywhere.*

apt, liable, likely   *Apt* and *likely* are interchangeable. Strictly speaking, though, *apt* means "having a tendency to": *Horace is apt to forget his lunch in the morning. Likely* means "probably going to": *Horace is leaving so early today that he's likely to catch the first bus.*
   Liable normally means "in danger of" and should be confined to situations with undesirable consequences: *Horace is liable to trip over that hose.* Strictly, *liable* means "responsible" or "exposed to": *The owner will be liable for Horace's injuries.*

are, is   Use *are* with a plural subject (*books are*), *is* with a singular subject (*book is*).

as   Substituting for *because, since,* or *while, as* may be vague or ambiguous: *As we were stopping to rest, we decided to eat lunch.* (Does *as* mean "while" or "because"?) *As* should never be used as a substitute for *whether* or *who*. *I'm not sure whether* (not *as*) *we can make it. That's the man who* (not *as*) *gave me directions.*

as, like   In formal speech and writing, *like* should not introduce a full clause (with a subject and a verb) because it is a preposition. The preferred choice is *as* or *as if: The plan succeeded as* (not *like*) *we hoped. It seemed as if* (not *like*) *it might fail. Other plans like it have failed.*

as, than   In comparisons, *as* and *than* precede a subjective-case pronoun when the pronoun is a subject: *I love you more than he* (*loves you*). *As* and *than* precede an objective-case pronoun when the pronoun is an object: *I love you as much as* (*I love*) *him.* (See also p. 116.)

assure, ensure, insure   *Assure* means "to promise": *He assured us that we would miss the traffic. Ensure* and *insure* often are used interchangeably to mean "make certain," but some reserve *insure* for matters of legal and financial protection and use *ensure* for more general meanings: *We left early to ensure that we would miss the traffic. It's expensive to insure yourself against floods.*

at   The use of *at* after *where* is wordy and should be avoided: *Where are you meeting him?* is preferable to *Where are you meeting him at?*

at this point in time   Wordy for *now, at this point,* or *at this time.*

awful, awfully   Strictly speaking, *awful* means "awe-inspiring." As intensifiers meaning "very" or "extremely" (*He tried awfully hard*), *awful* and *awfully* should be avoided in formal speech or writing.

a while, awhile   *Awhile* is an adverb; *a while* is an article and a noun. *I will be gone awhile* (not *a while*). *I will be gone for a while* (not *awhile*).

bad, badly   In formal speech and writing, *bad* should be used only as an adjective; the adverb is *badly. He felt bad because his tooth ached badly.* In *He felt bad,* the verb *felt* is a linking verb and the adjective *bad* describes the subject. See also pp. 123–24.

being as, being that   Colloquial for *because,* the preferable word in formal speech or writing: *Because* (not *Being as*) *the world is round, Columbus never did fall off the edge.*

beside, besides   *Beside* is a preposition meaning "next to." *Besides* is a preposition meaning "except" or "in addition to" as well as an adverb meaning "in addition." *Besides, several other people besides you want to sit beside Dr. Christensen.*

better, had better   *Had better* (meaning "ought to") is a verb modified by an adverb. The verb is necessary and should not be omitted: *You had better* (not *better*) *go.*

between, among   See *among, between.*

bring, take   Use *bring* only for movement from a farther place to a nearer one and *take* for any other movement. *First take these books to the library for renewal; then take them to Mr. Daniels. Bring them back to me when he's finished.*

but, hardly, scarcely   These words are negative in their own right; using *not* with any of them produces a double negative (see p. 126). *We have but* (not *haven't got but*) *an hour before our plane leaves. I could hardly* (not *couldn't hardly*) *make out her face.*

but, however, yet   Each of these words is adequate to express contrast. Don't combine them. *He said he had finished, yet* (not *but yet*) *he continued.*

can, may   Strictly, *can* indicates capacity or ability, and *may* indicates permission: *If I may talk with you a moment, I believe I can solve your problem.*

censor, censure   To *censor* is to edit or remove from public view on moral or some other grounds; to *censure* is to give a formal scolding. *The lieutenant was censured by Major Taylor for censoring the letters her soldiers wrote home from boot camp.*

center around *Center on* is more logical than, and preferable to, *center around.*

climatic, climactic *Climatic* comes from *climate* and refers to the weather: *Last winter's temperatures may indicate a climatic change. Climactic* comes from *climax* and refers to a dramatic high point: *During the climactic duel between Hamlet and Laertes, Gertrude drinks poisoned wine.*

complement, compliment To *complement* something is to add to, complete, or reinforce it: *Her yellow blouse complemented her black hair.* To *compliment* something is to make a flattering remark about it: *He complimented her on her hair. Complimentary* can also mean "free": *complimentary tickets.*

conscience, conscious *Conscience* is a noun meaning "a sense of right and wrong"; *conscious* is an adjective meaning "aware" or "awake." *Though I was barely conscious, my conscience nagged me.*

contact Often used imprecisely as a verb instead of a more exact word such as *consult, talk with, telephone,* or *write to.*

continual, continuous *Continual* means "constantly recurring": *Most movies on television are continually interrupted by commercials. Continuous* means "unceasing": *Some cable channels present movies continuously without commercials.*

could of See *have, of.*

credible, creditable, credulous *Credible* means "believable": *It's a strange story, but it seems credible to me. Creditable* means "deserving of credit" or "worthy": *Steve gave a creditable performance. Credulous* means "gullible": *The credulous Claire believed Tim's lies.* See also *incredible, incredulous.*

criteria The plural of *criterion* (meaning "standard for judgment"): *Our criteria are strict. The most important criterion is a sense of humor.*

data The plural of *datum* (meaning "fact"). Though *data* is often used as a singular noun, most careful writers still treat it as plural: *The data fail* (not *fails*) *to support the hypothesis.*

device, devise *Device* is the noun, and *devise* is the verb: *Can you devise some device for getting his attention?*

different from, different than *Different from* is preferred: *His purpose is different from mine.* But *different than* is widely accepted when a construction using *from* would be wordy: *I'm a different person now than I used to be* is preferable to *I'm a different person now from the person I used to be.*

differ from, differ with   To *differ from* is to be unlike: *The twins differ from each other only in their hairstyles.* To *differ with* is to disagree with: *I have to differ with you on that point.*

discreet, discrete   *Discreet* (noun form *discretion*) means "tactful": *What's a discreet way of telling Maud to be quiet? Discrete* (noun form *discreteness*) means "separate and distinct": *Within a computer's memory are millions of discrete bits of information.*

disinterested, uninterested   *Disinterested* means "impartial": *We chose Pete, as a disinterested third party, to decide who was right. Uninterested* means "bored" or "lacking interest": *Unfortunately, Pete was completely uninterested in the question.*

don't   *Don't* is the contraction for *do not,* not for *does not: I don't care, you don't care,* but *he doesn't* (not *don't*) *care.*

due to   *Due* is an adjective or noun; thus *due to* is always acceptable after a verb to refer back to the subject: *His gray hairs were due to age.* Many object to *due to* as a preposition meaning "because of" (*Due to the holiday, class was canceled*). A rule of thumb is that *due to* is always correct after a form of the verb *be* but questionable otherwise.

due to the fact that   Wordy for *because.*

eager, anxious   See *anxious, eager.*

effect   See *affect, effect.*

elicit, illicit   *Elicit* is a verb meaning "bring out" or "call forth." *Illicit* is an adjective meaning "unlawful." *The crime elicited an outcry against illicit drugs.*

ensure   See *assure, ensure, insure.*

enthused   Used colloquially as an adjective meaning "showing enthusiasm." The preferred adjective is *enthusiastic: The coach was enthusiastic* (not *enthused*) *about the team's victory.*

et al., etc.   Use *et al.,* the Latin abbreviation for "and other people," only in source citations for works with more than three authors: *Jones et al.* (see pp. 224, 231, 253–54). *Etc.,* the Latin abbreviation for "and other things," should be avoided in formal writing and should not be used to refer to people. When used, it should not substitute for precision, as in *The government provides health care, etc.*

everybody, every body; everyone, every one   *Everybody* and *everyone* are indefinite pronouns: *Everybody (everyone) knows Tom steals. Every one* is a pronoun modified by *every,* and *every body* a noun modified by *every.* Both refer to each thing or person of a specific group and are typically followed by *of: The game commissioner has stocked every body of fresh water in the state with fish, and now every one of our rivers is a potential trout stream.*

everyday, every day *Everyday* is an adjective meaning "used daily" or "common"; *every day* is a noun modified by *every*: *Everyday problems tend to arise every day.*

everywheres Nonstandard for *everywhere.*

except See *accept, except.*

except for the fact that Wordy for *except that.*

explicit, implicit *Explicit* means "stated outright": *I left explicit instructions. Implicit* means "implied, unstated": *We had an implicit understanding.*

farther, further *Farther* refers to additional distance (*How much farther is it to the beach?*), and *further* refers to additional time, amount, or other abstract matters (*I don't want to discuss this any further*).

fewer, less *Fewer* refers to individual countable items (a plural count noun), *less* to general amounts (a noncount noun, always singular). *Skim milk has fewer calories than whole milk. We have less milk left than I thought.*

flaunt, flout *Flaunt* means "show off": *If you have style, flaunt it. Flout* means "scorn" or "defy": *Hester Prynne flouted convention and paid the price.*

flunk A colloquial substitute for *fail.*

fun As an adjective, *fun* is colloquial and should be avoided in most writing: *It was a pleasurable* (not *fun*) *evening.*

further See *farther, further.*

get This common verb is used in many slang and colloquial expressions: *get lost, that really gets me, getting on. Get* is easy to overuse; watch out for it in expressions such as *it's getting better* (substitute *improving*) and *we got done* (substitute *finished*).

good, well *Good* is an adjective, and *well* is nearly always an adverb: *Larry's a good dancer. He and Linda dance well together. Well* is properly used as an adjective only to refer to health: *You look well.* (*You look good,* in contrast, means "Your appearance is pleasing.")

good and Colloquial for "very": *I was very* (not *good and*) *tired.*

had better See *better, had better.*

had ought The *had* is unnecessary and should be omitted: *He ought* (not *had ought*) *to listen to his mother.*

hanged, hung Though both are past-tense forms of *hang, hanged* is used to refer to executions and *hung* is used for all other meanings: *Tom Dooley was hanged* (not *hung*) *from a white oak tree. I hung* (not *hanged*) *the picture you gave me.*

Usage

hardly   See *but, hardly, scarcely.*

have, of   Use *have,* not *of,* after helping verbs such as *could, should, would, may,* and *might: You should have* (not *should of*) *told me.*

he, she; he/she   Convention has allowed the use of *he* to mean "he or she": *After the infant learns to creep, he progresses to crawling.* However, many writers today consider this usage inaccurate and unfair because it excludes females. The construction *he/she,* one substitute for *he,* is awkward and objectionable to most readers. The better choice is to use *he or she,* to make the pronoun plural, or to rephrase. For instance: *After the infant learns to creep, he or she progresses to crawling. After infants learn to creep, they progress to crawling. After learning to creep, the infant progresses to crawling.* See also pp. 57–58 and 119.

herself, himself   See *myself, herself, himself, yourself.*

hisself   Nonstandard for *himself.*

hopefully   *Hopefully* means "with hope": *Freddy waited hopefully for a glimpse of Eliza.* The use of *hopefully* to mean "it is to be hoped," "I hope," or "let's hope" is now very common; but since many readers continue to object strongly to the usage, try to avoid it. *I hope* (not *Hopefully) Eliza will be here soon.*

idea, ideal   An *idea* is a thought or conception. An *ideal* (noun) is a model of perfection or a goal. *Ideal* should not be used in place of *idea: The idea* (not *ideal) of the play is that our ideals often sustain us.*

if, whether   For clarity, use *whether* rather than *if* when you are expressing an alternative: *If I laugh hard, people can't tell whether I'm crying.*

illicit   See *elicit, illicit.*

illusion   See *allusion, illusion.*

implicit   See *explicit, implicit.*

imply, infer   Writers or speakers *imply,* meaning "suggest": *Jim's letter implies he's having a good time.* Readers or listeners *infer,* meaning "conclude": *From Jim's letter I infer he's having a good time.*

incredible, incredulous   *Incredible* means "unbelievable"; *incredulous* means "unbelieving": *When Nancy heard Dennis's incredible story, she was frankly incredulous.* See also *credible, creditable, credulous.*

individual, person, party   *Individual* should refer to a single human being in contrast to a group or should stress uniqueness: *The U.S. Constitution places strong emphasis on the rights of the individual.* For other meanings *person* is preferable: *What person* (not *individual) wouldn't want the security promised in that advertisement? Party* means "group" (*Can you seat a party of four for dinner?*) and should not be used to refer to an individual except in legal documents. See also *people, persons.*

infer   See *imply, infer.*

in regards to   Nonstandard for *in regard to, as regards,* or *regarding.*

inside of, outside of   The *of* is unnecessary when *inside* and *outside* are used as prepositions: *Stay inside* (not *inside of*) *the house. The decision is outside* (not *outside of*) *my authority. Inside of* may refer colloquially to time, though in formal English *within* is preferred: *The law was passed within* (not *inside of*) *a year.*

insure   See *assure, ensure, insure.*

irregardless   Nonstandard for *regardless.*

is, are   See *are, is.*

is because   See *reason is because.*

is when, is where   These are faulty constructions in sentences that define: *Adolescence is a stage* (not *is when a person is*) *between childhood and adulthood. Socialism is a system in which* (not *is where*) *government owns the means of production.* See also pp. 141–42.

its, it's   *Its* is the pronoun *it* in the possessive case: *That plant is losing its leaves. It's* is a contraction for *it is: It's likely to die if you don't water it.* Many people confuse *it's* and *its* because possessives are most often formed with *-'s;* but the possessive *its,* like *his* and *hers,* never takes an apostrophe.

-ize, -wise   The suffix *-ize* changes a noun or adjective into a verb: *revolutionize, immunize.* The suffix *-wise* changes a noun or adjective into an adverb: *clockwise, otherwise, likewise.* Avoid the two suffixes except in established words: *I'm highly sensitive* (not *sensitized*) *to that kind of criticism. Financially* (not *Moneywise*), *it's a good time to buy real estate.*

kind of, sort of, type of   In formal speech and writing, avoid using *kind of* or *sort of* to mean "somewhat": *He was rather* (not *kind of*) *tall.*

　　　Kind, sort, and *type* are singular and take singular modifiers and verbs: *This kind of dog is easily trained.* Agreement errors often occur when these singular nouns are combined with the plural adjectives *these* and *those: These kinds* (not *kind*) *of dogs are easily trained. Kind, sort,* and *type* should be followed by *of* but not by *a: I don't know what type of* (not *type* or *type of a*) *dog that is.*

　　　Use *kind of, sort of,* or *type of* only when the word *kind, sort,* or *type* is important: *That was a strange* (not *strange sort of*) *statement.*

lay, lie   *Lay* means "put" or "place" and takes a direct object: *We could lay the tablecloth in the sun.* Its main forms are *lay, laid, laid. Lie* means "recline" or "be situated" and does not take an object: *I lie awake at night. The town lies east of the river.* Its main forms are *lie, lay, lain.* (See also pp. 88–89.)

Usage

leave, let   *Leave* and *let* are interchangeable only when followed by *alone; leave me alone* is the same as *let me alone.* Otherwise, *leave* means "depart" and *let* means "allow": *Jill would not let Sue leave.*

less   See *fewer, less.*

liable   See *apt, liable, likely.*

lie, lay   See *lay, lie.*

like, as   See *as, like.*

like, such as   Strictly, *such as* precedes an example that represents a larger subject, whereas *like* indicates that two subjects are comparable. *Steve has recordings of many great saxophonists such as Ben Webster and Lee Konitz. Steve wants to be a great jazz saxophonist like Ben Webster and Lee Konitz.*

likely   See *apt, liable, likely.*

literally   This word means "actually" or "just as the words say," and it should not be used to qualify or intensify expressions whose words are not to be taken at face value. The sentence *He was literally climbing the walls* describes a person behaving like an insect, not a person who is restless or anxious. For the latter meaning, *literally* should be omitted.

lose, loose   *Lose* means "mislay": *Did you lose a brown glove? Loose* means "unrestrained" or "not tight": *Ann's canary got loose. Loose* also can function as a verb meaning "let loose": *They loose the dogs as soon as they spot the bear.*

lots, lots of   Colloquial substitutes for *very many, a great many,* or *much.* Avoid *lots* and *lots of* in college or business writing.

may, can   See *can, may.*

may be, maybe   *May be* is a verb, and *maybe* is an adverb meaning "perhaps": *Tuesday may be a legal holiday. Maybe we won't have classes.*

may of   See *have, of.*

media   *Media* is the plural of *medium* and takes a plural verb: *All the news media are increasingly visual.*

might of   See *have, of.*

moral, morale   As a noun, *moral* means "ethical conclusion" or "lesson": *The moral of the story escapes me. Morale* means "spirit" or "state of mind": *Victory improved the team's morale.*

most, almost   See *almost, most.*

must of   See *have, of.*

myself, herself, himself, yourself   The *-self* pronouns refer to or intensify another word or words: *Paul helped himself; Jill herself said so.* The *-self* pronouns are often used colloquially in place of personal pronouns, but that use should be avoided in formal speech and writing: *No one except me* (not *myself*) *saw the accident. Our delegates will be Susan and you* (not *yourself*).

nowheres   Nonstandard for *nowhere.*

number   See *amount, number.*

of, have   See *have, of.*

off of   *Of* is unnecessary. Use *off* or *from* rather than *off of: He jumped off* (or *from,* not *off of*) *the roof.*

OK, O.K., okay   All three spellings are acceptable, but avoid this colloquial term in formal speech and writing.

on account of   Wordy for *because of.*

on the other hand   This transitional expression of contrast should be preceded by its mate, *on the one hand: On the one hand, we hoped for snow. On the other hand, we feared that it would harm the animals.* However, the two combined can be unwieldy, and a simple *but, however, yet,* or *in contrast* often suffices: *We hoped for snow. Yet we feared that it would harm the animals.*

outside of   See *inside of, outside of.*

owing to the fact that   Wordy for *because.*

party   See *individual, person, party.*

people, persons   In formal usage, *people* refers to a general group: *We the people of the United States. . . . Persons* refers to a collection of individuals: *Will the person or persons who saw the accident please notify. . . .* Except when emphasizing individuals, prefer *people* to *persons.* See also *individual, person, party.*

per   Except in technical writing, an English equivalent is usually preferable to the Latin *per: $10 an* (not *per*) *hour; sent by* (not *per*) *parcel post; requested in* (not *per* or *as per*) *your letter.*

percent (per cent), percentage   Both these terms refer to fractions of one hundred. *Percent* always follows a numeral (*40 percent of the voters*), and the word should be used instead of the symbol (%) in general writing. *Percentage* usually follows an adjective (*a high percentage*).

person   See *individual, person, party.*

persons   See *people, persons.*

phenomena   The plural of *phenomenon* (meaning "perceivable fact" or "unusual occurrence"): *Many phenomena are not recorded. One phenomenon is attracting attention.*

plenty   A colloquial substitute for *very: The reaction occurred very* (not *plenty*) *fast.*

plus   *Plus* is standard as a preposition meaning "in addition to": *His income plus mine is sufficient.* But *plus* is colloquial as a conjunctive adverb: *Our organization is larger than theirs; moreover* (not *plus*), *we have more money.*

precede, proceed   The verb *precede* means "come before": *My name precedes yours in the alphabet.* The verb *proceed* means "move on": *We were told to proceed to the waiting room.*

prejudice, prejudiced   *Prejudice* is a noun; *prejudiced* is an adjective. Do not drop the *-d* from *prejudiced: I was fortunate that my parents were not prejudiced* (not *prejudice*).

pretty   Overworked as an adverb meaning "rather" or "somewhat": *He was somewhat* (not *pretty*) *irked at the suggestion.*

previous to, prior to   Wordy for *before.*

principal, principle   *Principal* is an adjective meaning "foremost" or "major," a noun meaning "chief official," or, in finance, a noun meaning "capital sum." *Principle* is a noun only, meaning "rule" or "axiom." *Her principal reasons for confessing were her principles of right and wrong.*

proceed, precede   See *precede, proceed.*

question of whether, question as to whether   Wordy substitutes for *whether.*

raise, rise   *Raise* means "lift" or "bring up" and takes a direct object: *The Kirks raise cattle.* Its main forms are *raise, raised, raised. Rise* means "get up" and does not take an object: *They must rise at dawn.* Its main forms are *rise, rose, risen.* (See also pp. 88–89.)

real, really   In formal speech and writing, *real* should not be used as an adverb; *really* is the adverb and *real* an adjective. *Popular reaction to the announcement was really* (not *real*) *enthusiastic.*

reason is because   Although colloquially common, this expression should be avoided in formal speech and writing. Use a *that* clause after *reason is: The reason he is absent is that* (not *is because*) *he is sick.* Or: *He is absent because he is sick.*

respectful, respective   *Respectful* means "full of (or showing) respect": *Be respectful of other people. Respective* means "separate": *The French and the Germans occupied their respective trenches.*

rise, raise   See *raise, rise.*

scarcely   See *but, hardly, scarcely.*

sensual, sensuous   *Sensual* suggests sexuality; *sensuous* means "pleasing to the senses." *Stirred by the sensuous scent of meadow grass*

*and flowers, Cheryl and Paul found their thoughts growing increasingly
sensual.*

set, sit *Set* means "put" or "place" and takes a direct object: *He sets
the pitcher down.* Its main forms are *set, set, set. Sit* means "be seated"
and does not take an object: *She sits on the sofa.* Its main forms are *sit,
sat, sat.* (See also pp. 88–89.)

shall, will *Will* is the future-tense helping verb for all persons: *I will
go, you will go, they will go.* The main use of *shall* is for first-person
questions requesting an opinion or consent: *Shall I order a pizza? Shall
we dance? Shall* can also be used for the first person when a formal effect is desired (I *shall expect you around three*), and it is occasionally
used with the second or third person to express the speaker's determination (*You shall do as I say*).

should of See *have, of.*

since *Since* mainly relates to time: *I've been waiting since noon.* But
since is also often used to mean "because": *Since you ask, I'll tell you.*
Revise sentences in which the word could have either meaning, such as
Since you left, my life is empty.

sit, set See *set, sit.*

so Avoid using *so* alone or as a vague intensifier: *He was so late. So*
needs to be followed by *that* and a clause that states a result: *He was so
late that I left without him.*

somebody, some body; someone, some one *Somebody and someone*
are indefinite pronouns; *some body* is a noun modified by *some;* and
some one is a pronoun or an adjective modified by *some. Somebody
ought to invent a shampoo that will give hair some body. Someone* told
Janine she should choose some one plan and stick with it.

someplace Informal for *somewhere.*

sometime, sometimes, some time *Sometime* means "at an indefinite
time in the future": *Why don't you come up and see me sometime? Sometimes* means "now and then": *I still see my old friend Joe sometimes. Some
time* means "span of time": *I need some time to make the payments.*

somewheres Nonstandard for *somewhere.*

sort of, sort of a See *kind of, sort of, type of.*

such Avoid using *such* as a vague intensifier: *It was such a cold winter. Such* should be followed by *that* and a clause that states a result: *It
was such a cold winter that Napoleon's troops had to turn back.*

such as See *like, such as.*

supposed to, used to In both these expressions, the *-d* is essential: *I
used to* (not *use to*) *think so. He's supposed to* (not *suppose to*) *meet us.*

sure   Colloquial when used as an adverb meaning *surely: James Madison sure was right about the need for the Bill of Rights.* If you merely want to be emphatic, use *certainly: Madison certainly was right.* If your goal is to convince a possibly reluctant reader, use *surely? Madison surely was right.*

sure and, sure to; try and, try to   *Sure to* and *try to* are the preferred forms: *Be sure to* (not *sure and*) *buy milk. Try to* (not *Try and*) *find some decent tomatoes.*

take, bring   See *bring, take.*

than, as   See *as, than.*

than, then   *Than* is a conjunction used in comparisons, *then* an adverb indicating time: *Holmes knew then that Moriarty was wilier than he had thought.*

that, which   *That* always introduces restrictive clauses: *We should use the lettuce that Susan bought* (*that Susan bought* limits the lettuce to a particular lettuce). *Which* can introduce both restrictive and nonrestrictive clauses, but many writers reserve *which* only for nonrestrictive clauses: *The leftover lettuce, which is in the refrigerator, would make a good salad* (*which is in the refrigerator* simply provides more information about the lettuce we already know of). Restrictive clauses (with *that* or *which*) are set off by commas; nonrestrictive clauses (with *which*) are not. See also pp. 151–52.

their, there, they're   *Their* is the possessive form of *they: Give them their money. There* indicates place (*I saw her standing there*) or functions as an expletive (*There is a hole behind you.*) *They're* is a contraction for *they are: They're going fast.*

theirselves   Nonstandard for *themselves.*

then, than   See *than, then.*

these kind, these sort, these type, those kind   See *kind of, sort of, type of.*

thru   A colloquial spelling of *through* that should be avoided in all academic and business writing.

time period   Since a *period* is an interval of time, this expression is redundant: *They did not see each other for a long time* (not *time period*). *Six accidents occurred in a three-week period* (not *time period*).

to, too, two   *To* is a preposition; *too* is an adverb meaning "also" or "excessively"; and *two* is a number. *I too have been to Europe two times.*

too   Avoid using *too* as an intensifier meaning "very": *Monkeys are too mean.* If you do use *too*, explain the consequences of the excessive quality: *Monkeys are too mean to make good pets.*

toward, towards   Both are acceptable, though *toward* is preferred. Use one or the other consistently.

try and, try to   See *sure and, sure to; try and, try to*.

type of   See *kind of, sort of, type of*. Don't use *type* without *of*: *It was a family type of* (not *type*) *restaurant*. Or, better: *It was a family restaurant*.

uninterested   See *disinterested, uninterested*.

unique   *Unique* means "the only one of its kind" and so cannot sensibly be modified with words such as *very* or *most*: *That was a unique* (not *a very unique* or *the most unique*) *movie*.

usage, use   *Usage* refers to conventions, most often those of a language: *Is "hadn't ought" proper usage? Usage* is often misused in place of the noun *use*: *Wise use* (not *usage*) *of insulation can save fuel*.

use, utilize   *Utilize* means "make use of": *We should utilize John's talent for mimicry in our play*. In most contexts, *use* is equally or more acceptable and less stuffy.

used to   See *supposed to, used to*.

wait for, wait on   In formal speech and writing, *wait for* means "await" (*I'm waiting for Paul*), and *wait on* means "serve" (*The owner of the store herself waited on us*).

ways   Colloquial as a substitute for *way*: *We have only a little way* (not *ways*) *to go*.

well   See *good, well*.

whether, if   See *if, whether*.

which   See *that, which*.

which, who   *Which* never refers to people. Use *who* or sometimes *that* for a person or persons and *which* or *that* for a thing or things: *The baby, who was left behind, opened the door, which we had closed*.

who's, whose   *Who's* is the contraction of *who is*: *Who's at the door? Whose* is the possessive form of *who*: *Whose book is that?*

will, shall   See *shall, will*.

-wise   See *-ize, -wise*.

would have   Avoid this construction in place of *had* in clauses that begin *if* and state a condition contrary to fact: *If the tree had* (not *would have*) *withstood the fire, it would have been the oldest in town*. See also p. 100.

would of   See *have, of*.

Usage

you   In all but very formal writing, *you* is generally appropriate as long as it means "you, the reader." In all writing, avoid indefinite uses of *you,* such as *In one ancient tribe <u>your</u> first loyalty was to <u>your</u> parents.* See also p. 122.

your, you're   *Your* is the possessive form of *you:* <u>*Your*</u> *dinner is ready.* *You're* is the contraction of *you are:* <u>*You're*</u> *bound to be late.*

yourself   See *myself, herself, himself, yourself.*

Index

Page numbers in **boldface** refer to main definitions in the text.

Index

Index

Index

Index

Index

FINDING WHAT YOU NEED IN THIS BOOK

Use a directory.

❖ The "Guide to the Book": an overview with questions in everyday language that are commonly asked about the book's main topics (inside the front cover).

❖ The table of contents: a detailed outline of the book's chapters (next page).

❖ Detailed outlines of the material covered in each part of the book (tabbed dividers).

Use the index.

An alphabetical list of all topics, terms, and problem words and expressions (beginning p. 311).

Use the elements of the page.

❶ Running head (header) showing the topic being discussed on this page.

❷ Chapter number and title.

❸ Key term for this discussion, defined in the text.

❹ Examples, always indented, often showing revision.

❺ ESL designation, highlighting material especially for those using English as a second language.

❻ Page tab, containing the code of the nearest section heading (**26a**) and the symbol or abbreviation for the topic being discussed (**pn agr**).

❼ Section heading, containing a main convention or topic. It is labeled with the section code, **26a**: the chapter number (**26**) and the section letter (**a**).

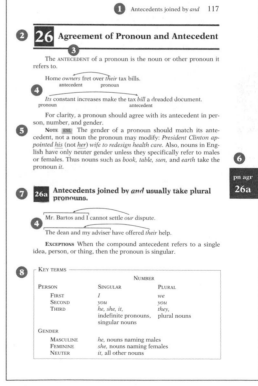

❽ Box defining secondary terms used on the page (always at the bottom of the page). Refer to these white boxes whenever a term is unclear. Otherwise, ignore them.

CONTENTS